National Youth Theatre

Monologues

75 Speeches for Auditions

Edited and Introduced by Michael Bryher

www.nickhernbooks.co.uk

www.nyt.org.uk

A Nick Hern Book

National Youth Theatre Monologues
first published in Great Britain in 2018
by Nick Hern Books Limited, The Glasshouse, 49a Goldhawk Road,
London W12 8QP, in association with the National Youth Theatre

Cover: Seraphina Beh in the 2016 National Youth Theatre production
of *Pigeon English*, adapted by NYT alumnus Gbolahan Obisesan, at the
Ambassadors Theatre, London. Photo by NYT alumna Helen
Murray/ArenaPAL. Design by October Associates

Designed and typeset by Nick Hern Books
Printed and bound in the UK
by Ashford Colour Press, Gosport, Hampshire

A CIP catalogue record for this book is available
from the British Library

ISBN 978 1 84842 676 4

For Judy Browne

Contents

Foreword

Over fifty years of new writing for the first official youth theatre in the world is something we can all be proud of.

I say 'all', and it is said with little humility, because wherever we go and whoever we work with, it appears that someone somewhere has either seen or been involved in a National Youth Theatre production. Ever since the NYT's birth in 1956, this company has led the way in youth drama, from the inspiring early days of making Shakespeare accessible to young actors and audiences alike, to more recent times and the hard-hitting, risk-taking stories written by emerging young writers who soon became household names.

Throughout our illustrious highs and sometimes fragile lows, what sets us apart from other companies is our unique ability to find raw and exciting talent both on and off stage. It's important to stress the off stage, because these plays would not have been produced without our young cohort of backstage and technical talent. Or their directors, to many of whom NYT have given their first break, like Matthew Warchus, current Artistic Director at London's Old Vic.

We champion diversity and individuality, and many of the speeches chosen in this anthology reflect that stand-out quality. It is the what we *are* that informs the what we *say* – and our vast national reach of diverse voices is wrapped neatly into these pages of monologues that will help you find your own individual voice when making that all-important impression.

This collection features a speech from the first play to be commissioned by NYT in 1967. It was the 'summer of love', and a simmering youth might have been feeling amorous, but *Zigger Zagger* reflects the anxiety and anger of Britain's young, set against

11

their (sometimes violent) passion for the beautiful game. It might well be one of our 'classics', but it still delivers some thrilling and chilling resonance today.

When commissioning new work I often seek a brave voice keen to explore the extremities of a character's mind and actions, whilst retaining the plot. Admittedly, the road to opening night can involve acrimonious bust-ups followed by kiss-and-make-ups between director and writer. I can recall stories of writers 'being banned' from rehearsal and technical sessions in the theatre, and others where directors have simply gone 'It's either them or me!' On such rare occasions, I choose the writer every time. After all, it is their words we are illuminating.

Many of writers featured here were 'first-timers' with NYT. It's with some pride that I flick through these speeches and remember the moment I first met James Graham. I went to see his play *Albert's Boy* at the Finborough Theatre – and couldn't believe it when the young boy (twenty-two, but looking fourteen) at the bar, awkwardly sipping a pint, introduced himself as the writer of something truly sophisticated and appealing. I offered him a commission on the spot. *Tory Boyz* was the first play he wrote for NYT and the first time he ever received payment for his immense skill. I had asked James to write a play that highlighted the homophobic bullying that stalked the Westminster lobbies, and to mirror it with the likelihood that the first gay PM would be a Tory – and a deceased one at that. Ten years on, the play still resonates today, as do so many of the speeches in this book.

Often writers find their voice by happy accident or simple frustration at not being cast in plays they feel they are right for. Some are lucky enough to do both. At sixteen, Sarah Solemani was a bundle of talent and opinion that deserved to be seen and heard. I had to give Sarah her first writing break just a few years later because she is so damn funny and observant. *Eye/Balls* packed a punch and put a female character at the heart of the double bill that again showed astonishing complexity for someone so young. It was clear Solemani was an important champion for female voices and remains so today.

Over the past fifteen years, I've commissioned more female writers than male simply because I've felt a desire to hear their stories more. For instance, Stephanie Street's sensitive adaptation of Mohsin Hamid's *The Reluctant Fundamentalist* puts love and grief at the heart of the play because she can. *Blue Moon Over Poplar*, Rebecca Lenkiewicz's story of incest amongst the post-war rubble in London's East End, feels real and raw because she dares to write of uncomfortable beauty in an ugly world.

None of the plays in this collection could have been commissioned or produced by NYT without our brilliant supporters, past and present, to whom we're extremely grateful. A special mention must go to the Pureland Foundation for their support of our new writing for young people, and our other principal supporters, The David Pearlman Charitable Foundation and Arts Council England.

Whilst compiling this book, the NYT lost Judy Browne, one of our inspiring alumna and practitioners, so it seems fitting to honour her name with this collection of speeches. She was never short of a speech herself.

I can't mention all of the writers I've loved working with, simply because this is not meant to be a love letter. Sadly some of them didn't even make the cut here because their plays didn't have suitable monologues. But thanks to Michael Bryher's keen eye, we have a collection of voices for you to enjoy. I hope it will help you find your own individual voice – and an audience to share it with.

Paul Roseby
Chief Executive and Artistic Director
National Youth Theatre of Great Britain

Introduction

No matter who you are or where you're from, no matter what you look like or sound like, no matter what your background is or what school you go to – whether you love musicals, Shakespeare, TV, or even if you've never been to the theatre before, *you* could pursue a career as an actor. And perhaps reading this book might be the beginning of your journey. Welcome to the National Youth Theatre's volume of audition monologues.

At the National Youth Theatre (NYT), we know that auditions can be scary and nerve-racking, but they can also be exhilarating and sometimes even fun. We have put this book together to give you the tools to help you choose the right speech for you, so that you can prepare properly and be ready for anything that might happen in an audition room – and you may even enjoy yourself along the way!

It doesn't matter if you've never done any acting before; if you're a passionate, motivated person who is interested in the world around you, and you want to give it a try, go for it. There are speeches in this book that could work in all different types of audition, so have a look and see if you can find one that inspires you.

What this book is for

The bad news is that there is no secret recipe for the perfect audition. There's no definitive list of dos and don'ts; it depends on who you are auditioning for, what the role is and whether it's for a play, musical or screen. The good news, however, is that there are lots of ways that you can prepare yourself so that no matter what situation you find yourself in, you can still do your best. This book will provide guidance and advice for navigating a variety of auditions including NYT, drama schools and castings, and whilst it is impossible to supply you with all the right answers, it will definitely help you to ask the right questions.

We've selected seventy-five monologues from plays that the National Youth Theatre has commissioned or produced over more than fifty years and from a wide variety of writers. Before each monologue is a commentary that will give you context from the play, as well as notes and advice about how you might approach the speech should you choose to perform it. You may feel that you want to do a speech differently from the way that's been suggested – that's fine! This book isn't intended to limit how you perform the monologues we've chosen, instead it should be a starting point so that you can feel confident approaching any speech.

There is also a section with exercises that you can use to deepen your understanding of the speech, as well as a glossary at the back (in case there are any words you don't understand).

Back to Basics

Different types of auditions

Let's go back to basics: an audition is an interview in which you will be asked to do some kind of performance.

If you're auditioning for **drama school** the process varies depending on where you've applied. Often you will be asked to learn and perform between one and four speeches each lasting somewhere between one and three minutes.

Two or three of these speeches should be taken from a modern play (some schools are happy with anything written after 1900 and some schools will want the play to have been written no earlier than 1990 – check the individual guidance) and one or two should be classical speeches by Shakespeare (or another Elizabethan/Jacobean playwright like Christopher Marlowe or Ben Jonson).

Some drama schools will give you a list of classical speeches to choose from, and others will let you choose yourself, but all of them will let you choose your own modern speech. It is always worth having a range of speeches that vary in tone to draw from; you might want to have one speech that allows you to be emotionally vulnerable, and another that will allow you to show a lighter, more comedic side. Alternatively, you could pick one character that is quick thinking and witty, to perform alongside another character who is in a state of emotional turmoil and finds it hard to articulate their emotions.

Whatever you choose, try and play to your strengths, and pick speeches that you enjoy performing.

Some schools also include a workshop in the first-round audition, which might cover voice work, movement exercises or improvisation; others might only invite you to take part in a longer process if you get a recall.

The number of recall rounds depends on the school, but all the information for the individual school will be detailed on their website. There will also be a slightly different process if you are applying to a musical-theatre course or a course in applied theatre, so make sure you *carefully* read the individual guidance for each course you are applying for. This might sound complicated, but all you need to do is make sure that you have prepared the right number and type of speeches for each audition, which means looking carefully at the individual school's guidance, and giving yourself a few months to get ready.

If you're auditioning for a production of a **musical** or a musical-theatre course, the process will involve singing, acting and probably a dance audition too. Just like having monologues in your memory, it is also worth having a variety of songs that you can sing at an audition which suit your range, tone and personality.

Even if you are only applying for an acting course, most drama schools will also ask you to sing something (by yourself without accompaniment), so it's worth keeping this in mind in case they ask you to sing.

If it's a full musical production you're auditioning for, you should also consider what type of musical it is and match the song you sing at the audition to that style; for example, if you are auditioning for a Sondheim musical, make sure you pick something that has an emotional journey and allows you to show your acting ability, whereas if you are auditioning for a Broadway musical you may want to pick something more showy.

Sometimes you will be asked to learn multiple songs and scenes from the show you are auditioning for; as with drama-school auditions, this can involve a lot of preparation, but it will be worth it if you get the part.

For a **screen** role, you might be asked to learn several scenes from a TV or film script. Screen auditions are different from stage auditions – they rarely require monologues and instead you will be given an extract from the script of the programme or film you're auditioning for, and you'll often be filmed as you perform it in the audition.

It's important that you try and learn the lines for a screen audition so that the camera captures everything you do (rather than filming the top of your head as you look down at the script). If you only receive the script the day before the audition (which isn't uncommon), try your best to learn it but, if that's not possible, make sure you know it well enough to be able to bring it to life in the audition.

The casting director or their assistant will read in the other characters, and they will often sit just to the side of the camera so that your full face is captured within the shot (but don't be afraid to ask if your body position and eyeline are okay for the camera).

Auditioning for screen roles can feel a little intimidating, but if you prepare well you should feel confident to give the most truthful performance you can.

Usually these days, if you're auditioning for a **theatre** role, you will be asked to read from a scene of the play you're auditioning for. There is slightly less expectation to learn the lines than for a screen audition, but if you can learn them, do; your performance will be more alive if you aren't constantly looking at the script, and you will find that you can invest so much more in the character and the relationship.

Remember that there are lots of other people out there who would love to get this job too, so make sure that you prepare as much as you can and give yourself the best chance.

That being said, if you've only *half* learnt the lines, make sure you have the script in hand – an audition is there to test your suitability to play the character, not to test how good your memory is.

The director may give you notes and redirect you in the scene or they may not. Try not to read anything into this decision, but if they *do* redirect you, remember that this isn't because they thought you were bad the first time; they may also want to see how you respond to direction. Listen to their notes and try to take them on as you give it another go. If you don't understand what they are saying then ask them to clarify, but otherwise try your hardest to make the piece of direction you've been given come to life.

As with all theatre auditions, it is so important that you *read the whole play* so that you know where in the story the scene you're performing comes, what the tone of the play is, who your character is and what they want.

It's often a good idea to come to the audition with a few questions either about the play or the production, to show that you have engaged with the play and are interested in the project.

For the **National Youth Theatre**'s intake auditions we ask that you prepare one speech, but for our castings we might want two or three speeches and a song too. Since we are an ensemble-based company, we will want to know if you can work as part of a team, so we also run workshops as part of our audition process where you are asked to move, play, improvise and work as an ensemble.

We are slightly different from drama schools or auditions for a play or film – we are just as interested in you as a person as your ability to act. We value independent spirits and young people who have something to say about the world, so as well as preparing a speech for us, make sure you come in and tell us about what makes you *you*!

As you can see, there's no one rule to how an audition will run – each drama school, director or theatre company is different and will be looking for different things. As a result, it's really important that you are 100 per cent prepared for any circumstance, so no matter what you're auditioning for, it's always worth having no fewer than two different modern monologues, at least one Shakespeare prepared, and a song which you can sing easily without accompaniment.

What is the auditioner looking for?

This is the golden question, and again there is no easy answer. As I've already said, different types of audition will ask you to prepare different things, and even within those types, different auditioners may be looking for different things; for example, one drama school may want you to be able to sing as well as move and act, whereas another will place less emphasis on your musical ability; one director may value a playful approach where another is looking for intensity for a certain part. So how can you know how to give them exactly what they want? Well, in short, you can't. But there are lots of things you *can* do to present the best version of yourself, and deliver a speech that is emotionally committed and truthful.

What is a monologue?

Very simply, a monologue is a part of a play where a character talks, uninterrupted, for anywhere upwards of a minute. Monologues can occur within scenes where a character is talking to another character, or they can be addressed to the audience – sometimes whole plays can be monologues.

When taken from a scene, a monologue often marks an important moment for the character as they have so much to say that they need to speak for a long time. No matter what the context, when a character speaks for a prolonged period of time, they are always trying to affect and change the person (or people) they are talking to, and in doing so, they go through some kind of change themselves. For example, in Al Smith's *The Astronaut Wives Club*, which features in this book, Mary Engle wants all the other women at the party to understand why she wants to expel Sandra from the club, and in doing so Mary moves through explosive anger, to vulnerability and finally to a sense of dignified defiance.

In several of the speeches in this anthology the character is talking directly to the audience, so 'who' they are talking to is a trickier question to answer. Even when this is the case, they still want to change the audience in some way, but you have to think about who the audience is: do they represent the character's best friend, or perhaps a counsellor the character has visited to talk about their situation? Maybe the audience could be someone on a bus that the character has just struck up a conversation with? In Eddie's speech in James Graham's *Relish*, the audience might represent a new member of the kitchen staff, or perhaps they could be the people eating in the restaurant. You might instead decide that the play is 'metatheatrical' and that the audience is just an audience, but even if this is the case, make sure you know how the character wants to affect them.

Not every monologue has to be deep and meaningful – comic speeches are great as well, but the same principles apply: who is the character talking to? How do they want to change them? What change do they go through themselves?

Where do I start?

Don't be scared. It might be that you've known you want to act since you can remember, or perhaps you've never done any acting at all before. If you feel that you would like to try acting, then go for it – what's the worst that can happen? At the root of acting is play (they are called *plays* after all), so try and approach finding a speech with a sense of adventure.

This book is designed to help you find the right speech for you. It can be a daunting prospect to find the perfect speech from the many thousands of plays that exist, so we have selected a list of speeches that can act as a starting point in your journey towards being an actor. The plays featured in this book encompass all walks of life – there are characters from all backgrounds, so you should be able to find a part that you connect with. These speeches have also all been performed by young actors in NYT productions, so you can be assured that you will find something that suits you.

The speeches in the book have been ordered alphabetically by play, so you might want to just read it from cover to cover and see which speeches leap off the page for you. Alternatively, you might want to start by looking at the gender of the characters, and read all the speeches that match your gender identity as a way of narrowing it down. You may then also look at the age guidance to help you find the speeches that will suit your playing age. When you have found a few speeches that you can identify with, you should definitely read the plays that they come from in order to get to know the character better, which might make choosing easier.

Once you have chosen the speech (or speeches) that you want to learn, you can start to begin 'working' on them. This introduction will take you through a process for bringing your speech off the page and turning it into a compelling and truthful performance through guidance, advice and various exercises.

Choosing a Speech

Preparation

First things first: give yourself plenty of time. Don't leave it until the last minute; remember that you need enough time to find a speech that you like, read the play, learn it and rehearse it enough so that when you get to the audition, you aren't worried that you'll forget your lines. Make sure that you are clear on how many speeches you need to prepare. The amount of time you give yourself is up to you, but I would suggest beginning your search *at least* two months before your audition date.

Then ask yourself: 'What am I auditioning for?' If you're auditioning for a drama school, they will supply information about what they're looking for, along with some simple dos and don'ts. Follow their guidance! If they ask you to do a speech no longer than three minutes, don't go over the time limit. If they suggest that you choose a monologue written after 1990, don't prepare a speech written in 1975. Breaking the rules might make you stand out, but for all the wrong reasons!

Probably the most important thing when choosing a speech, however, is that you are excited by it. There should be something about the character that really interests you – perhaps you have had similar experiences or maybe you love the speech because the character is totally different to you but for some reason you're drawn to them – whatever the reason, you should feel an instinctive connection to the speech and enjoy performing it.

You may also want to consider whether the speech 'suits' you – does it play to your natural strengths? If you are good at comedy does it allow you to show this? Does it let you emotionally connect? Perhaps it enables you to reveal a part of your personality that might otherwise remain hidden. It is worth thinking about what your natural strengths are, and whether the speech works with them. If you don't know, try asking friends, family or teachers what your strengths are, and pick a speech that will allow you to showcase them.

You should also consider:

Age

The most important thing to consider when you are choosing a speech is whether you can *connect* to the character, regardless of how old you are or they are. Most of the characters in this volume are 'younger', but their ages vary and some characters are slightly older.

It's worth remembering that every monologue in this book has previously been played by a young person, and when older characters have been included, this is because they offer chances to play compelling characters in high-stakes situations. In Dominic McHale's *Tallman*, for example, Mum is a character who had children when she was young and is full of guilt and resentment towards her daughter, while in *Dancing at Lughnasa* by Brian Friel, Kate is a woman on the edge of losing control. Neither of these characters would require you to play an 'old' person, but both of them allow you to explore rich emotional journeys, and play strong objectives.

So don't think too much about how old the character is, and instead consider whether you feel that you can truthfully represent them in performance.

Gender

At NYT we celebrate individuals of all gender identities and recognise that the gender identification you choose to adopt is defined by you and only you. We are happy for anyone to perform any speech, regardless of gender. In our production of Gbolahan Obisesan's adaptation of *Pigeon English*, for example, the male role of Harri was played by a female actor (Seraphina Beh – see the cover of this book!). In this anthology, we have ordered the speeches alphabetically by play title, and have also listed the age and gender of the character as originally intended by the writer to make it as easy as possible for you to find the right speech for you.

Background

NYT produces work about people from all backgrounds, and we try to make sure that our membership reflects the diversity of the country. In this anthology there are characters from a wide range of backgrounds, but again, the most important thing is that you are excited by the speech, rather than feeling that you have to perform a character that comes from the same place as you do.

Looking elsewhere

If you decide not to choose a speech from this volume, you can still use many of the commentary suggestions as hints and tips about how to approach your chosen monologue/s. Here are a few other things to think about when researching other plays and speeches:

Try to find an uninterrupted speech, as these tend to flow the best. Some of the speeches in this book have been put together from a section of dialogue, but only when the interjections from the other characters don't alter the thought process of the character speaking. For example, in James Graham's *Tory Boyz*, Nicholas's speech has been put together from a scene in which he's talking to Sam, but Sam's interjections don't alter what Nicholas wants to say, and so it can be read as one flowing speech without the rhythm feeling disjointed.

Don't take a speech from an Internet site that has lists of monologues on it that have been self-published. These speeches can often be badly written, and won't show you in your best light. Instead, search for plays that have been performed on stage at professional producing theatres. At NYT, we would recommend theatres like the Royal Court, the National Theatre, Live Theatre, the Bush, the Traverse, Birmingham REP and Manchester Royal Exchange, to name a few, or writers that have been published by Nick Hern Books, Faber & Faber, Methuen Drama or Oberon. If a play or a writer has been professionally performed or published by one of these organisations, it suggests that the writing is of a high quality and will allow you to perform to the best of your ability.

Be wary of characters who are 'mad' or shouting angrily throughout as it is sometimes difficult to see what you're really capable of. The best audition speeches show variety and take the character (and you, the actor, and your audience) on a journey.

It doesn't matter if the audition panel have seen the speech one hundred times before; if you can connect to it with a sense of bravery and truth, your performance will be rich and alive. So don't worry if you find out someone else is doing the same speech as you.

Read the play. Read the play. Read the play.

Once you've found a speech that you think you might like to perform, read the play. The notes in this book give a comprehensive overview of what happens in each play, but this is no replacement for you reading it yourself. Reading the whole play will really help you prepare your monologue – it will give you context, it might help clarify the style of the piece, and it will give you a sense of understanding and ownership of the character. Many of the speeches in this book have been published and several of the others are available to read on the NYT's website, so make sure you read the play – if you can't afford to buy it, try going to a library or ask if they have a copy at your school or college. At the end of the commentary before each speech is information on where you can find the play.

Preparing the Speech

Thinking about the character

This can be the hardest part for any actor: once you've found a speech, and read the whole play, what next? Obviously you have to try and learn it, but you also have to rehearse it, and 'work on it' in some way. We'll now go through some things you can think about, and some simple techniques that you can use to help you develop a sense of character and connection. These suggestions broadly come from the Stanislavskian tradition of naturalism, which is widely used by many directors in British theatre. It's worth saying, however, that there are other of ways you can approach acting and performance, from methods like the Meisner Technique (which built on the teachings of Stanislavsky) to the teachings of Jacques Lecoq and Philippe Gaulier which focus on the physical world of the actor and clowning instead, so if this approach isn't for you – that's fine.

A simple way to think about a character in a play is by asking three questions: 'Who am I?', 'Where am I?' and 'What am I doing?' You can unpack these three simple questions as little or as much as you want, but they are always a good starting place.

Who am I?

Or put another way, who is the character you're playing? The best way to work this out is by reading the play. You will get a sense of the character from reading the whole text and noticing how they respond in certain situations, who they have relationships with, and what they say. A good way of being specific about this is by doing the character lists exercises starting on page 43. Once you have made note of all the details about your character, you can start to get a clear picture of who they really are.

Some of the characters featured in this book appear in their plays only once – for example, Mrs Tiresias in *The World's Wife* – or they say very little through the rest of the play, so in this instance it's your job to imagine them as a fully rounded person. To help you do this, you can try and answer the questions on pages 47–9 or even draw your character (see page 49). You want to get a complete sense of who the character is, so anything you can do to help that will only add to your performance.

Where am I?

In order to answer this question, you may need to do some research to find out when and where the play is set, and what culture the character comes from.

Being an actor is like being a detective. Each of these monologues is a window into another world; some of these worlds might be familiar to you – for example, Evan Placey's *Consensual* is primarily set in a school – and others may not. Don't be put off by something you don't immediately understand, if a play is set in another historical time or geographical place, do some research to find out what life was like. Part of being an actor is being nosey; you have to be interested in how other people live, think and feel – people who may be very different to you.

If you are performing Razia's speech from *Razia Sultan* by Jamila Gavin, for example, it might help you to understand the character better if you know more about thirteenth-century India. Your aim should be to find out about what the daily life of the character might have been like. Where did they live? What kinds of relationship might they have had? What was the wider society like? Try to let your research inform the immediate world of the play – so if you are doing Razia's monologue, where might she have delivered this speech? What might the buildings have looked like that she stands on the steps of? Does this influence your understanding of the tone of the speech?

Equally, if you don't understand a particular word or phrase that a character says, look it up and maybe even try and use it in conversation to see how it feels. Actors need to be inquisitive and brave; don't be put off by something that you don't understand – see it as an opportunity to learn something new.

Try to make your research fun: think about whether there are any films or TV programmes that might help you imagine a character – for example, if you are considering King Ethelred's speech from *Silence*, watching *Game of Thrones* may help you imagine the world of the play. If you are thinking about Shirley's speech from *Blue Moon Over Poplar*, try looking at some images of Teddy Girls to give you a sense of her world. Images are just as useful as text when researching a character's situation, so you may find it useful to create a mood board for your character (see page 50).

Some characters will require you to do some research to get to grips with their historical situation, and some will require you to think carefully about the emotional state they're in. Rachel's speech from Jack Thorne's *When You Cure Me* deals with the aftermath of a brutal sexual assault, so you may need to research the after-effects of such an incident. Or if you are going to do Aswan's speech from *Inside*, you may want to find out more about life in prison.

Research is an important part of most acting processes, and will help you to imagine the world of the character, but don't feel that you have to present your research through your performance. All of your findings should inform your characterisation – you should think about them when rehearsing and they will then bubble under the surface; then, once you are performing, you want to focus on the character in the moment and what they want.

What am I doing?

This is perhaps the most important question of all. You may have also heard the phrases: 'What do I want?' or 'What is my motivation?' Let's try to unpack these questions so that they're easier to think about – this can sometimes feel a little complicated, so take from it anything that you find useful.

Acting is all about doing. You might think that your aim as a performer is to effectively portray emotion, and whilst this is definitely part of it, at the heart of acting is *action*.

So what does this mean? Well, just as in life, when you want to achieve or obtain something or have an effect or get a reaction from somebody, you act upon this impulse – or perform an action – in order to try and get what you want, and you either achieve your goal or not, which results in some kind of feeling. Unlike in life, however, most plays involve situations of heightened tension, and so the outcome of what the character does is usually pretty important, which leads to big emotions. But emotion shouldn't be your goal – action should. If you just play emotion, your performance will be two-dimensional.

In order to fully get to grips with what your character *does*, first you need to think about what they *want*. It is up to you how deep you go into this (books like *Different Every Night* by Mike Alfreds will take you through a detailed system of objectives), but in this instance, I am just going to talk about what the character wants in the speech. In the commentary for each speech I have suggested some options for what the character 'wants', but I would encourage you to read the play and see if you agree with me. For example, in Al Smith's *The Astronaut Wives Club*, Mary Engle wants the other women to understand her frustration that her husband will never land on the moon, and so she attacks and ridicules Sandra. Through her desire to be understood (her *want*), what she does is attack (her *action*), which gives rise to bitterness and anger (her *feeling*).

In many of the speeches, the character will be talking to other characters and trying to affect them, so make sure you have thought carefully about who they are talking to, and how this other person is responding during the speech. It is worth thinking about how the other character might be reacting line by line during the speech, as you might find it gives your character extra motivation to speak.

Speeches are always more engaging, dynamic and emotionally truthful if the performer has thought clearly about what the character wants, who they are talking to and what they are doing to achieve that goal.

A note of caution

I've talked here about being clear on what the character 'wants'. Keep in mind that sometimes characters don't know exactly what they want. Sometimes they want conflicting things, and they aren't always in control of what they are saying, but there is always an impulse of some kind that drives them forward. So you may have to take the speech line by line to think about what they are *doing* in that moment, which might then change in the next moment.

Change

Not only is the character trying to change the world outside by pursuing what they want, they are also changing themselves. Think really carefully about how the character is different at the end of the speech from the beginning – how has saying this speech changed them? Are they relieved? Upset? Angry? Exhausted? It might be useful to think of a word to describe the character at the beginning of the speech, and then another word to describe them at the end of the speech, and make sure you are charting how they change as the speech progresses.

Emotional intensity

It is often the case that a monologue will come at a point of heightened emotion in a character's journey through the play. Generally, however, you don't have the luxury of this build-up in an audition scenario, so you need to think about how you are going to access this level of emotional intensity quickly. You may want to run around for ten seconds to get your heart rate up, or quickly press against a wall to engage your body. Alternatively, you might think back to a memory in your own life which allows you to access whichever emotion you need. If you do this, however, look after yourself; don't dredge up painful parts of your own life if you are feeling fragile or might not be able to deal with what comes up. Whatever you choose, try building this process into your rehearsals for the monologue, so you know what works for you *before* the audition.

Spontaneity

Keep in mind that the character doesn't know they are going to be speaking for two minutes – they haven't set out to do 'a speech'. In fact, if they wanted, they could stop at any moment; but they don't – for whatever reason they keep on going. So try not to think of it as a 'speech' and instead try and bring the moment to life, and let each line of thought spark the next line until the character finishes – either because they have nothing left to say, or because they have been cut off by another character.

Style

In this anthology there are plays of all different styles: gritty naturalism, storytelling, verse, tragedy and comedy. No matter what the style, make sure you think of your character as a person communicating with someone else, trying to effect change in them.

Staging

It's fine to keep your staging simple; as long as you are playing strong actions, and are emotionally connected and committed, you will be engaging and interesting to watch. Try to stage your monologue with a minimum of fuss – you may be able to use chairs, but that's it. Most auditioners will request that you don't use props, as they can often be distracting, but if you do use a prop, keep it simple, safe and make sure you've practised with it.

The chances are you will have rehearsed your speech in a small room – like your bedroom – which is fine, but do try and connect to your body when performing. This means working on what you are doing physically within the speech as well as with your voice. So think about whether your character might stand or sit during the speech – does this change at any point? If they are feeling angry or joyful, think about how you might communicate this physically. Or if they are experiencing emotional uncertainty, how might this express itself in your body? It is important that you practise your speech physically so that you know what it feels like to inhabit the character fully.

You don't have to recreate the exact staging in the play if it doesn't work in an audition setting; for example, in the speech from *When You Cure Me*, Rachel is meant to be lying on the floor, but if this means the auditioner can't see you, you will have to prop yourself up (or you may find it easier to use a chair). Make sure that, whatever staging decisions you choose, allow the audition panel to see and hear you.

Accents are allowed but, to be blunt, only do one if you're good at it – you don't want the panel to be distracted by a dodgy accent. If the speech is written in a dialect and requires a specific accent, make sure you are confident with that accent, and if you're not, choose another speech.

Miming

Be very wary of doing lots of miming. If your character is telling a story in which they drove a car or drank tea or went for a swim... do they really need to mime it? Think to yourself – would the character do this? In Luke Barnes's *The Class*, Wayne pretends to be all the animals he talks about, which is fine because he's ridiculing them, but if a character is talking about going through a door, do they really need to mime going through a door in order for an audience to understand that that's what is happening? Most of the time, the answer is no, and we would much rather see you imagining it, so that you draw us into your world, rather than showing us the mechanics of what they did.

Doing the Audition

Preparing for the day

You've now done lots of character work and the audition date is approaching.

Learn your lines. Learn your lines. Learn your lines.

This is the question actors get asked more than any other – how do you learn your lines? And again, unfortunately, there is no simple answer. You just have to find the best way for you.

Some people learn their lines visually, through reading the text, covering it up and trying to remember what was written. You can gradually build this up, one sentence at a time; so at first you are only remembering a section of a line, then a whole line, then two, three, four... until you've memorised the whole speech.

Other people like to record their lines and listen back to them on their headphones.

It is also possible to learn lines through saying them out loud and going through the character's physical journey as they say them.

Whichever way suits you best, make sure you know your lines inside out. Auditions can be nerve-racking as it is, so you don't want to be going into the room worried that you might forget your lines. A way of trying to make sure this doesn't happen is to practise in front of other people. This could be a friend, a teacher or your family, but make sure you have spoken the lines out loud in front of someone before the audition (preferably more than once). This way you'll have already experienced the nerves of doing the speech and you'll be better prepared for the real thing.

Logistics

There is no point in doing all this work on your speech if you don't manage to turn up for the audition in the right place at the right time.

Organisations like NYT and drama schools will audition thousands of people every year, so they are good at communicating all the information you need in order to get to your audition – make sure you read it carefully. If you get a casting audition for a play or musical, and you aren't sure about a detail of the audition – for example, where it will be taking place, or if it hasn't been specified whether the character has a specific accent – make sure you ask well in advance and prepare accordingly. If you are travelling a long way, be sure to plan your route so that you get there in plenty of time rather than arriving sweaty and flustered. Get a good night's sleep the night before and make sure you eat some breakfast! Also, always bring a bottle of water, a snack, and clothes and shoes that are appropriate for moving in.

The individual audition

Every audition will be different, and it will depend on where you're auditioning as to exactly how it will run, but at some point you will have an individual audition, in which you will meet the person or panel of people auditioning you, who might include the director or casting director. If you're auditioning for NYT, there may also be an actor, writer or theatre-maker, and they will see your speech.

Bear in mind that you might be in a small room or a big room, there might be noise coming in from outside, and the auditioner might ask for you to address the speech to them or to pretend they aren't there – but now it's your job to transport yourself and the panel into the world of the character. When they ask you to perform the speech, make sure you take a little bit of time to focus your mind and prepare your body so that you can access the performance that you've prepared.

Go for it!

This might sound like a strange thing to say, but it's now time to forget all of the work you've done on the speech, and just go for it. Leading up to the audition, practise, practise, practise, and then when you get into the room, breathe, relax, throw caution to the wind and enjoy yourself. Audition panels don't want to see you remembering the historical context of the speech; they want to see you alive in the moment, making bold instinctive choices. Trust that any work you have done will be bubbling under the surface, and go for it!

Taking direction

A big part of being an actor is working with a director. They will want to know that if you were to work with them, you will be open to collaboration and taking direction. Sometimes they may ask you to repeat part or all of the speech, but with a different emphasis. It may be that this redirection asks you to bring out a certain aspect of the character, or change something about your characterisation, or it may be that you are asked to do something silly like imagine you are in a Western or running away from an angry bear. Actors can get stuck in the way they have practised the speech and are unable to break out of their habits, so in your preparation at home, it's always worth mixing it up a bit and trying the speech in a way that is totally different to how you usually do it.

If you get redirected, don't assume that it means you've done a bad job, and equally, if you don't get redirected, don't think that the auditioner didn't engage with what you did – it's just the luck of the draw.

The 'chat'

Auditions can last anything from five minutes to a whole day. There might be one person auditioning you, or there might be a big panel of people, and they might ask you about your life, your experience and your interests, so be prepared to talk about yourself. Often, the people auditioning will want to know what makes you tick: what fires you up, what your passions are – and they don't have to be anything to do with theatre! In fact, most directors and casting directors love it when people have a diverse range of interests, experience and hobbies. The NYT company is made up of people who are interested in the world and who have a bold and individual outlook; we want to see your personality, your vibrancy, your passion for life shining through!

Workshop auditions

Workshop auditions aren't uncommon these days, especially for drama schools or professional jobs that require devising. They are a chance for a director to work with you in a more relaxed way, and to get to know how you might work in a rehearsal setting. An NYT intake audition will always start with a workshop, which may involve some games, movement, voice exercises and devising. We try to make our auditions as open and friendly as possible, so that you can relax and give the best performance you can.

Access

At NYT we strive to remove any barriers that may prevent young people from accessing our work, such as organising BSL interpreters and other additional support staff where appropriate. As well as asking all applicants what their access requirements are in advance of their auditions, from 2019 we'll be offering Relaxed Accessible Auditions for young people with a disability who would prefer to audition in a more supported environment. Our Relaxed Accessible Auditions have been designed in consultation with our disability partner Diverse City, with whom we work on a wider programme across the organisation to make our opportunities accessible for young people with disability. They have also been directly informed by our pilot programming with young people from Highshore School in Southwark. This includes specialist training for the directors who deliver our auditions. If you have any questions or concerns about accessing NYT auditions you can contact us on info@nyt.org.uk or 020 3696 7057.

After the audition

Waiting to hear about an audition can be horrible! Sometimes you might hear the next day if it's a casting for a part, sometimes it could be a week, and sometimes it could be a few months. Hard as it may seem, once it's over, try and put it out of your mind. Sometimes these processes take a really long time, so hang in there. As an actor, you *always* have a right to know when you might hear the result, so don't be scared of asking on the day when that might be, but often it will take a while, so it's best to try and forget about it until closer to the time. It might be a good idea to organise something fun to look forward to immediately after an audition to distract yourself.

When the result arrives, if it's a 'Yes', WELL DONE! You've done a fantastic job and should be proud of yourself. If, on the other hand, it's a 'No', try not to be too downhearted; this doesn't mean that you're not talented, it just means that you weren't right this time. It's fine to feel disappointed, so allow yourself a little time to get over it, but if you want to be an actor, you will have to be resilient – think about what you've learnt, and keep going!

Top Tips

There's lots of information here about how to approach choosing a speech, how to rehearse it and what the day might be like. Some of it is obvious, and some of it you may not have thought of before, but try not to feel overwhelmed.

Here are a few things that are always worth remembering:

- It's worth having at least one or two modern monologues and one Shakespeare speech learnt, as well as a song that you can sing unaccompanied – just in case. Although at the NYT we only ask for one modern speech.

- Come prepared by making sure you've read the play your speech comes from, and learn the lines thoroughly.

- Think carefully about whom the character is talking *to* and how they are trying to affect them.

- Try and perform the speech in front of someone before you come to the audition – it will make the prospect of doing it again much less scary.

- Be on time! There's no point doing all this work if you miss the audition.

- Get ready for redirection – think of it as an opportunity to test yourself and try something new.

- Be prepared to talk about yourself and your interests, no matter what they are. Actors need to be inquisitive people with a wide range of experiences, who are interested in the world around them.

- If it doesn't work out this time, try and learn from your mistakes and give it another go next time. Acting is a competitive industry with lots of rejection, so you need to be resilient.

- Be kind to yourself – if you put time and effort into preparing a speech, made it to the audition, and performed the monologue in front of total strangers, that is an achievement in itself. Well done!

As well as these top tips, there are snappy quotes dotted throughout the book from former NYT members, offering useful advice on how to handle auditions, along with lengthier interviews with the actors who first performed some of the speeches in the original NYT productions. These wise words should give you further inspiration on how you might approach your audition.

When you are using this book – reading the guidance and looking at the speeches, it's worth considering a final piece of advice, which Hamlet gives to the Players before they perform in front of the king in Act Three, Scene Two: 'Let your own discretion be your tutor.'

In other words: 'Follow your instincts and do whatever you feel is right for *you*.' If you don't find something I've said useful – ignore it! This book hasn't been written to tell you exactly what to do, but instead to give you some help and guidance if you're feeling stuck. The most important thing is that you feel that you have enough tools in your kit to be able to go to an audition feeling confident.

Don't worry about saying the right thing in the interview, or about what other people around you are doing; if they're more experienced than you are, or if they've chosen the same speech, none of that matters. What matters is that you enjoy yourself – acting in plays is all about being playful (the clue is in the word!), so try and think of it as the most exhilarating, high-stakes game you can play, and remember that whatever happens, it's not life and death.

And, above all else, be yourself. There's no one in the whole world who is the same as you – you are totally unique, and no one can do 'being you' like you can. So if you've put the work in beforehand, if you can find it within yourself to be brave and honest in the room, and make bold and clear choices in your performance, you'll be able to bring the best version of yourself – and what more can you do than that? Go for it, have fun, and good luck!

Commentary Guidance

Each monologue in this book is accompanied by a commentary that will help you understand the speech out of context. I've provided lots of basic information about the play, who wrote it, when NYT performed it and where it's set, but I've also suggested what the character might want in the speech and a few things to think about.

These notes aren't intended to tell you how to perform the speech, but they offer prompts to help you think about the character and their situation. They are only suggestions, however, so if you decide the character wants something totally different, that is fine – as long as you are being *specific*.

Here is a breakdown of what each section within the commentary contains:

Character Where the age and gender of the character has been supplied by the playwright, these are included here. You can use the information to help you choose a speech, but don't feel you have to portray a character of the same age and gender as you.

Where the playwright hasn't specified an age, I have given a short description of each character to give you an idea of who they are and how old they might be. Not all of the speeches in this book are spoken by characters under the age of twenty-five, but all of them have been performed by NYT members in the past, so you should be able to find enough speeches in here to suit your own playing age. At NYT, we are aware that everyone grows up differently, and just because you are fourteen it doesn't mean that you can't play a part that is older than you are (however, some drama schools will prefer that you pick a speech as close to your own age as possible, so keep this in mind).

Likewise, at NYT we don't mind what gender you identify as, and we are happy for anyone to play any gender. The most important thing to consider is whether the speech is within reach for you, and that you pick a character you feel you can portray truthfully. The top priority is that you connect with the character.

■ **Location** I have given an indication of generally where and when each play is set. If the play is set in another historical period or geographical place, you may want to do some research to find out more about the world in which the character lives.

■ **Accent** If a speech was written to be performed in a specific accent, I have included it here. Sometimes a speech is written in a dialect, which means some of the words in the speech will be specific to that accent. For example, Betty in *The Astronaut Wives Club* says, 'She had a book club and it was *goin' real swell*', and this might sound strange if performed in your own accent. Most of the speeches, however, can be performed in your own accent if you don't feel confident attempting the one described here.

■ **Scene** This section gives a bit of background about where the speech comes in the play, who the character is, and what has prompted them to speak. Having read this section, you should be able to understand each speech the first time you read it – however, it doesn't replace reading the whole play, which is essential if you decide to perform the monologue.

■ **Who is she/he talking to?** It is essential to think about who your character is talking to, and how they are trying to affect that other person or people. And make sure you have thought carefully about how any other character or characters (or the audience) might be receiving the speech.

■ **Where?** This section will give you an idea about the immediate surroundings of the character – whether they are inside or outside and what kind of space they are in – which should help you to imagine their physical world. You may want to think about the difference between someone speaking in a public place (for example, Freddie in *Consensual*) as opposed to a character speaking from a place they know well (like Boy in *Fluffy Rabbit*).

What does she/he want? It will really help you to think about what the character wants, as this will give you the vocal and emotional energy and focus to power through the speech. In this section, I have given several pointers for what I think the character might want, based on a close reading of the play, but don't take my word for it – read the play yourself, and see if you can make some of your own decisions.

Things to think about This section of the commentary gives a few extra hints and tips about how you might go about approaching the speech. I may draw attention to the language the character uses or suggest that you think about how the character changes throughout the speech. This section is designed to get you thinking deeply about the character and how you want to play them, but hopefully you will think of other questions to explore as well.

Where to find the play When you choose a speech, you should always read the entire play that it comes from, which will give you much more information about the character, their intentions, and their world.

Many of the speeches in this book are from plays that have been published, and the publisher's name is given in this section. Plays can be bought from specialist bookshops or online direct from the publisher (where you can often get a discount). When a play hasn't been published, you can access it on the NYT website:

www.nyt.org.uk/monologues
Password: nytspeeches

Exercises

Character lists

As mentioned on page 26, character lists allow you to develop a clear and detailed understanding of the character based on the play.

You can read the whole play, and make a note of the following things:

Facts about the character

The facts are things that you know to be *true* about the character; they can come from a variety of sources, like character descriptions by the author (if there are any), stage directions and things that the character does within the play. Don't worry if you don't find many facts, the most important thing is that they are facts and not opinions that you have come up with.

For example, in Simon Reade's adaptation of *Private Peaceful*, some of the facts about the character of Tommo could include:

- *He lives in Iddesleigh, Devon.*

- *He has two brothers – one called Charlie, one called Big Joe – whom he lives with, along with his mum.*

- *When Tommo doesn't want to go to school, he gets a piggyback from his brother Charlie; he clings on tight and tries not to weep or whimper.*

- *His father was killed in an accident when he saved Tommo from dying by pushing him out of the way of a falling tree, only to be struck himself.*

And so on.

What your character says about themselves

Make sure you are specific; write down exactly what your character says about themselves – and don't paraphrase it. When a character talks about what they think, believe or feel, make sure that you include these observations in your list, as it will help you clarify and understand their point of view. You don't have to write down big sections of text, only the sentences or phrases that are relevant to this list. It is also worth writing down the page number so you can easily go back to the quote if needs be. As with the facts, don't worry if the character doesn't say much about themselves.

- *'I want to feel alive.'* (Act One, Scene One, page 8)
- *'Big Joe is always happy, always laughing. I wish I could be happy like him. I wish I could be at home like him. I don't want to go, Charlie. I don't want to go to school.'* (Act One, Scene Two, page 9)
- *'All I can think is that I've killed my own father.'* (Act One, Scene Four, page 14)
- *'I don't believe in heaven.'* (Act One, Scene Thirteen, page 33)
- *'I'm not sure I ever really believed in God. At church I'd look up at Jesus hanging on the cross and wonder why God, who is supposed to be his father, and almighty and powerful, would let them do that to him, would let him suffer so much.'* (Act One, Scene Thirteen, page 33)

And so on.

What your character says about other people

You can choose to group these quotes either by character (that is, the person your character is describing) or list them in the order that your character says them in the play. You may find that some things go in both the lists above. This is fine as it will enlighten you about both your character and their relationships. Again, don't write down more than you need to, and put a page number next to each one so that you can refer to the context easily.

- About Big Joe: 'Big Joe doesn't have to go to school and I don't think that's fair at all.' (Act One, Scene Two, page 9)

- About Big Joe: 'Big Joe is always happy, always laughing. I wish I could be happy like him. I wish I could be at home like him. I don't want to go, Charlie. I don't want to go to school.' (Act One, Scene Two, page 9)

- About Charlie: 'Whenever you say "honest" Charlie, I know it's not true.' (Act One, Scene Two, page 9)

- About his father: 'Look, Joe: a swallow. It's Father trying to escape. He told us in his next life he'd like to be a bird, so he could fly free wherever he wanted.' (Act One, Scene Four, page 13)

And so on.

What other people say about your character

As with the previous lists, you can choose to organise this by character or by the order in which the quotes appear in the play.

- Grandma Wolf: 'You haven't been brought up properly, you Peaceful children. Your manners are terrible. You don't know right from wrong.' (Act One, Scene Eight, page 24)

- Molly: 'I love you Tommo. I love you both [you and Charlie].' (Act One, Scene Fifteen, page 39)

- Charlie: 'You love her don't you?' (Act One, Scene Seventeen, page 45)

And so on.

Imagery

If the play uses heightened language – such as Lorca's *Blood Wedding* or T. S. Eliot's *Murder in the Cathedral* – make a note if the character uses any imagery or metaphors. In plays like this, whilst the imagery isn't a *fact*, it can give clues to support some of the factual information that you are gathering in the other lists.

45

For example, in *Blood Wedding*, we know that the Bride returns home at the end of the play, distraught at the death of her lover, and in her speech she uses a great deal of imagery that helps us understand her mental state.

- *'Even though I'm mad they can bury me and not a single man will have looked at himself in the whiteness of my breasts.'*
- *'I was a woman burning...'*
- *'Your son was a tiny drop of water...'*
- *'The other one was a dark river, full of branches, that brought to me the sound of its reeds and its soft song.'*
- *'Your son, who was like a child of cold water, and the other one sent hundreds of birds that blocked my path and left frost on the wounds of this poor, withered woman, this girl caressed by fire.'*
- *'The other one's arm dragged me like a wave from the sea, like the butt of a mule, and would always have dragged me, always, always, even if I'd been an old woman and all the sons of your son had tried to hold me down by my hair.'*

The Bride uses these images and words to describe how she feels, not because she's 'feeling a bit poetic', but because no other words will do to encapsulate the way she feels. When she describes herself as a 'woman burning', we come to understand the burning intensity of her feelings for Leonardo, and the constant use of nature imagery helps us understand how primal and essential her feelings are. When we think about translating this imagery into performance, knowing how bold she was to run away with Leonardo, we might think about how alive and instinctive she is.

Depending on how much time you have, you can either read the play once for each list, or you can try and fill in all the lists on one reading.

Once you have made your lists, you can start to try and understand your character better. How do they see themselves? Is their image of themselves different to the way that other people see them? How does what they say about other people help create their worldview? What can you learn about their relationship to the person that they are talking to in the speech? Does their use of imagery tell you anything about their mental state?

Diary accounts

If your character talks about events that have happened in the past, or if they recall specific moments in the speech, try writing a diary account from that day to help you flesh out the details. For example, if you were to perform Sasha's speech from Jane Bodie's *Out of Me*, it might help you to write a diary account from the day that Sasha discovered that her dad was having an affair. If there are facts that you can include from your character lists – in this instance, that it was her birthday, and she was upstairs when she received the text from him – then use them to inform the memory that you create in your ficitonal account. Try and imagine the scene fully and incorporate as much detail as you can about what happened, where the character was, what they felt like, any sensory memories like touch, taste, sight, smell and sound, so that when the character references this moment in the speech, you have fully imagined what this moment felt like.

List of questions

You should now be able to make some decisions about your character based on what the playwright has written, but you may also feel that you need to flesh out the character even more. If your character only appears in this speech, or doesn't feature much in the play, you may not be able to do your lists at all. So here is a list of questions that you may be able to ask yourself about the character:

- What is their name?

- How old are they?

- Where were they born?

- Where do they live?

- What does their room look like?

- Do they have any family? Who?
- Are they in love?
- Who is the most significant person in their life?
- Who was their best friend as a child?
- What makes them happiest in the world?
- What makes them angry?
- When did they last smile, and why?
- When did they last cry, and why?
- Have they ever been in a fight?
- What colour is their hair?
- What colour are their eyes?
- Do they have a birthmark? If so, what and where?
- Do they have any scars? If so, what and where?
- What size are their feet?
- What do they carry in their bag on a day-to-day basis?
- What is in their pocket during the play?
- What is their most prized possession?
- Can you describe their average morning routine?
- Can you describe their routine on the morning of the speech?
- Do they have a nickname – if so, who gave it to them and why?
- If they were an animal, what animal would they be?
- If they were a colour, what colour would they be?
- If they were a song, what song would they be?
- Do they have a motto for life?
- Does your character have any secrets?
- What likeable qualities do they have?

- What qualities might other people find difficult about them?
- Complete the sentence for the character:
    I wish...
    I regret...
    I resent...
    I deny...
    I forgive...
- Can you write a diary entry for the character aged ten?
- Can you write a diary entry for the character the night before the scene that your speech is from?
- What is their superobjective for life?
- What is their objective in the play?
- What is their objective in the scene?
- What do they want in the moment they begin the speech?

As you are answering these questions, try to make sure that your version of the character fits within the world of the play. Why not also try making up your own questions, depending on the character you're playing?

Draw your character

Not everyone is good with words, so if you don't like writing, why don't you try drawing your character? Try to be really detailed about their physical appearance, and don't worry if it's different from yours. If you want to, you can annotate the picture; for example, if your character has a scar, you could describe where they got the scar, or if they have ginger frizzy hair, you might decide that they inherited this from a parent, and you could describe who that is.

You could also try drawing a version of your character, but inside the outline of their body, you could write all of their secrets – everything that they don't readily reveal about themselves. On the outside, around their body, you could write words that describe how they present themselves to the world; for example, if you were choosing to perform Harri from *Pigeon English*, inside the drawing you might write *'I'm in love with Poppy'* or *'I'm scared of X-Fire and the Dell Farm Crew'*, and outside, you might write something like *'I am the man of the house.'*

When you've done this, you could try performing the speech and imagining that these inner thoughts are located in a specific part of your body – so what does it feel like when Harri's secret that he is in love with Poppy lives in his tummy? Or what does it feel like when his feeling that he has to be the 'big man' comes from his chest?

Doing an exercise like this may give a physical specificity to your performance that didn't exist previously.

Character mood board

A character mood board can include a variety of things, but should help to give you a sense of the character's world. Here are a few things you can include:

- Pictures that you've found of people who look like your character.

- Clothes that your character might wear.

- Drawings of your character.

- Pictures of other characters in the play.

- Quotes or phrases from the play that stick out for you (you could take these from your lists).

- Colours that encapsulate a moment or scene within the play.

- Pictures of locations or settings within the play – specifically where the speech is set.

- If the play is set in another time or place, pictures that help evoke that period – these could be adverts, art or clothing.

You don't have to justify your choices, as long as they feel right for you, they will help give you a sense of the world of the character.

2:18 Underground

Laurie Sansom & the NYT company

Devised by Laurie Sansom and the NYT company, *2:18 Underground* was first performed at the Edinburgh Festival Fringe and the Lyric Hammersmith in 1999. Like a lot of NYT's work at the turn of the millennium, the content of the show was devised by the members of the company, using their experiences and imaginations to create the play. *2:18 Underground* presents a Tube carriage full of passengers travelling from King's Cross to Angel and imagines what their lives might be like. On the way it asks big questions about what kind of journeys we all go on as we head towards our final destination.

2:18 Underground contains a wide variety of characters who happen to be on the Northern Line for the same two minutes and eighteen seconds (which is the time it takes to travel by Tube between King's Cross and Angel). It is a weird and wonderful play that jumps from location to location and character to character, dipping into each one's life along the way and often using songs to punctuate the scenes. The character of Robin acts as a kind of conductor throughout the play, introducing other characters, playing games of 'Confessions' with them and encouraging them to tell the audience more about themselves. In the first scene, however, he announces that when the Tube gets to Angel, one of the characters will throw themselves under the next train; so even though the play contains a great deal of humour and some eccentric characters, it is underpinned by a feeling of tension as we begin to imagine which of the characters might be the one who wants to take their own life.

Ariadne

Character A young woman of working age.

Location London, 1999.

Accent Your own.

Scene The play opens with a big ensemble scene where all the characters recreate the ordered chaos of the London Underground with a multitude of people moving in every direction. Ariadne ('Ari') Goodge is the first character we meet in detail. Robin, our narrator, has informed us that she is on her way back to work after an intense lunch with her flatmate, Pat, whom we meet later on the play. In this speech she tells us about her life, where she works – even what she's reading!

Who is she talking to? The audience.

Where? In an imaginary space.

What does she want? Robin has just introduced Ari to the audience, so you first need to think about who the audience might represent for Ari: a close friend? A date? She clearly wants to draw the audience into her world and tell them both about the new stage she's entering in her life, but does she feel comfortable talking to them? Is she embarrassed by any of what she says? Or does she want to impress them?

Things to think about On the surface, Ari seems to be fine, but there might be more going on underneath the surface: for example, what do you think happened when she broke up with John? Is she really fine, or is there more to it than meets the eye?

When you read the play, look for the scene entitled 'Confessions', and find out what Ari says about herself. How might this shed new light on the speech?

Ari tells us all the details of her life: what kind of person do you think she is? See if you can think of three words to describe her.

This isn't a speech in which the character goes on a massive emotional journey so it is important that you bring energy and detail to your performance. It does give you the chance, however, to create a light-hearted, perhaps eccentric character, so think about how you can be both playful and truthful in your characterisation.

There is another speech in the play by Angel, which you may also want to look at.

▨ Where to find the play This play can be read on the NYT website (www.nyt.org.uk/monologues, password: nytspeeches).

Ariadne

Hi, I'm Ari… I work for Tokyo Mitsubishi International plc in the operations department, (so that's product control, P&L* and risk reporting). I'd say that I'm entering a new stage in my life. I think I measure my life in stages.

So at sixteen or seventeen I was going through my rebellious stage – dyed black hair, DM boots and a boyfriend who fancied himself as Axl Rose. He used to pick me up in his Ford Fiesta accompanied by the dulcet tones of 'Paradise City'.

Then Manchester Uni, where I studied business management and accountancy. Hah, wild crazy university years. And then… work. But now I'm entering a new stage in my life. I'm really into art and books. I've just read *An Intimate History of Mankind* by Theodore Zeldin. I'm also really into Yoga classes, and I've also turned minimalist – I went minimalist shopping and bought a bright white sofa and ice-blue ashtrays. The thing is, I've bought so many minimalist things my flat really isn't minimalist any more. I'm also trying to cut down on the amount I drink. Just the odd bottle of New World Chardonnay when I'm trying to relax.

This is my flatmate, Pat. He's an architect, a friend from uni. I didn't actually know him that well before he moved in. I was going to ask him to move out, but after last night that's not really an option. I used to live with Tara but she's just got married. I've now been a bridesmaid four times…

But I'm single. I've just split up with John – totally mutual decision. We're just at different stages. So, yeh, everything's fine.

That's it.

* 'P&L' means Profit and Loss, and refers to the money going in and out of a company.

Character A man with a wife and young child.

Location London, 1999.

Accent Your own.

Scene The audience has encountered Neil in several of the scenes already – for example, in the scene with Oster, Neil says that he is on his way to visit his wife, although he doesn't say why. This speech comes later in the play, after Robin, our narrator, encourages Neil to open up about where he is going and what he is thinking. Neil begins to explain how his wife and child have 'left' him, and he is on his way to see them now; to begin with, we imagine that they are divorced, but gradually it becomes apparent that his wife and child died in a car crash, and he is on his way to visit their graves.

Who is he talking to? The audience.

Where? In an imaginary space.

What does he want? In the first line of the speech, Neil says that he needs someone to help him 'feel again', so in revisiting the incidents that led up to his wife's death, he is trying to reconnect with his emotions. It is clear that Neil feels guilty about what happened, so perhaps he wants to apologise to both of them. Maybe he also wants the audience to tell him that it wasn't his fault, or to understand how sorry he is. Neil might think that if he talks about everything that has happened, it might stir some emotion in him – it might help him to feel.

Things to think about As with all speeches to the audience, it will help you to have an idea about who the audience might represent for Neil – maybe they are just strangers, and he is feeling so low that he will talk to anybody, or perhaps they could represent an old friend; it will help you to think about who they are.

Try and imagine what happened when Neil heard his wife and child were involved in a car crash; where was he when he heard? What happened in the aftermath? How has his life changed since then?

Even though Neil says he cannot feel, there is a great deal of emotion bubbling under the surface; make sure you fully imagine everything that has happened to him.

Be careful not to let the speech become a general wash of depression: are there moments where the pace changes? Think about how Neil changes through the speech.

Where to find the play This play can be read on the NYT website (www.nyt.org.uk/monologues, password: nytspeeches).

Neil

Can somebody help me? Can somebody help me to feel again? Because I can't.

About ten years ago I bought up this grotty little office just off Soho. My wife sorted out all the refurbishments inside, you know, got the place looking really nice. Which was pretty amazing really seeing that she was five months pregnant with our little boy, Daniel. I think things really started to change when I decided to expand the business. With the increase in clients I found myself becoming a bit more ruthless.

Still, I suppose it doesn't matter now. You see, my wife and child, they've – well, they've left me now.

It was Sunday, and my little boy kept on asking me to play football with him. 'No.' I was too busy with work. I told my wife to take him to the park. They wanted to walk but I told them to take the car. I told them to take the car.

(*He watches the crash.*)

I didn't buy another car, after that. I take the Tube these days, or I walk. I haven't been to visit them since the crash. There's a woman on the Tube today who reminds me a little bit of my wife and there's a little boy sitting next to her. I've been staring at them since King's Cross. They probably think I'm really weird.

Can someone help me, please? Can somebody help me to feel? Because I can't. I just can't.

The Astronaut Wives Club

Al Smith

The Astronaut Wives Club was first staged at Soho Theatre in 2006 as part of the fiftieth anniversary Sextet season. The Sextet season comprised six new commissions to celebrate the NYT's golden jubilee year, each focusing on a different decade ranging from the '50s up to the '00s. Al Smith's play imagines a fictional meeting in the 1970s between a group of women who existed in real life and were known as 'The Astronaut Wives Club'.

It's a summer afternoon in Florida, 1971, and the 'Astronaut Wives Club' has assembled in Sandra Wilder's back garden. Sandra is the young fiancée of NASA astronaut Alfred Worden, who is currently on the Apollo 15 mission orbiting the moon, and the women have assembled to support Sandra through this tense time. The play begins at a nerve-racking moment when Apollo 15 has travelled to the dark side of the moon and lost radio contact. As the women wait for the spacecraft to regain radio contact, the conversation between them becomes fraught and tensions begin to bubble – not least because NASA rules state that astronauts must be married in order to go on a mission, and Alfred divorced his previous wife to be with Sandra. Mary Engle, the glamorous wife of Joe Engle, finds this particularly maddening, as Alfred was chosen for the mission over her own husband. Subtle power games and barbed exchanges turn into full-blown arguments when Mary is challenged about her status within the group – her husband having never been to space – and she storms out in a fit of rage.

Betty Grissom

Character An older woman, widowed.

Location Florida, 1971.

Accent American.

Scene This speech comes at the end of the play, immediately after Mary Engle's speech (page 62). At the start of the play, Betty seems to be warm and softhearted, but as the action progresses she begins to show her inner strength, challenging Mary Engle's bullying behaviour, which prompts Mary's dramatic exit at the play's climax. The women are left in stunned silence, when Betty begins to tell a story which at first seems to come from nowhere. Gradually, however, she reveals how her husband died in a cockpit fire four years earlier, and talks about the deep sacrifices she made to be the wife of an astronaut. Her sunny attitude early in the play quickly transforms as she lays bare the scars of losing her husband.

Who is she talking to? The five women who are left.

Where? Sandra's garden.

What does she want? In her speech, Betty says that she started the group, so perhaps she wants to show her status to the other women. She tells the story of when her husband died and she wants the other women to understand how deeply this hurts. But does this mean that she wants sympathy? Does she want the women to respect her because she has had to make the ultimate sacrifice? Or does she want to shock the women into realising that being an astronaut's wife is an empty, hollow occupation? Maybe she wants them to understand that it is the *wives* of astronauts who have to be truly strong to deal with the uncertainty and danger of their husbands' professions.

Things to think about Betty's speech is written in an American idiom. Do you want to perform it in an American accent, or do you want to perform it in your own accent?

Although Betty is much older, don't feel that you have to do an impression of an older person; instead, let the speech come to life by connecting with her situation and emotion.

Throughout the play Betty has been drinking Scotch – what might this tell us about her character?

Betty is telling a story that has a deep emotional connection to her past; make sure you think not only about how this affects her, but also about where she is and who she is talking to. Why is she telling the other women this story? How might the situation she's in affect how she tells the story? How does she want to make *them* feel?

Where to find the play This play can be read on the NYT website (www.nyt.org.uk/monologues, password: nytspeeches).

Betty Grissom

I was over at Joan Aldrin's place – she had a book club and it was goin' real swell – we was readin' *Up the Down Staircase* – real good book, I really liked it. (*Beat.*) Annie Glenn was there, Nancy Conrad – we'd all been old pals since we started the club – our men bein' the Original Seven and all. We'd finished up, and just as I got to the door, I saw the pastor's car pull up – big thing, cranky old Buick, real well shined. (*Beat.*) And you know the feelin' girls? We'd all seen that car pull up outside them houses down at Patterson Wright and Pax River so many times – we all knew what it meant but up until then we'd never been burnt. (*Beat.*) Here's the pastor all rolled up, and I watch through the netting as he gets out, and walks up the path. I look back at Joan, she ain't seen 'im comin', so I go over to take her hand, to sit her down for what's next. Annie's opened the door and let him in. (*Beat.*) He looked at us, looked at us all, and said my name. Betty Grissom. (*Beat.*) Just then, Deke telephoned – must've figured out where I was. Pastor sat with me as Deke told me the news. Nice thing 'bout Deke is he'll always give it to ya straight. 'Roger Chaffe, Ed White and Gus'd been testing the rockets on the launch pad' he said, 'there's been a fire. A fire in the cockpit', he said, 'a real intense fire and Gus is dead, they're all dead.' (*Beat.*) He said it couldn't have lasted more than a half minute. A half minute. (*Beat.*) Later on, I found out that Deke had heard it all over the intercom. All of it. Says he screamed my name. (*Pause. The telephone starts to ring. Sandra gets up to go.*) Don't hope for fairness girls – there's no such thing. We all get abandoned, we all do. What part can you or I play in getting a man to the Moon and back? Nothin'. (*Beat.*) What you're here for is to soften the blow when he falls back to Earth. So sit back, let 'em fire him into the arms of his mistress, and hope you can welcome him, with wide smiles and open arms, when he comes crawling home out of the night.

Mary Engle

■ **Character** A young woman, new to the club.

■ **Location** Florida, 1971.

■ **Accent** American.

■ **Scene** This speech comes at the climax of the play when Mary Engle cannot contain her frustration any longer. As she lets rip, we discover why she has been treating Sandra with such contempt throughout the play – she believes it should have been her husband on Apollo 15 and not Alfred, as he and Sandra are not married, which should have stopped him from going into space under NASA's rules.

■ **Who is she talking to?** There are six other women with Mary and in this speech she is addressing all of them.

■ **Where?** In Sandra's back garden.

■ **What does she want?** Ultimately Mary wants the status of being an astronaut's wife; she has stuck by her husband (despite his cheating) for fifteen years, and feels she has been denied the respect that comes with having a husband who has gone into space. This, however, won't happen, so she also wants to undermine Sandra, to insult her and belittle her, and for the other women to understand how unfairly she has been treated. As the speech reaches its climax, she desperately wants to reclaim some self-respect from the situation.

■ **Things to think about** When Engle first arrives, she is angry that no one told her that her hair was out of place – she is a woman who cares about how she looks and the image she presents to the world; how might you communicate this physically?

To whom does she direct the speech? Sandra? All of the women?

See if you can be specific about which sections she says to whom.

How long has it taken Mary to get this angry? From the moment she arrives in the play? Even longer? This will inform the strength of feeling in your performance.

Unusually, this character is based on a real person; can you find pictures of her online or pictures of other women from the time to help you imagine how the character might look?

The speech is written in an American idiom, so decide if you want to perform it with the accent.

Where to find the play This play can be read on the NYT website (www.nyt.org.uk/monologues, password: nytspeeches).

Mary Engle

The hell I'm not! Take a good hard look at her, girls. She's right in front of your eyes, runnin' all over your territory, and you caint even see it. You've all got Air Force Marriages, you all should know the rules.

That no unmarried man goes into Space, Sandra. No unmarried man! The number one prerequisite for astronaut selection, girls – no unmarried man – they can't fly without us. Had they stuck to that rule, this tart and her fella'd be outta the picture, and my Joe'd be on the Moon.

Would you really have spent fifteen years of your life tagged onto those cheating assholes if you knew that come the chance for lift-off they'd change the goddamn rules and send 'em up anyways?! It's bad enough that we all know what goes on, but to bring it home? These are our fucking homes, girls! She opens her legs in some goddamn bar, and we open up our arms for her. No unmarried man, Marilyn, what the hell happened to that rule?! (*Clearly.*) He left Pammy for this hooker and they gave him his ride anyway! This whole thing's a fuckin' car-wreck and she's sittin' right in front of you, huh? It's a betrayal of absolutely fuckin' everything, *absolutely everything*!! Fifteen years girls! You didn't go livin' in some shitty tract home washin' his goddamn jocks and smilin' for *Life* and *Time* just to see yourself cut out when he finally gets his ride, did you?! Well neither the hell did I! Call yourselves women, where's your damned self-respect!

Who gives a shit if he never comes back. (*To Mary and Lurton.*) I'm sorry girls. (*She leaves.*)

Balls

Sarah Solemani

Balls was performed as part of the double bill *Eye/Balls* at Soho Theatre in 2009. Set in Dublin, *Balls* is a funny, provocative play that explores the intertwined love lives of a group of friends on a stag weekend.

When the play opens, Simon and his mates are getting ready to go on his stag-do to Dublin, but what he doesn't know is that his fiancée, Tess, and two of her best friends are planning to follow them so that Tess can keep an eye on her husband-to-be. As the play progresses, a web of past relationships are unearthed and the characters become more and more entangled in each other's lives until it reaches a crescendo in a strip club called 'The Tobacco Drum'.

Carly

Character A young woman on holiday with her friends.

Location Present-day Ireland.

Accent Your own.

Scene Tess has arrived in Dublin with her two friends Carly and Jess. They are standing on a street corner and Tess is spying on Simon and the 'stags' through the window of a Travelodge using binoculars. The three girls have been there for a while, and as boredom sets in, Carly and Jess suggest that instead of spying on Simon they should go and explore Dublin. Carly then reveals that she has never been out of London before and tells of the time as a young girl when she was about to go on holiday with her mum, only for the police to arrive and charge her mum with shoplifting before having her sectioned, and taking her into psychiatric care.

Who is she talking to? Her two friends, Tess and Jess.

Where? On a street corner in Dublin.

What does she want? The speech comes out of nowhere – a few seconds before, Carly has been describing the intimate details of waxing bikini lines. To begin with, Tess and Jess presume this will just be an amusing story about an awful family holiday, and so the tragic end to the speech is unexpected. Carly starts to tell the story in order to justify why she wants to explore the city, but by the end, she has inadvertently revealed to her friends the reason she grew up living with her nan.

Things to think about Part of the joy of the speech is how understated it is. Enjoy playing with the contrast between the serious content of the speech, and Carly's light-hearted attitude.

Despite the subject matter, Carly is not overly dramatic about the way she tells the story – a few seconds afterwards she begins flirting with Danny, a strip club owner who jeers at them on the street. But how is she different at the end of the speech from the beginning?

Does Carly know that she is going to tell the whole story when she begins talking?

See if you can picture the scene when the police arrive in detail in your head: how old was she? What did/does she think of 'Steve'? Where was she when the police knocked on the door? How did she feel when the police took her in for questioning?

■ **Where to find the play** This play can be read on the NYT website (www.nyt.org.uk/monologues, password: nytspeeches).

Carly

I'd quite like to see a bit of Dublin while I'm here. I've never been out of London before.

Well there was one time, before I lived with my nan, my mum booked a holiday to Spain. I was so excited, finally, I could use the swimming costume with an inflatable ring built in so I wouldn't drown. My nan had bought it years before when we were going to Southend but had to cancel at the last minute. I kept it under my bed. It was pink with little skull and crossbones. Mum wasn't sure if Steve was coming, he'd been coming and going for a while but had been going a lot so more we knew not to rely on him. She was so excited. She'd cleaned out the fridge and bought these special wipes you use for your hands before you eat fruit. She'd braided my hair for my passport photos so we were all set. Then the morning before we were due to fly, the community police officer came round to the flat. Said Mum had been seen on CCTV putting economy nappies in her duffel coat. She denied it, told them to go, said we had a flight to catch to Spain and her daughter hadn't been out of London before and anyway if she had gone to the trouble of shoplifting, it certainly wouldn't have been economy nappies. They didn't listen, they said she'd been caught on CCTV in another shop putting tins of puréed beef in her purse. She denied it but they pulled out a warrant. Sure enough, under her bed was this stash, not just nappies, puréed foods, but toys, talcum powder and a second-hand safety gate.

She couldn't explain it. She just said it was an outrage how expensive things for babies are. She said nappies should be free on the NHS.

She wasn't very well. They took her off for questioning and then thought it'd be for the best if she rested, you know, with people to look after her. After that I moved in with my nan. We never got to go away.

Lauren O'Rourke played the part of Carly in the Soho Theatre production of *Balls* in 2009, and she currently works as an actress. Screen roles include *The Inbetweeners Movie* (Film 4), *Drifters* (E4), *Miranda* (BBC), *This is England '90* (Channel 4) and *White Gold* (BBC 2).

If you could give one piece of advice about auditions, what would it be?

Prepare, prepare, prepare, and then be yourself. Auditions can be terrifying! The last thing you want is to be worrying if you know your lines! If you have prepared, the lines will be in there, then you can relax. However, an audition is not a memory test so don't worry if you do slip up. Being yourself is also so important, so always show who you really are!

What is your abiding memory of NYT?

Performing at Soho Theatre in London. My first run in a professional theatre! I felt like a fraud! It was such an amazing experience, and made me realise that this is what I had to do for a living. I still walk past that theatre sometimes and remember the buzz I would have every night. I will also always remember the great people I met and worked with – friends for life! It provided a network of young people in the same industry who I can still always turn to for advice.

How did NYT affect your future life and career?

Without NYT I would not have a career. It opened doors for me. I never even dreamed that being an actress was an option – that happened to other people. It made me realise that I did have a knack for performing, something I was good at. There wasn't a lot of opportunities for me when I was younger living in Birmingham, but NYT gave me access to them! I met great people in NYT who have always helped and guided me along my way. I always think how different life would be had I not applied.

Besieged: A Play About War and the Everyday

Aisha Zia

Presented alongside *Ripple* at the Arcola Theatre in 2016, *Besieged* is a vivid and mercurial play by Aisha Zia, which explores the way that war penetrates our everyday lives. This ranges from the small conflicts in day-to-day decision making, to an image of London as a war-torn battleground.

Besieged doesn't stick to a single narrative but follows multiple characters through their lives as they try to make sense of the modern world; from Pete and Jenny, a couple who exist in a mist of hopelessness and inactivity, to Kaz and Anna, who cannot agree about whether or not education will help them achieve their life goals. It is divided into three acts named: 'I Am', 'Fear' and 'The Siege'. In 'I Am', the named characters (along with a nameless ensemble) go through their repetitive daily routines; in 'Fear' the play bombards us with voices telling us of their fears for the future; then in the final act, 'The Siege', war has come to London, and the cast have to battle through to find meaning and hope in a cruel world.

Anna

Character A young woman of unspecified age.

Location London, present day.

Accent Anna is not from Britain, but it is not specified where she is from, so her accent is up to you.

Scene Anna appears throughout the play, so there are clues about what she is like as a character, but this speech stands alone as a window into her life. This speech appears in 'I Am' (Act One). Anna is on the streets in London, talking to an ensemble member about how she has travelled to London with her mother. In an almost dream-like fashion, she describes parts of her life: at the beginning she talks of going to the park and the distress of losing sight of her mother as she plays; later she describes her mother's disgust at the relationships Anna has with men. The play is often ambiguous, leaving us to fill in the gaps with meaning and intention, and in this speech it is unclear exactly when these incidents have happened. What is clear is that Anna is a complex and intense character who is trying to discover where in the world she fits in.

Who is she talking to? A member of the ensemble. It is up to you to decide who you want this to be: is it someone she knows well? Or a stranger?

Where? On the streets of London, but it is up to you to decide where. Is it a public place, or somewhere secluded? What time of year is it? Is it night or day?

What does she want? It is not immediately clear what Anna wants; much will depend on who you think she is talking to. Anna is very direct and open in the speech, so maybe she wants whomever she is talking to to understand exactly what her life is like. At the end of the speech Anna says that she is alone, so maybe she wants some company and to feel less lonely. Perhaps she also wants her behaviour to be recognised and approved, and in turn she wants to hurt her mother.

■ **Things to think about** You will have to make a lot of decisions about where the character is and what they are doing in this speech – remember that it's fine to keep it simple.

In the first scene, Anna says that she forces herself to be late for things. What clues might this give us about her character? Is she bold? Is she trying to be cool? Does she want to be noticed?

The stage direction says that Anna is on the street – is she homeless? What kind of quality would speaking in the street give to the speech? Alternatively you could ignore this stage direction and imagine she is in a private space.

Try and be specific about the different incidents she describes: is she talking about specific memories? Is she talking about dreams? Is she making any of it up?

In Act Two Scene One, Anna screams 'I need to be loved' twice. How might this inform your understanding of the speech presented here?

This speech is quite long – you may need to cut some lines to fit into the time limit.

■ **Where to find the play** This play can be read on the NYT website (www.nyt.org.uk/monologues, password: nytspeeches).

Anna

No. No I'm not. I'm not from here. I travelled. With my mother. From another place. From far away. Some place different. Some place old. Some place. I don't know.

And I hate her. At home I hate her.

And she doesn't know yet. I'm so tired. We go to the park and there's a slide. I go on it. I get to the top, I slide down, but there's no one there at the bottom. I look around and there's no one. – I can see the trees and the breeze shakes the leaves, it's autumn, I can feel that. I can feel the seasons changing, just so naturally, but my mother isn't there. I feel the breeze and I feel. I just feel for a second. With no one there.

What? Where are you? Mum?

I call in the dark. Mum! Mum! But she can't see me. I don't know why. I think it's because of what I'm wearing, my denim shorts, or because I cut my hair too short, it could be my blue mascara or the red lipstick, smudged. I'm crying. Still calling but she looks away. And there's a lot of traffic now. As I get older.

Books, cars, boys.

The boys especially, she doesn't get. I fuck them. And I enjoy it. Mum hates that. She's never going to get it. And I like it. They like it too. Mum does not like that. Black. White. Jewish. I don't judge love. Class. Just go out, get on, and go for it. The one. Stupid. On the dance floor. In the bar. I'm dancing, in my bra. And I'm smiling. Dancing, with some boy.

(*Dancing.*)

'Show some respect!' She says. And she's there. At the bar.

I love him. I say. I love him. And she drags me home by the hair; she pulls me by the bra. In front of everyone, I'm humiliated.

We're so different now. We don't even speak any more. I'm not from here.

We look the same, my mother and I. The same round face, the same soft brow the same hair. Brown eyes, five foot six inches, size seven feet but.

No respect.

And she hates me. She hates me.

We don't see each other.

And I'm alone.

Helen Mirren

Use your wonderful youth and who you are. A lot of the time you can look at other actors and go: 'They're so brilliant at doing that, why can't I do that?' But you are a complete individual and there's no one else on the planet like you. You by nature of being you will make it your own, so just believe in that and let that happen.

Black & White

Al Smith

Black & White was first performed by the pilot NYT REP company in 2012. It was written by Al Smith in response to the phone-hacking scandal at the *News of the World* and the subsequent Leveson inquiry that followed in 2012. Just as the public inquiry sought to scrutinise and challenge the culture, practices and ethics of the British media, *Black & White* examines the lives of five young journalists and asked what lengths will reporters go to for a story, and post-Leveson, has anything changed?

The play begins in the 'Cub Reporter Room' of the *Sunday Sun*, a dingy, windowless office, occupied by five aspiring journalists all competing for a junior post at the paper. The characters include Tash and Levi, who were the co-editors of the Cambridge University paper and are looking for their first professional gig; Matt, a junior showbiz reporter for the *Yeovil Standard* who has his sights set higher; and Corrina, who currently writes for her parish magazine. In the first scene they are all told by Bella, who works for the *Sun*, that whoever presents the most 'newsworthy' story to the editor by the end of the week will be hired. We then follow each character as they test their moral boundaries in pursuit of the most salacious story.

Corrina

Character A nineteen-year-old woman.

Location London, 2012.

Accent Your own.

Scene As the play unfolds, several of the characters push the boundaries to get their story – Tash sleeps with a politician's son to unearth some damaging secrets, and Matt rummages through Pippa Middleton's bin bags to dig up some dirt – but Corrina seems to be quite different. Described as an Alpha Christian, she finds the lengths that her competitors go to deplorable. As the end of the week closes in, however, Corrina starts to realise that perhaps she wants this job more than she thought, and, after wrestling with her conscience, she uses the disappearance of a friend as the subject for her story. This speech is her pitch to the editor, right at the end of the play, and in it she attempts to justify using her inside knowledge about her friend's possible abduction to further her career by recounting a parable she has heard about a Babylonian king who can prove that the difference between black and white is just a matter of perspective.

Who is she talking to? The editor of the *Sunday Sun*.

Where? In the editor's office.

What does she want? The fact that Corrina has decided to pitch the story of her missing friend suggests that what she really wants is a job at the *Sunday Sun*. So she wants to impress the editor, and convince them that she is the best candidate. There's more going on in this speech, however: she also wants to tell the story of the painted wall in order to ease her sense of guilt. She wants to convince herself that exploiting her friend is not immoral – that it is in fact a reasonable course of action.

■ Things to think about At first this speech can seem a little strange; she seems to be telling a random, irrelevant story about an ancient king. But think carefully about why she is telling this story, and how it relates to her, both in terms of her religious beliefs and her friendship.

Think about the pressure of this moment – Corrina feels that her career as a journalist hangs on this moment. She is in the editor's office, and only has a few minutes to prove herself.

How do you think the editor reacts to the parable she tells? Make sure she is trying to convince and persuade the editor with her pitch.

Look up the 'Alpha course' (the type of Christianity Corrina follows) so you can understand the importance of her moral sensibility.

■ Where to find the play This play can be read on the NYT website (www.nyt.org.uk/monologues, password: nytspeeches).

Corrina

Father Angus... gave this sermon once. He started with a question. A kid in our parish had been stabbed. He didn't die or anything, he was okay, but it kicked up a lot of fuss – was right to. Kid who got stabbed was white, kid who did the stabbing was black and there's a lot of tension that way where I'm from. They all gather in the church the families, one side black, the other white, and he gives this sermon. He talks of a painter in Babylon who told the king he could prove there was no difference between black and white. He paints a wall a mile long, at one end jet black, at the other, bright white with every colour from one to the other perfectly blended from left to right. The king comes to the wall and laughs at him. He can see every colour in the spectrum. And then the painter pulls out a board, this big. (*Holds out her arms wide.*) Two holes are cut out of it, one on the left, one on the right. He places it up against the deepest black of the wall and asks the king to tell him if there's a difference between the colours in the two holes. No. No difference. The painter then moves the board a metre along, so the hole on the left is now over where the hole in the right was, and the hole on the right's now moved a metre further down the wall. He asks again. Any difference? Again, the king says no, cos the relative change is nothing. He repeats this all the way down the wall – it takes him the whole day, but not once does the king see any difference between the colours he can see in through the board. Eventually they get to White and the painter's proved it's exactly the same as Black. (*Beat.*) It's just... how you look at it. (*Beat.*) I have a friend who's gone missing. She's not been seen for a week, I think she's dead. A week ago, I would have told you she was off limits. Be wrong to sell a story about a friend. Now? I can't tell the difference. It's not that I don't know the difference, it's just I can explain it away. It's just how I look at it. She is a story. She'll make me a bright future. She's not gonna have one, so what's so bad about making something of the loss? She'll put me on the map. In black and white.

Blood Wedding

Federico García Lorca
translated by Gwynne Edwards

Originally written in Spanish by Lorca in 1932, this translation by Gwynne Edwards was performed by NYT at the Bloomsbury Theatre in 1991. It is inspired by the true story of a young woman running off with her cousin moments before she was about to get married, and the tragic events that followed. Set in rural Spain in the early twentieth century, Lorca's modernist play is steeped in myth, folk music and poetry, and offers us a rich and stylised drama that explores the depths of human emotion.

Blood Wedding centres on a wedding between two characters simply called Bridegroom and Bride. At the beginning of the play, the Mother of the Bridegroom is lamenting the murder of her husband and her other son at the hands of the Felix family. In the same scene, the Mother says that whilst she is happy at the prospect of the wedding (and the future prospect of grandchildren), a seed of doubt is sowed when she discovers from a neighbour that the Bride had a previous lover – Leonardo Felix. In the second act of the play it gradually becomes clear that the Bride is still in love with Leonardo, and no matter how hard she tries to honour her engagement to the Bridegroom, she elopes with Leonardo on her wedding day. In the third act, when their disappearance is discovered, a search party is sent out which results in both Leonardo and the Bridegroom being killed in a fight. The Bride returns home, distraught at the death of both men.

Bride

▪ **Character** A young woman of unspecified age.

▪ **Location** Spain.

▪ **Accent** Your own.

▪ **Scene** The Bride's speech happens in the final scene of the play. She has returned to the village, covered in the blood of her husband and her lover, and she attempts to assert her honour by convincing everyone that she is still 'pure', she didn't sleep with either man, and if they kill her she will die with her honour intact.

▪ **Who is she talking to?** Her mother-in-law.

▪ **Where?** In a church.

▪ **What does she want?** Bride is in a state of emotional turmoil; Leonardo, the man she passionately desired, has been killed, as has the Bridegroom, who she knew would be a good husband but whom she didn't love. She is in a desperate situation; she wants her mother-in-law to recognise that she felt powerless to resist Leonardo, but also that she knows her behaviour was wrong. She says that she wants to be killed for what she has done, but before that happens she wants recognition that she didn't act maliciously, and that she is pure.

▪ **Things to think about** The Bride has just travelled a long way – think about the energy that this will bring to the speech.

Think carefully about how the Bride changes throughout the speech: where does she feel sorry for what has happened, and where is she defiant? She wants both to submit herself for sacrifice, but also to be respected by the mother-in-law, so try to explore the full range of the speech.

This is a speech that contains rich, poetic imagery; make sure you don't fall into performing in a generally *romantic* way. Each image should feel fresh-minted, as if this is the only way she can truly express the way she feels.

The stakes in this speech are incredibly high; the Bride is ready to die for what she has done, so think about how you will access this level of emotion in an audition situation.

There are several translations of *Blood Wedding*; you might like to look at how this speech varies in different versions.

■ **Where to find the play** This play is published by Methuen Drama, an imprint of Bloomsbury Publishing Plc (www.bloomsbury.com).

Bride

(*To the Neighbour.*) Leave her. I came so that she could kill me, so that they could bear me away with them. (*To the Mother.*) But not with their hands; with iron hooks, with a sickle, and with a force that will break it on my bones. Leave her! I want her to know that I'm clean, that even though I'm mad they can bury me and not a single man will have looked at himself in the whiteness of my breasts.

Because I went off with the other one! I went! (*In anguish.*) You would have gone too. I was a woman burning, full of pain inside and out, and your son was a tiny drop of water that I hoped would give me children, land, health; but the other one was a dark river, full of branches, that brought to me the sound of its reeds and its soft song. And I was going with your son, who was like a child of cold water, and the other one sent hundreds of birds that blocked my path and left frost on the wounds of this poor, withered woman, this girl caressed by fire. I didn't want to, listen to me! I didn't want to! Your son was my ambition and I haven't deceived him, but the other one's arm dragged me like a wave from the sea, like the butt of a mule, and would always have dragged me, always, always, even if I'd been an old woman and all the sons of your son had tried to hold me down by my hair.

Blue Moon Over Poplar

Rebecca Lenkiewicz

Blue Moon Over Poplar was part of the Sextet season of plays performed at Soho Theatre in 2006. The Sextet season comprised six new commissions to celebrate the NYT's golden jubilee year, each focusing on a different decade ranging from the 1950s up to the 2000s. Rebecca Lenkiewicz's play is set in 1955, when the idea of the 'teenager' was a relatively new concept and young people were finding new ways to express themselves. The Teddy Boy/Girl style, which features in the play, was a working-class movement that combined Edwardian tailoring with American Rock 'n' Roll hairstyles and a rebellious attitude.

The play gives us a snapshot of the lives of a group of Teddy Boys/Girls in 1955, specifically Judy and her twin brother, Peter, who are part of the post-war generation that were beginning to explore changes in fashion and sexual freedom. Peter is a wannabe-intellectual with a tortured soul who is seen as a heart-throb to several of Judy's friends, even though he teases and taunts them. When he encounters a Jamaican immigrant named Margaret, however, his attitude changes and a more caring side comes out. But it is his relationship with his sister, Judy, which has the greatest hold over him; as he becomes more and more confused about his feelings for both women, his behaviour leads to potentially disastrous consequences.

Peter

■ **Character** A young man in his late teens.

■ **Location** London, in 1955.

■ **Accent** London or your own.

■ **Scene** After dancing together at the Four Feathers club, Peter and Margaret have gone outside to get some air. Peter fancies Margaret and has been flirting with her for a while, and soon they start to talk about their respective families. Margaret asks Peter about his brother, Eddie, who died a year ago, and Peter begins to tell her that although his family said Eddie died in his sleep, he actually committed suicide. As he talks, Peter begins to open up about how much his brother's death affected him, and how angry he is with the people that caused it.

■ **Who is he talking to?** Margaret.

■ **Where?** In the wreckage of a bombsite.

■ **What does he want?** At the beginning of the scene, it seems like Peter wants to kiss Margaret, but when he starts to talk about his brother, his objective changes. He wants to set the record straight about what caused his death, and let Margaret know how unjust it was. He also wants Margaret to see how noble and good Eddie was. Perhaps this is also a bit of a confession for Peter; through opening up about Eddie's suicide and the effect it had on him, he's justifying his own messed-up behaviour.

■ **Things to think about** At the beginning of the scene he is trying to woo Margaret; why does he begin to tell her this incredibly personal story – something that very few people know? Is he expecting to tell it? Maybe he has surprised himself?

Do you think he tells this story to many people? Why does he tell Margaret about it now?

Does he really want to kill his father? How hard is it for him to say that he does?

It is night time in this scene – what time of year do you think it is? A cold winter night or a hot summer one? How might this inform your performance?

■ **Where to find the play** This play can be read on the NYT website (www.nyt.org.uk/monologues, password: nytspeeches).

Peter

They told everyone Eddie died peacefully in his sleep. But he wasn't ill and he didn't die peacefully. Which is ironic really. Cos he was the most gentle guy you could ever wish to meet. He was a lot older than me and Jude. Eighteen when the war started. He got called up. And he told them he wouldn't fight.

So they said fair enough, do something else. For the war effort. But he said no. He wanted nothing to do with it. So he did time instead.

He came out. Okay. Bit battered and bruised by it all but still in one piece. Quieter. His girl had gone off with another guy. Fair enough. He could cope with that. But everything else you know. Mainly my old dad. He was so ashamed. Refused to walk down the street with him. Nine years he tried to live a normal life. Couldn't get the jobs he wanted because of what he'd done and couldn't hold the rubbish ones down for long cos of the other blokes. And all because he didn't want to put a bullet through another man's mind.

He just sort of faded away. Became invisible. Ended it all when everyone was out one Monday afternoon. Wrote me a note. And Judy. And one to my mum and dad. Weak heart they told the neighbours. Truth is he had a strong heart. Too strong. I'd like to kill the scum who made his life a misery. Especially my old dad. That's evil isn't it? Patricide.

Come on. I'll walk you to the trolley bus.

Mark Finbow was a member of NYT from 2003 to 2006. He played Peter in *Blue Moon Over Poplar* in 2005 as well as being involved in several other productions. He now runs The Keeper's Daughter, a drama school in Diss, Norfolk, and is also a freelance writer/director.

How did you prepare for the part of Peter?

I seem to remember Paul Roseby, the director, gave me a lot of freedom. My portrayal of Peter ended up somewhere between Jagger, Travolta and Boycie [from *Only Fools and Horses*]! I actually still have the script and it has incoherent scribbles all over it. It seems I wrote a lot.

What advice would you give a young actor playing Peter?

You can't hold back. You have to completely let your barriers down. Peter will give his opinion no matter who's listening – even if no one's listening. He's like a stand-up, but his bravado is all a front, of course. And this is a key moment where he lets his guard down.

If you could give one piece of advice about auditions, what would it be?

Prepare. Prepare. Prepare. But don't over-prepare!

What is your abiding memory of NYT?

An adventure. And friendship. I got to know lots of amazing people.

Shirley

■ **Character** A young woman in her late teens.

■ **Location** London, in 1955.

■ **Accent** London or your own.

■ **Scene** Shirley is also part of the gang, but she is much sassier than the others and is willing to challenge Peter's politics; for example, when he doesn't consider women's rights to be important. Throughout the play Shirley seems like a strong, independent woman until she breaks down in tears at the Four Feathers club. When Betty goes after her, the audience discovers a painful secret about Shirley's past that haunts her every day.

Shirley has run into the toilets of the club in tears and locked herself in the cubicle after overhearing Pat talking about how she doesn't want to have children. Betty knows that Shirley is upset because she had to give her baby up for adoption, and she says that she wants to try and make her feel better. Shirley begins to open up about what happened when she was forced to give up the baby and how desolate she feels now.

■ **Who is she talking to?** Betty.

■ **Where?** In the ladies' toilet of a nightclub.

■ **What does she want?** Shirley is full of conflicting emotions in this speech: she wants to punish herself for what she did, but she wants to connect to the memory of her son, to connect to the love she felt. Perhaps part of her wants to excuse what she has done – she has already seen that Betty is sympathetic to her, so she tries to convince Betty that she regrets her decision. She wants Betty to know that she did love her child, and that she didn't give him away because she was callous.

Things to think about Shirley probably plays this memory out every day in her head; make sure you can vividly see, smell, hear and feel everything that she talks about.

Think about the depth of feeling and emotion that Shirley is going through. In the rest of the play she is confident and assertive, but in this moment the floodgates open and she becomes vulnerable and raw.

Think about where she is: do you want to stage the monologue in the semi-public space of a toilets, or do you want to place it in a private space?

The play mentions lots of different songs; try listening to them to get into the world of the characters.

Where to find the play This play can be read on the NYT website (www.nyt.org.uk/monologues, password: nytspeeches).

Shirley

Giving's such a nice thing to do innit? For normal people. You give someone presents. Your dad gives you away at your wedding. But to give a child away. That's something quite particular isn't it? Unnatural.

He was ever so beautiful.

Funny little chin and neck he had. Like a drunk. All red and wrinkled. Fucking beautiful.

His eyes… I knew I'd only have seconds. I had to imprint him. On me. Ever so quick. And I did. And he'll never go away. Not from here.

They never let me hold him. He'd been with me all that time. Getting bigger. First time he moved was the most exciting thing. I used to touch my belly at night and talk to him when he was kicking about. Little chats. And all I wanted to do when he came out was hold him. Just for a bit. Just to say goodbye. 'None of that,' they said. And I cried so hard. So loud that the nurse said she'd slap me if I carried on. Looked the type that would too.

I couldn't stop. So I put my head into the pillow and screamed into it. My mouth was so wide it ached. Pillowcase stank of TCP and I wished the smell would kill me. That I could smother myself.

I miss him. I really miss him. Didn't even know him, but it feels as if someone's cut half my body away. I thought it would get easier. But it doesn't. It just gets worse. Every day. Sorry Bet. Sorry.

Jo Cassidy played the part of Shirley at Soho Theatre in 2006. Jo was in a number shows with NYT, and after working for several years as an actor on both stage and screen in shows like *Endeavour* (ITV), *Pete Versus Life* (Channel 4) and *Holby City* (BBC), Jo now works at The Grand Theatre in Blackpool, and is currently studying for a PhD in Drama Therapy.

How did you prepare for the part of Shirley?

I initially spoke to my grandparents who were brought up in the East End of London. They were a little older than the Teddy Girl I was playing but they still gave me some fabulous insights. Then, I did lots of research and kept pictures and news articles with me at all times in the rehearsal space.

What advice would you give a young actor playing Shirley?

I felt a strong connection to Shirley. She was a girl who was constantly playing tough but inside was so vulnerable and alone. She had to give up a child because society at the time told her to. The line 'They wouldn't let me hold him' has always stayed with me, even after all this time. I thought about what that would actually be like: how does a teenager process and deal with something like that? Finally, I would say, treat the facts playwright has given you as the foundations of the part, but decorate the 'house' with the rest of your own experiences.

If you could give one piece of advice about auditions, what would it be?

Be yourself, be confident in the knowledge that if you have put the work in, you are the best you are. SHINE! In any audition, the person auditioning you knows you are nervous – they are not there to catch you out, they are there to see you at your best. So if you make a mistake out of nerves, or if they ask you to do something again or in a different way, this is not a bad thing – this is them seeing something in you that they like and they are trying to pick out more.

What is your abiding memory of NYT?

I met some amazing people at NYT including friends I still speak to now, and directors and playwrights whom I continue to respect and admire. The one thing that has always stayed with me was the realisation that when I got to NYT I wasn't alone – there were people as passionate, crazy and as expressive as me from all walks of life. Coming from the North to stay in Tufnell Park when I was fifteen was huge, but I did it and it changed my life. The best memories and lessons I have ever learnt have been at NYT. Even now I encourage young people if they do ANYTHING with their summer, it should be to go for it!

How did NYT affect your future life and career?

I don't do as much stage acting as I used to: I now work as an assistant director at The Grand in Blackpool and run cabaret nights, which I compère in character. I also work in a special needs school, where I teach music and drama, and soon I will complete a PhD in drama therapy and drama for social change. I decided to focus my time into helping young people the way NYT helped me, and, funnily enough, a lot of the techniques I was taught at NYT I still use today!

The Class

Luke Barnes

Written by former NYT member Luke Barnes in 2012 for the Playing Up company, *The Class* was developed through a devising process and drew upon the experiences of the cast. *The Class* doesn't tell a specific real-life story, but all the characters have been influenced in some way by real-life situations.

The Class centres on the story of Lorraine, a young girl who is trying to make her way through life. Lorraine lives with her older sister, Sarah, because their father has left home and their mother committed suicide. In the opening scenes of the play we learn that Lorraine is being bullied at school for being fat, while at home she is being physically and mentally abused by her sister. She decides to run away, finding refuge at Andy's house – a classmate who has recently been expelled – and becomes pregnant after sleeping with him. When he finds out, Andy attacks Lorraine in the school canteen in an attempt to kill the baby, but is prevented from doing so by Wayne. The character of Wayne appears throughout the play in a series of monologues, but he isn't an active character in the plot until the end of the play, when he heroically defends Lorraine – with whom he is in love.

Wayne

■ **Character** A school-age boy in his teens.

■ **Location** Present-day Britain.

■ **Accent** Your own.

■ **Scene** Wayne is in love with Lorraine from afar. In a series of monologues he speaks to the audience about his interest in nature, and in previous speeches he likens different classmates to different animals. In this speech he explores the pack mentality of his classmates, suggesting that they are just puffed-up bullies; he laments that he wishes that he could stand up to them.

■ **Who is he talking to?** The audience.

■ **Where?** At home.

■ **What does he want?** Wayne wishes he could defend Lorraine from the bullies that are picking on her. He dreams of standing up to them and scaring them away. In this speech he wants to belittle them and show them up for being cowards; however, he later admits that every time he comes to confront them he loses confidence. He wants to let the audience feel his inner power and anger, but also for them to understand why he has never stepped up.

■ **Things to think about** The title of the speech is 'Wayne's World';* this suggests that he is sharing his innermost thoughts with us, so try to draw the audience in.

When Wayne talks about animals, he is really talking about his classmates. Try and imagine who might be a toucan or a peacock, and how much he hates these people.

---

* *Wayne's World* is a 1992 comedy film, starring Mike Myers and Dana Carvey as rock 'n' roll fans whose public-access television programme is bought out by a major television producer.

Some of Wayne's speeches happen in school, and one happens at the bus stop, but this one takes place at home; where might he be when he speaks? What time might it be? What has he just been doing before he begins to speak?

Chart how Wayne's speeches change throughout the play: does he grow in confidence? If so, how is he feeling at this point in the play?

There are several speeches from Wayne in the play; have a look at all of them – you may find one you prefer.

■ **Where to find the play** This play can be read on the NYT website (www.nyt.org.uk/monologues, password: nytspeeches).

Wayne

Wolves eat more if there's more food there. And goldfishes can grow bigger the bigger the space they're in. This is like the IDIOTS in my class, the more there is to pick at they will, and they'll gnaw the skin off your bones and gorge themselves on your intestines… At least they give the impression they will.

The toucan, I don't know if you know it, it's the little one with a massive yellow beak, sort of walks around like this. Sort of waddles around like Benny Hill. The toucan has a massive beak like Owen Wilson, huge, yellow and scary but in reality it's an absolute pussy and can't even use it. Just like the people in my class, all mouth and no balls. Like the peacock, thrusts out that beautiful tail, all eyes and colours, and terror but really it's just a fucking stupid bird that can't even walk… It's the fucking Nicki Minaj of birds, the peacock.

The toucan picks fruit up with its beak and throws it around to impress girls like this… and the peacock flashes its tail like this…

You can learn a lot about humans from animals you know. That's all we are, animals, just different types of monkey.

I want to flash my tail and scare off all the idiots, I want to throw fruit around to impress girls… I just… I just can't fucking speak, any time anything happens, any time anything happens in school I just get this fucking thing in my throat, it just like closes up and what comes out is just a mumble, my jaw tenses all of it and it's because I've got this stupid voice in the back of my head going 'you're thick, don't let them hear what you say, everyone will know you're thick' and my words just mumble out, they just fucking roll and I hate it. All I want to do is stand up in that circle and go 'I have something to say, now fucking listen'. But it's hard isn't it?

Cold Comfort Farm

Stella Gibbons
adapted for the stage by Paul Doust

Cold Comfort Farm was performed in the 1992 season at the Greenwich Theatre. Adapted from Stella Gibbons's 1930s comic novel, the play revolves around a young metropolitan woman, Flora Poste, who goes to live with her rural relatives on a remote farm in Sussex, after being orphaned and left penniless. *Cold Comfort Farm* is a surreal parody of romantic, rural melodrama, which offers vividly drawn characters and plenty of comic set pieces.

The play begins with Flora Poste explaining how she has been recently orphaned, and despite rumours of great wealth in the family, she's been left penniless. The only thing she can do is go and live with her mother's relatives, the Starkadders, on their dilapidated farm. When she arrives, she decides to tidy the farm up and help improve her relatives' lives. What follows is a farce-like plot, packed with a multitude of larger-than-life characters including: Mr Neck, the fast-talking Hollywood producer; Uncle Amos, a lunatic cult leader; and Aunt Ada, the mad old woman who tyrannises the family. By the end of the play, Flora has achieved her goal of reorganising everyone's lives, and they all live happily ever after.

Flora

■ **Character** A nineteen-year-old woman.

■ **Location** A farm in Sussex, in 1946.

■ **Accent** Your own.

■ **Scene** This speech happens towards the end of the play, when Flora is having a showdown with Aunt Ada Doom. Just as she intended, Flora has managed to improve the lives of her relatives by finding opportunities and love matches for all of them – including Elfine, who is to marry Richard Hawk-Monitor the following morning. As a result, Aunt Ada will soon be left on Cold Comfort Farm alone, and so, in retaliation, she vows to undermine Flora's plan and put a stop to Elfine and Richard's wedding. In this speech Flora challenges Aunt Ada, saying that she sees through Ada's 'madness' and asserts that her own plan *will* be successful.

■ **Who is she talking to?** Aunt Ada.

■ **Where?** In the kitchen of Cold Comfort Farm.

■ **What does she want?** Aunt Ada is the main obstacle to Flora getting what she wants – namely to bring order and tidiness to Cold Comfort Farm. Her main goal in this scene is to keep Elfine's wedding plans on track, and she goes about achieving this by unmasking Aunt Ada's 'artificial' madness, by challenging her malicious behaviour, and asserting her will to make this marriage happen. Flora wants Aunt Ada to submit to her command and for her version of dignified and civilised behaviour to win out.

■ **Things to think about** The speech begins with Flora mimicking Aunt Ada's 'crazed ecstatic laughter'; make sure you have a clear idea of how Aunt Ada behaves in order to recreate this moment.

98

Although the play is broadly a comedy, in the first scene Flora states that she is 'entirely serious about almost everything'. Can you find comedy in Flora's 'seriousness'?

Despite the fact that Flora values order above all else, think about how passionate she becomes as the speech progresses – does she surprise even herself with this outburst?

Like all of the characters in *Cold Comfort Farm*, Flora is eccentric. Have fun with the speech. Think about how someone like Flora might look physically, or what her voice is like; you might like to use the last image of a 'haughty' deer as inspiration.

Flora references several other characters' personalities in the speech – like the fact that Elfine may have children who love poetry – so make sure you have read the whole play so that you understand exactly what she is referring to.

Where to find the play This play is published by Samuel French (www.samuelfrench.co.uk).

Flora

(Flora bursts into a crazed conniption of ecstatic laughter, gesticulating with wild glee. She concludes her outburst with a shriek of anger. Ada stares at Flora.)

Yes, you see – I can do it too. But I choose not to. In very much the same way as you choose to be mad. Yes – choose. You have chosen, Aunt Ada, just about the most convenient form of madness possible. Oh, yes! It allows you absolute control with not a whiff of responsibility! Oh, you can shriek and gesticulate as derangedly as you please! Gibber in dialect 'til the cows come home – with or without their horns; but from me, Aunt Ada, you cannot hide the fact that you are a shrewd old bird, as calculating as an abacus, with a determined mind as sharp and penetrating as a needle! But I have rescued Elfine from you – and there is nothing you can do about it. She will marry Richard – she *will* – and she will bear him a fine family of pleasant, ordinary, acceptable children. She will not bear them with venom and with loathing; nor with any sort of piston plunging in her sinews. She will bear them with love! These children may, of course, burn a little with poetry in their secret souls – but that is only to be expected, and not entirely without merit. But not for one instant will your artificial lunacy cloud their sunny lives! I have prised open your visor, old woman – and there is nothing there! This is my Victory! Lay down your malice and accept defeat! For my hands are on the handles of the sword, and I shall not turn back!

My victory is Elfine and my victory is in sight! My victory is a victory of dignified application! My victory, Aunt Ada, is the victory of Civilised Thought over your own grubbing philosophy of farmyard and bin! My victory is a splendid deer stepping haughtily over a ploughed field!

Mr Neck

■ **Scene** The speech comes from the opening scene of the play; Flora and her potential boyfriend, Charles, have arrived at Cold Comfort Farm and she is explaining her family history and why she has come to live here. Meanwhile, Mr Neck, a Hollywood producer friend who has been waiting outside, bursts into the scene, and impatiently tells Charles that they have to get going on to Paris, as he is on the search for a new leading male actor. When he gets inside, however, he becomes distracted and starts to imagine the farmhouse as a location for a film set.

■ **Who is he talking to?** Flora and Charles.

■ **Where?** Inside a grubby farmhouse kitchen.

■ **What does he want?** Initially Mr Neck wants to fetch Charles and leave for France; however, as soon as he sees inside the house, he wants Flora and Charles to listen to his stream-of-consciousness as he talks at length on a variety of subjects.

■ **Things to think about** Mr Neck thinks very quickly. No sooner has he made one statement than he is on to the next. What does that tell you about him?

Be careful to make sure that when Mr Neck asks a question, he really asks it – even though he doesn't give anyone time to answer.

Mr Neck is a larger-than-life character and this is a larger-than-life play. Have fun with his over-the-top theatricality, but also try to make him as real and rounded a character as you can.

Perhaps try and think of people that you have met in real life, or even that you have seen on screen, who have an overwhelming enthusiasm like Mr Neck, as a way of developing your characterisation.

■ **Where to find the play** This play is published by Samuel French (www.samuelfrench.co.uk).

Mr Neck

I've been out in that bi-plane nearly... Oh, now wait a minute! Wait a minute! Gee, but this'd make some location! Boy, what a location! I've got to come back here sometime – when I've found myself a new actor! Flora sweetheart – speak to your folks here for me will you? Tell 'em a big Hollywood producer wants to shoot a picture. Tell 'em I'll pay anything! Anything! Hey, that's it! I'll send 'em on a vacation of a lifetime! The South of France! The hotel *I'm* staying at, okay? (*He hands a brochure to Flora.*) The Hotel Miramar! See? Just look at the life they lead out there! All those old dames just lying around in the sun? You put an old bird on the side of that pool – and she feels a million years younger. Oh, yes! I seen it happen! I tell you babes, there's only one place in this whole world near half as beautiful as the Hotel Miramar – and that's right here in Sussex. Hautcouture Hall! I met the family on this Search of Star stuff. I was looking for someone English, you know, but earthy. So I fixed to test the kid – Dick. Richard Hawk-Monitor. But it didn't work out. Not that he wasn't a dish! Oh, boy – what a dish! But he was too damned... *British*. See? British Reserve. And British Reserve is *not* what they want. Not any more. No – what they want now is *Passion*! I want a fella who can take that screen in the palm of his hand and have the dames just melt right through the floor! A big, husky stiff! Red blood! I need a guy who looks great in a tuxedo – but even better half out of it! Know what I mean? Hence – I gotta go to France! Well I've looked every other place! And if I don't find him soon, I'm sunk! So – come on now, Charlie! Wake up! Smell the coffee! I've *hired* you and your wings to fly me over there, haven't I? Let's fly! Know what I mean? So long, toots – see you again!

Consensual

Evan Placey

Consensual is about consent in sexual relationships – who gives it, when, and how the boundaries can blur. Written by Evan Placey, it was first performed as part of the 2015 REP season at the Ambassadors Theatre in London's West End, and revived by the 2018 REP company at Soho Theatre. Exploring ideas around sex, power and personal responsibility, *Consensual* depicts a complex situation in which the truth is not clear-cut.

In the first scene of the play, Freddie, a twenty-two-year-old man working in Barclays Bank, confronts his old teaching assistant, Diane, and accuses her of grooming him for sex – an accusation she strenuously denies. It's his word against hers, but as the play unfolds, it seems that both Freddie and Diane may not be fully admitting what happened that night seven years ago. The action in the first act takes place against the backdrop of a school environment – where Diane, a pregnant teacher, is giving Sex and Relationship Education (SRE) lessons around the idea of consent. In the second half of the play, we are taken back to the night in question. It becomes clear that Freddie was not lying – they did have sex – but the questions around the issue of consent become increasingly difficult to answer.

Character A twenty-nine-year-old female teacher.

Location Present-day Britain.

Accent Your own.

Scene This speech happens at the climax of the first act. Diane has just found out that she has been sacked because she admitted to another teacher that she once had sex with a student (Freddie), and that teacher then reported her. Diane has come to Freddie's flat to confront him about what happened that night; she says that she doesn't remember everything and starts to doubt herself. She is clearly in a state of distress, and, at the end of the speech, blood begins to run down her leg – she could be giving birth or having a miscarriage.

Who is she talking to? She is talking to Freddie, the young man who has accused her of grooming him for sex when he was fifteen.

Where? Outside Freddie's flat.

What does she want? Diane is in a state of emotional turmoil. She has been fired from her job, she is having difficulties with her husband, and she is heavily pregnant. Freddie's reappearance in her life has given her many questions and brought back memories of a difficult time in her life, and she wants to know; what *did* happen that night – does she want to confide in him? Maybe she also wants him to admit that she didn't do anything wrong and that he's making it up. At the end of the speech she apologises to him over and over again, so maybe she is admitting that she did exploit him, and she wants him to know how sorry she is.

■ **Things to think about** Diane is heavily pregnant in this speech, so how will this affect her physicality? (Be careful not to let miming pregnancy take over.)

Diane is waiting for Freddie outside his flat; just like in the first scene when they meet in a pub, they are not in a private space. Does the public setting of the speech affect Diane, or is she so consumed in her thoughts that she doesn't notice?

Read the second act of the play. What do you think really happened – who did what to whom, and who may have been in the wrong? Once you have decided this, think about what Diane does and doesn't know, and what she can and can't remember. If you decide that she isn't sure, that is fine, but be specific about what details you think she *can* recall.

■ **Where to find the play** This play is published by Nick Hern Books (www.nickhernbooks.co.uk).

Diane

I don't know how I got here.

I mean I walked but. I didn't walk with the intention of arriving here. Did I come here before? I must have. But why? To drop off some missing work or – don't answer that. It doesn't matter.

There's this student at school, Georgia, and she...

I lost my job. Today.

Because of you. Well because of. Actually I'm technically suspended but I'll resign before they fire me. One of my colleagues reported me to the Board of Governors. The woman I was mentoring actually. Because that's what happens. The mentee, the student – they all grow up and have minds of their own. And everything you taught them they use against you. I guess it's my fault. I told her what happened.

What did happen?

Freddie?

Because every time I.

There's the way I remember things. The way I want to remember things. And the way things happened. And I don't think I can tell them apart.

And maybe neither can you.

The only thing I can absolutely remember is the first time I saw you. You'd come into the office with your tie loose and askew, your shirt untucked, and a pen in your mouth, drawings on your hands, and you said – 'I think we're gonna be stuck together for a while. I apologise in advance.' And you smiled.

And I thought right then – or maybe it was later, maybe it's in hindsight that I thought what I think I thought then. I thought: 'If I were fifteen.'

So maybe I deserve all this. Because at the very least I thought it.

And when you'd come see me I liked it. I liked that you needed me.

Do you still smoke? Can I have a cigarette?

For a long time I hated you. I still hate you I think.

You knew what you were doing. Irrespective of me.

But.

I once confronted a man on the street because he threw some rubbish on the ground. I was honestly gobsmacked. And his response was: 'So what? What difference will my one piece of litter do? The world is collapsing with or without me picking up that piece of litter.'

Whether or not you knew what you were doing, I… (*She starts crying.*) I…

I need to…

I'm sorry.

I'm so very sorry…

(*She's hysterical now.*)

I'm so very sorry. I'm sorry, I'm sorry, I'm…

No I don't want you to say anything. I didn't come here to…

(*She looks down. Touches between her legs. Heavy bleeding.*)

Lauren Lyle played the part of Diane in the NYT REP production of *Consensual* in 2015. She works as an actress and has performed at the Old Vic Theatre and the Royal Court. Screen roles since REP include Chloe Demichelis in Jimmy McGovern's *Broken* (BBC) and Marsali MacKimmie Fraser in *Outlander* (Starz/Sony).

How did you prepare for playing Diane?

I plotted Diane's life events, and developed a family background for her, as well as researching the commitments and consequences that teachers face. I also found contrasting energies and rhythms for each half of the play; one for when she is older, pregnant and experiencing tremendous stress, and another for the second half when she is younger, more free and starting adulthood.

What advice would you give a young actor playing Diane?

Don't judge Diane. Try to understand, accept and believe why she has done the things she has done.

If you could give one piece of advice about auditions, what would it be?

Don't worry about what anyone else is doing. It's your time to focus on the work you've done and be confident in your own unique skills. No one does *you* better than *you*.

What is your abiding memory of NYT?

The euphoric exhaustion I would feel every day after rehearsals having known I'd worked as hard as I could on a project that I was so proud of, with the most supportive and talented team around me.

How did NYT affect your future life and career?

Having begun a foundation of a career on my own, I joined NYT and it has launched me onto a path by which I am now a professional actor. I learnt invaluable lessons every day during REP, from supportive professionals and from my friends. I believe the importance of working incredibly hard, and together, is essential in order to make a career of acting.

Freddie

Character A twenty-two-year-old man.

Location Present-day Britain.

Accent Your own.

Scene This speech is taken from the first scene of the play. Freddie has asked Diane to meet him, and she has suggested they meet a pub. It is clear that something has happened between the pair, but we are not sure what. Then Freddie tells Diane that his father has died, and that on his deathbed his father revealed to Freddie that he never loved him. As Freddie becomes more emotional, he accuses Diane of grooming him. Diane denies it, and is clearly uncomfortable with the situation, so gets up to leave. It is then that Freddie announces that he has told the police, which sets in motion the rest of the play.

Who is he talking to? Diane, his old teaching assistant from school, whom he hasn't seen for seven years.

Where? In a pub at lunchtime.

What does he want? Freddie wants lots of different things in this speech; he is a complex character, and it is up to you to decide why he acts in the way he does. When he tells Diane about his father dying, does he want sympathy? Does he want Diane to admit that she took advantage of him? Does he want to make her feel bad for ignoring him after they had sex seven years ago? Does he want to destroy her life because he feels let down by her?

Things to think about Place is an important consideration in this speech: how does the public setting affect the way that Freddie talks to Diane?

Freddie talks about having regrets in this scene; apart from the scar on his tummy, what else might he regret – his own actions on the night in question?

Freddie's thoughts jump about from subject to subject early on in the scene – what does this suggest about how he is feeling?

Why does he tell Diane that his father has died? What effect does he want this revelation to have on her?

Does Freddie believe that Diane took advantage of him? Read the second act of the play, and think about his motives for contacting her again.

■ **Where to find the play** This play is published by Nick Hern Books (www.nickhernbooks.co.uk).

Freddie

My dad died.

(*A glass somewhere in the bar breaks. They both watch.*)

A week ago. Bastard finally drank himself to death.

You probably don't remember, but one time, we were in your office. I was crying. Told you my mum was gone, had a brother who did fuck all, and had a dad who didn't love me. And you told me he did, of course he did. He was just too afraid to show it. You probably don't remember.

The night he died he's lying in hospital drugged up and he takes my hands. Like properly takes them. (*He takes her hands.*) And he says, swear to god, 'I love you son. I know I was never very good at sayin it. Maybe cos my dad never said it to me, so was too scared to. But I love you.

'Jake. I love you Jake. Not like that faggot brother of yours. I tried, god knows I tried. But the thing with Freddie is he wants it too much. You can smell it when he walks into a room. He just so desperately wants to be loved that I couldn't stand to look at him. Like one of them manky wet foxes you'd find by the bins, staring up at you longing in their eyes. Just makes you want to kick the shit out of them.'

(*Pause.*)

Dad was right. People can smell it on me. The fellas at work, always taking the mick cos they know I'll take it. My last girlfriend. Who told me I was too needy.

So how did you know?

How did you, why did you choose me?

(*Diane goes to speak.*)

Dammit, can you just – ! If I knew what it is that people see in me, what they smell on me that –

If I knew what you saw in me so you knew you could…

You know…

Groom me. If I knew what it was that you saw, so that you knew that you could groom me, that you could…

You made it so I became dependent on you. So you could exploit that trust, that dependency. And take advantage of me.

Oscar Porter joined NYT in 2012. He was part of the REP company in 2015 and played the part of Freddie in *Consensual* at the Ambassadors Theatre. He also performed in *Wuthering Heights* and *The Merchant of Venice*. He now works as a professional actor.

How did you prepare for the part of Freddie?

I read the play loads of times until I really understood why Freddie does what he does. I tried to think of times when I experienced similar things in my life to what he goes through. I also watched real-life cases of student–teacher relationships which were really interesting. I think I just tried to completely immerse myself in the world of the play so I knew Freddie as well as I could before we went on stage.

What advice would you give a young actor playing Freddie?

Really enjoy and relish it! It's a cracking part. A lot of the issues in the play are quite heavy so I reckon it's good to try and find the light in it all. Freddie genuinely believes in everything he does, so even if you as the actor don't agree with him, you still have to find a way of understanding him.

If you could give one piece of advice about auditions, what would it be?

Never apologise for yourself.

What is your abiding memory of NYT?

In my Intake Course I was dying whilst in the middle of a Rikki Beadle-Blair Workout. I was on the floor attempting to plank when I looked up to see a bearded man planking next to me who I hadn't spoken to before, also struggling. We both looked at each other as if to say 'Well this is incredibly painful and unpleasant' and bonded in this moment. This man is now one of my closest friends.

Dancing at Lughnasa

Brian Friel

Written in 1990, *Dancing at Lughnasa* was performed by NYT at the Arts Theatre in 1998. When writing about the play, Friel said that it was an exploration of 'family life – make-believe – remembering and remaking the past – betrayal groping towards love'.* It is a beautiful, spare play which looks in microscopic detail at the lives, loves, tensions and regrets that engulf five sisters living on the edge of poverty in rural Ireland in the 1930s.

A loosely autobiographical play, *Dancing at Lughnasa* is set in Donegal in 1936 during harvest time (also known as the festival of Lughnasa). The play is narrated by Michael as an adult, looking back at one summer in his childhood when he was seven. He recalls how he lived with his mother, Christine, and her four sisters Maggie, Agnes, Rose and Kate, and the play follows their fortunes over one tumultuous summer. In the opening piece of narration, Michael describes this as a time of change: the family purchase their first ever radio; Uncle Jack has returned in disgrace from his missionary post in Uganda after adopting the local customs; while Michael's father, Gerry, also shows up causing distinct unrest amongst the sisters. The arrival of these two characters sets in motion a chain of events that alter the family dynamic forever, and through a mixture of narration and action, we watch as hopes and dreams are dashed, and lives are haunted by the promise of what might have been.

* '*Dancing at Lughnasa*: The evolution of a masterpiece, step by step', David Ward, *Guardian*, 1 April 2014.

Kate

■ **Character** A woman of unspecified age, the eldest sister in the family.

■ **Location** Ballybeg, a village in County Donegal, Ireland, in 1936.

■ **Accent** Irish.

■ **Scene** Gerry, Christine's ex-lover and Michael's father, has just arrived, sending the sisters into a frenzy: Christine quickly falls back in love with him, whilst Agnes secretly holds a flame for him and Kate cannot stand his presence, knowing the bewitching and destabilising effect he has on her sisters. Added to which, former missionary Uncle Jack seems to have adopted the un-Christian culture of the Ugandan natives causing controversy among the locals of Ballybeg. The parish priest suggests that Uncle Jack's behaviour might result in Kate losing her job as a teacher in the local school. As the main breadwinner of the house, Kate is beginning to feel that her world is crumbling around her, and she cannot contain her thoughts and feelings any longer; she unburdens herself to her sister, Maggie.

■ **Who is she talking to?** Maggie, her younger sister by two years.

■ **Where?** In their kitchen.

■ **What does she want?** Kate wants to keep the family unit together. She works hard as a school teacher, and feels that despite her best efforts, she cannot keep control of everything and everyone. She wants to reach out to Maggie for help. Kate is caught between wanting Maggie to confirm all of her suspicions about how their lives are disintegrating and also wanting Maggie to comfort and reassure her. Perhaps, for a short period, Kate wants to relinquish control to her sister, and for a moment not be the person who is responsible for everything.

117

■ **Things to think about** In Act One the sisters all lose themselves in a frenzy of dancing. Look at Kate's involvement in this moment – what does it tell us about her?

Kate is described as a very proper woman and has a specific role in relation to all her sisters. Read the play and see how she behaves around them, and then contrast that to Kate in the speech. Where is she different and where is she similar?

Kate is going through a moment of emotional struggle, so as well as exploring her internal feelings, think carefully about how she is trying to affect and change Maggie with her outpouring.

■ **Where to find the play** This play is published by Faber & Faber (www.faber.co.uk).

Kate

You work hard at your job. You try to keep the home together. You perform your duties as best you can – because you believe in responsibilities and obligations and good order. And then suddenly, suddenly you realise that hair cracks are appearing everywhere; that control is slipping away; that the whole thing is so fragile it can't be held together much longer. It's all about to collapse, Maggie.

That young Sweeney boy from the back hills – the boy who was anointed – his trousers didn't catch fire, as Rose said. They were doing some devilish thing with a goat – some sort of sacrifice for the Lughnasa Festival; and Sweeney was so drunk he toppled over into the middle of the bonfire. Don't know why that came into my head…

And Mr Evans is off again for another twelve months, and next week or the week after Christina'll collapse into one of her depressions. Remember last winter? – all that sobbing and lamenting in the middle of the night. I don't think I could go through that again. And the doctor says he doesn't think Father Jack's mind is confused but that his superiors probably had no choice but to send him home. Whatever he means by that, Maggie. And the parish priest did talk to me today. He said the numbers in school are falling and that there may not be a job for me after the summer. But the numbers aren't falling, Maggie. Why is he telling me lies? Why does he want rid of me? And why has he never come out to visit Father Jack? (*She tries to laugh.*) If he gives me the push, all five of us will be at home together all day long – we can spend the day dancing to Marconi. (*Now she cries.*)

But what worries me most of all is Rose. If I died – if I lost my job – if this house were broken up – what would become of our Rosie?

Rachael Stirling played Kate in NYT's 1998 production of *Dancing at Lughnasa*. Since then she has gone on to work extensively in films including *Snow White and the Huntsman* (Universal) and *The Young Victoria* (GK Films) as well as on TV, in shows such as *The Detectorists* (BBC) and *Doctor Who* (BBC). She has been twice nominated for an Olivier Award, in 2010 and 2011, and has worked extensively in the West End.

How did you prepare for the part of Kate?

I remember our rehearsals took place in the summer of 1998. We were steeping ourselves in Ulster culture, in the lyricism, the music and the poetry of the area. Then the Omagh bombing took place while we were rehearsing, which brought the reality of all the politics of Ulster – its heritage, its history and its current reality, into high definition.

Kate is the eldest; she has shouldered most of the responsibility of the sisters, and this is a rare moment of insight into her own fears, which normally she keeps hidden. The language does so much that I remember being totally still during the speech in the end, letting the words do the work. You have to work hard to realise the mundane reality of life in that house. Chekhov serves as a good comparison to the sisters' sense of loss and longing in Friel's play, so reading *Three Sisters* or *The Cherry Orchard* was useful research.

Concentrate on the details of their everyday existence, down to who does what in the kitchen, what each sister's role is within the household, and how Kate keeps a hold on everyone therein. She is alone, and isolated in many ways.

The accent demands most preparation because it can be a tough one to become accustomed to. I worked and worked until it felt natural to me, and a couple of the cast were from Ulster, so we just kept it up as much as possible, in and out of rehearsal. You don't need to over-emote. Here is a woman trying to keep it all in, her heroism and pathos come from seeing her trying to keep control, and at the last moment, failing to do so.

What advice would you give a young actor playing Kate?

Whatever you do, don't play her age... As I've said, immerse yourself in her everyday reality. Really work out how she feels about all of the other characters she mentions here, especially if you are performing the speech in isolation from the play. Read and read and re-read the entire text until you own her attitude to all the other people she speaks of. And practise the accent until you don't have to think about it at all any more. It may be hard at first, but it will reap rewards in performance. I can still do the accent to this day – it sticks with you, so work at it and it may serve you at an audition later on too.

If you could give one piece of advice about auditions, what would it be?

Prepare properly, so if you don't get it, it isn't for lack of preparation. Have a sense of humour about it; we ALL fail to get the part, we ALL give ghastly auditions, but we all love what we do which is why we go through this torture in the first place. I remember an audition for the part of a doctor in a horror film where the casting director told me to pretend I was trapped in a cave by crouching under a desk and re-enacting a life-saving operation on another (invisible) character under selfsame desk, using Sweet'N Low sachets and scissors and sellotape. I didn't get the part. But I did make an interesting saccharine sculpture. And I did laugh a lot afterwards. You may not get the part because you are too tall, too short, too posh, too Northern. Don't take it personally. Keep the faith and keep on trucking.

How did NYT affect your future life and career?

I did my course, followed by three seasons of plays at the NYT, every summer while I was at university; it gave me as close an experience of being a working actor as it is possible to have; performing in a theatre to genuine audiences, with genuine critics, and the truest insight into the professionalism it demands.

By the time I left university, I knew that an actress was what I wanted to be.

■ **Character** A man of unspecified age.

■ **Location** Ballybeg, a village in County Donegal, Ireland, in 1936.

■ **Accent** Irish.

■ **Scene** This speech is taken from a longer section of narration towards the end of the play as Michael begins to tell us of what happened to his family. At the beginning of the speech he describes the fate of two of his aunts, Agnes and Rose, after they leave Ballybeg, and in this speech he talks about what happened to his father.

■ **Who is he talking to?** The audience.

■ **Where?** In an imaginary space.

■ **What does he want?** Whilst Michael's narration looks back on the past and has a reflective quality to it, it is important to think about what he wants in order to give the speech its own dynamic. With this section of the speech he may want to lay the memory of his father to rest, or he may want to shame his father by highlighting his bigamy. Or maybe he wants to honour his father by giving a true account of him – maybe by telling the audience about his father's other life, he feels that he is making amends for never having revealed the truth to his mother.

■ **Things to think about** How does Michael feel about his father? Is he angry with him? Does he pity him? Does he feel numb? Or all of these things and more at various points throughout the speech?

In his notes on the play, Friel suggested that the narrator of the play couldn't just be 'a fact-teller – a link man' and said that 'All these enacted events must have had an adjusting effect on him.'

Make sure you read the whole play and think about how the action has affected Michael in this speech.

It will be useful to think about where Michael is physically when delivering the speech, and whom he is talking to. Throughout the play his narration has a kind of dreamlike quality to it, but make sure you aren't lulled into a vague haziness.

One way to root the speech will be to think carefully about the individual moments he describes: the moment his father left, the times he returned, how he felt when he received the note from his half-brother, and perhaps the moments when he considered telling his mother. Having a sense of these moments will give texture to the speech.

■ Where to find the play This play is published by Faber & Faber (www.faber.co.uk).

Michael

My father sailed for Spain that Saturday. The last I saw of him was dancing down the lane in imitation of Fred Astaire, swinging his walking stick, Uncle Jack's ceremonial tricorn at a jaunty angle over his left eye. When he got to the main road he stopped and turned and with both hands blew a dozen theatrical kisses back to Mother and me.

He was wounded in Barcelona – he fell off his motor-bike – so that for the rest of his life he walked with a limp. The limp wasn't disabling but it put an end to his dancing days; and that really distressed him. Even the role of maimed veteran, which he loved, could never compensate for that.

He still visited us occasionally, perhaps once a year. Each time he was on the brink of a new career. And each time he proposed to Mother and promised me a new bike. Then the war came in 1939; his visits became more infrequent; and finally he stopped coming altogether.

Sometime in the mid-fifties I got a letter from a tiny village in the south of Wales; a curt note from a young man of my own age and also called Michael Evans. He had found my name and address among the belongings of his father, Gerry Evans. He introduced himself as my half-brother and he wanted me to know that Gerry Evans, the father we shared, had died peacefully in the family home the previous week. Throughout his final illness he was nursed by his wife and his three grown children who all lived and worked in the village.

My mother never knew of that letter. I decided to tell her – decided not to – vacillated for years as my father would have done; and eventually, rightly or wrongly, kept the information to myself.

DNA

Dennis Kelly

Originally written in 2008 for the National Theatre Connections, *DNA* was then performed by NYT during the 2016 REP season, at our Holloway Road base in 2017, and again in 2018 at Southwark Playhouse. Perhaps the most popular play for young people of the past decade, *DNA* tells the story of a group of teenagers who think they have murdered someone. Exploring ideas around bullying, cruelty and collective responsibility, Dennis Kelly's dark comedy is full of big characters making life-and-death decisions.

One afternoon, a group of bored teenagers start to taunt and bully one of their peers, Adam. It starts when they challenge him to eat some leaves and gradually progresses through various forms of violence until they find themselves, drunk on vodka, throwing stones at him as he balances precariously on a grille above a disused shaft. When Adam falls through the grille, the group presume that he is dead, and begin to panic. They decide to enlist the help of Phil – a quiet and calculating young man – and Leah – an unstoppable chatterbox, who is besotted with Phil – to cover up the murder. Phil's plan to make it look like an abduction initially seems to work, and they all think they have got away with it; however, Adam reappears several weeks later, injured and traumatised. At this point the group are faced with another dilemma: do they take Adam back home and admit to their original crime or commit an even bigger one?

Leah

■ **Character** A school-age girl in her teens.

■ **Location** Non-specific, present day.

■ **Accent** Your own.

■ **Scene** This speech comes from the beginning of the play, before Leah and Phil are embroiled in the cover-up for Adam's murder. We find Leah chatting to Phil as he sits eating an ice cream on a playing field. Phil does not, however, respond or even react to Leah despite being asked lots of questions. As the speech progresses, Leah begins to answer her own questions on Phil's behalf, and as she does so begins to tie herself in knots excusing the fact that she doesn't have many friends, and fretting over whether he thinks she talks too much.

■ **Who is she talking to?** Phil.

■ **Where?** On a playing field.

■ **What does she want?** At this point in the play, Leah could want several things from Phil, but she certainly wants his approval and to be his friend. Halfway through the speech she almost admits to thinking he's perfect, so maybe she wants him to fancy her or even fall in love with her. Even though this may be true, however, it seems that Leah doesn't want Phil to know the extent of her feelings, so she also wants to seem cool – as if she doesn't care.

■ **Things to think about** Leah's thought patterns move very quickly – make sure you know your lines *really* well so that you can change from one thought to the next with ease.

Sometimes Leah doesn't even finish her thoughts, for example when she says: 'you know it's not the collapse of my, because I do have, I could walk out of here.' What might it be 'the collapse' of?

Her world? Her self-esteem? Make sure you have fully understood each of Leah's thoughts and imagined what she *would* have gone on to say – even if she doesn't actually say it.

This is a long speech to fit into two minutes; make sure you keep to time, or, if that's not possible, trim some lines out.

Leah has several speeches of this kind peppered through the play – have a look at the others and see if you like any of them.

■ **Where to find the play** This play is published by Oberon Books (www.oberonbooks.co.uk).

Leah

What are you thinking?

(*No answer.*)

No, don't tell me, sorry, that's a stupid, that's such a stupid –

You can tell me, you know. You can talk to me. I won't judge you, whatever it is. Whatever you're, you know, I won't, I won't...

Is it me?

Not that I'm –

I mean it wouldn't matter if you weren't or were, actually, so –

Are you thinking about me?

(*No answer.*)

What good things? Phil? Or...

I mean is it a negative, are you thinking a negative thing about –

Not that I'm bothered. I'm not bothered, Phil, I'm not, it doesn't, I don't care. You know. I don't...

What, like I talk too much? Is that it? That I talk too much, you, sitting there in absolute silence thinking 'Leah talks too much, I wish she'd shut up once in a while' is that it, is that what you're, because don't, you know, judge, you know, because alright, I do. There, I'm admitting, I am admitting, I talk too much, so shoot me. So kill me, Phil, call the police, lock me up, rip out my teeth with a pair of rusty pliers, I talk too much, what a crime, what a sin, what an absolute catastrophe, stupid, evil, ridiculous, because you're not perfect actually, Phil. Okay? There. I've said it, you're not...

You're a bit...

You're...

(*Pause. She sits.*)

Do I disgust you? I do. No, I do. No don't because, it's alright, it's fine, I'm not gonna, you know, or whatever, you know it's not the collapse of my, because I do have, I could walk out of here, there are friends, I've got, I've got friends, I mean alright, I haven't got friends, not exactly, I haven't, but I could, if I wanted, if I wanted, given the right, given the perfect, you know, circumstances. So don't, because you haven't either, I mean it's not like you're, you know, Mr, you know, popular, you know, you haven't, you know, you haven't, you know, you haven't, but that's, that's different, isn't it, I mean it is, it is, don't say it isn't, really, don't, you'll just embarrass us both because it is different, it's different because it doesn't matter to you. Does it. Sitting there. Sitting there, all...

all...

Sarah Solemani

Make sure you perform your speech in front of someone you know before the audition. It's so embarrassing doing it in front of people you know, but do it because it'll never be as embarrassing as the first time and you'll discover things in the writing you can't see by just reading it. It'll also give you a chance to conquer your nerves. The more prepared you are, the more psychologically you are in control of your nerves and they're good nerves to use.

Catrin Walker-Booth was a member of NYT from 2013 to 2017. She played the part of Leah in Dennis Kelly's *DNA*, Lady Montague in *Romeo and Juliet*, and Kyle in *Pigeon English* during the 2016 REP company's season at the Ambassadors Theatre. Since graduating from the REP company, Catrin has gone on to work as an actress before training further at the Royal Welsh College of Music and Drama.

How did you prepare for the part of Leah?

Leah's speeches are really challenging because of her constant changes of thought. I knew that to really tap into such a vibrant and enigmatic character, I needed her lines to be in my body – rather than just my head – so I made myself learn her speeches on my feet. I'd walk around my bedroom/the NYT studio/my living room talking to myself like a nutter! Wherever I got to a shift, I'd change direction. Leah's thoughts seem sporadic on the surface but, once I physicalised them, the jumps between them became much more logical. She's always thinking, her mind always whirring away, and I found it a really useful way of exploring what it must be like to live in her head. I made sure that I never learnt her speeches sitting down, just because she has such an active mind! I suppose it did help that we're similar in some respects.

What advice would you give to a young actor playing this part?

I'd beg them not to judge Leah. She feels she has to fill the void of silence between her and Phil which means she talks an awful lot. She comes out with gloriously bizarre concepts, and you could argue she makes questionable choices in the play, but all of these discussion points are for the audience. As an actress playing her, I'd suggest that working out what motivates her to behave the way she does is far more useful to you than colouring her actions with your own opinion.

If you could give one piece of advice about auditions, what would it be?

Have fun! To help myself enjoy auditions more, I tell myself: the panel have spaces for actors in their play/company/project, and need to fill them. You are nothing more than a possible solution to that problem, and can but generously offer your help. Whether you're the right solution is out of your control, so... play! Have fun.

What is your abiding memory of NYT?

The REP company warming up together as an ensemble before a show during our run at the Ambassadors. We were quite naughty, always very loud, and usually singing!

How did NYT affect your future life and career?

NYT has given me a family, whose hands I know will be there for me to hold through the rest of my life and career.

Richard

▓ **Character** A school-age boy in his teens.

▓ **Location** Non-specific, present day.

▓ **Accent** Your own.

▓ **Scene** This speech comes right at the end of the play, and Richard, one of the group who committed the crime, is trying to persuade Phil to come and hang out with everyone again. Throughout the speech, Richard describes how everyone has changed since the traumatic event, and it seems that Phil has also been affected, as he now spends his days on the playing field staring into space. Towards the end of the speech Richard tells the story of being caught in a cloud of cotton seeds, and how this made him consider life on other planets.

▓ **Who is he talking to?** Phil.

▓ **Where?** On the playing field.

▓ **What does he want?** Richard says he wants Phil to come down from the playing field, but you need to think about why. Earlier in the play, Phil brings stability and leadership to the group, so maybe Richard wants Phil to come and take charge again – especially given that everyone else seems to have fallen apart. In the second half of the speech, Richard also talks about his feeling that there is alien life out there, and he considers how aliens live their lives. Why does he say this? Is he actually trying to consider their own behaviour in the past few months? Maybe he wants Phil to tell him that what they did was okay?

▓ **Things to think about** Read the whole play, and think about where Richard fits into the group's pecking order. What does this tell you about the character, and how might that inform the way you perform this speech?

How does Richard feel about all the individual people he describes? For example, John Tate joining the Jesus Army, or Cathy becoming the top-dog in school – is he dismissive? Worried? Surprised?

This is a philosophically tricky speech, but you need to decide why you think Richard tells the story about alien life, and what reaction he wants from Phil.

This is a long speech to fit into two minutes. You may want to cut it down, or finish the speech early.

There are several other speeches in this play that you may also want to take a look at.

Where to find the play This play is published by Oberon Books (www.oberonbooks.co.uk).

Richard

Everyone's asking after you. You know that? Everyone's saying 'where's Phil?' 'what's Phil up to?' 'when's Phil going to come down from that stupid field?' 'wasn't it good when Phil was running the show?' What do you think about that? What do you think about everyone asking after you?

(*No answer.*)

Aren't you interested? Aren't you interested in what's going on?

(*No answer.*)

John Tate's found God. Yeah, yeah I know. He's joined the Jesus Army, he runs round the shopping centre singing and trying to give people leaflets. Danny's doing work experience at a dentist's. He hates it. Can't stand the cavities, he says when they open their mouths sometimes it feels like you're going to fall in.

(*Pause.*)

Brian's on stronger and stronger medication. They caught him staring at a wall and drooling last week. It's either drooling or giggling. Keeps talking about earth. I think they're going to section him. Cathy doesn't care. She's too busy running things. You wouldn't believe how things have got, Phil. She's insane. She cut a first year's finger off, that's what they say anyway.

Doesn't that bother you? Aren't you even bothered?

(*No answer.*)

Lou's her best friend, now. Dangerous game. I feel sorry for Lou. And Jan and Mark have taken up shoplifting, they're really good at it, get you anything you want.

Phil?

Phil!

You can't stay here forever. When are you going to come down?

(*Pause.*)

Nice up here.

As I was coming up here there was this big wind of fluff. You know, this big wind of fluff, like dandelions, but smaller, and tons of them, like fluffs of wool or cotton, it was really weird, I mean it just came out of nowhere, this big wind of fluff, and for a minute I thought I was in a cloud, Phil. Imagine that. Imagine being inside a cloud, but with space inside it as well, for a second, as I was coming up here I felt like I was an alien in a cloud. But really felt it. And in that second, Phil, I knew that there was life on other planets. I knew we weren't alone in the universe, I didn't just think it or feel it, I knew it, I know it, it was as if the universe was suddenly shifting and giving me a glimpse, this vision that could see everything, just for a fraction of a heartbeat of a second. But I couldn't see who they were or what they were doing or how they were living.

How do you think they're living, Phil?

How do you think they're living?

(*No answer.*)

The Dream Ticket

Christopher Short

First presented at the Cochrane Theatre in London in August 1987, *The Dream Ticket* examines the history of protest within the Labour movement dating back to the 1930s. Featuring a large ensemble cast, the play tells the story of two groups of women who fought for their rights against a backdrop of political resistance. It poses questions about the effect that protest can have and asks whether theatre is an irrelevance in political struggle, or whether it can be an important tool in telling stories and empowering people.

The play operates in two timeframes concurrently, the main plot taking place in 1987 during a by-election in a Northern constituency called Whittingdale East. Within the local Labour party there are squabbles between different factions about who will stand as a candidate. Meanwhile, a group of women have staged a sit-in at the local cigarette-paper factory when their jobs come under threat. One of the candidates for the Labour nomination hears about the women's plight, and in order to gain some publicity for himself, encourages them to stage a play to further their cause. After some discussion about what the subject matter should be, they discover a diary that belonged to Mavis's gran, Kitty, which contains her account of when she marched to London with a group of women to protest against Ramsay MacDonald's government in 1930. As the play unfolds, the audience watches the story of the sit-in and rehearsals in 1987, whilst also seeing scenes and speeches from the play that the women have staged, which is set in 1930. The two stories have many similarities, and the audience is invited to compare the journeys that the two different groups of women go on, and notice the differences both in attitude and outcome.

Kitty

■ **Character** A woman of working age.

■ **Location** Britain, 1930s.

■ **Accent** Northern or your own.

■ **Scene** This speech comes from the 'play-within-the-play' element of the show, when the women in 1930 are marching to London. In these speeches and scenes, we hear about their lives, thoughts and feelings, as well as how hard their journey has been. Many of the women have been sceptical about whether the march will achieve anything, but Kitty is convinced that change is coming. At this point in the play, the women have marched from the North of England, and are on the outskirts of London. Kitty talks of the feeling of elation on being close to Hyde Park, where they plan to join other protesters.

■ **Who is she talking to?** The audience.

■ **Where?** In an imaginary space.

■ **What does she want?** Kitty wants to inspire the audience and enthuse them about the journey she has taken. She wants them to understand the hardships of the journey, but also communicate the sense of elation she felt in the moment she describes.

■ **Things to think about** Kitty is the chairwoman of the Women's Department of the National March Council, and it was she who organised a march to London to protest against Ramsay MacDonald's government, so we know that she is a strong, dynamic and persuasive woman.

We don't know a great deal else about Kitty, but in one of her speeches, she explains her motives for instigating the march – see if you can glean as much information about her before you think about your characterisation.

Just like she does in the play, Kitty goes on a journey through this speech. Make sure you have thought about all the different moments she describes, so that you can find all the different emotions within the speech.

Where to find the play This play can be read on the NYT website (www.nyt.org.uk/monologues, password: nytspeeches).

Kitty

'Good luck, give MacDonald hell!' the people had cheered. Occasionally, the sun shone. Spikes gave us corned beef sandwiches or bread and cheese. We'd sung songs as we went happy on our way. There were times – many times – when we thought we wouldn't make it, when the Moon seemed closer than London. But there was always someone ready with a joke, a song, an outstretched hand. 'Come on, lass. Think of the hungry kids in Walmsley Street' and up you'd get; and carry on, left–right, head held high, swing those arms, look out Labour! Until we got here. When at last we saw what we'd hoped, prayed and dreamed of, we could hardly believe. Thank God in Heaven. 'Central London – four miles.' Tears in my eyes. We hugged each other, crying, laughing, drunk with success. Nothing could stop us now! Deep breath, don't look at the cameras. Oh, it had been worth every agonising step. For this, this feeling: yes we might have helped win food and relief for the functionless and the only brotherhood is that of work. But to be alive, just alive is a little, little thing, unless passion is expended and fruitfulness achieved.

Dumped

Daragh Carville

Dumped was performed by an NYT company at the Edinburgh Fringe in 1998. Set on a barren patch of wasteland on the outskirts of an Irish city, it features a collection of characters whose relationships are slowly breaking down. At times *Dumped* has an almost surreal quality; it is a black comedy that explores the fracturing lives of a group of people living on the edge of society.

The action of the play takes place in and around a large yellow skip on a barren patch of land. In the opening scene we meet Nick, a *Big Issue* seller and his goth girlfriend, Liz. Nick and Liz's relationship is on the rocks – he loves rummaging through the skip every day to see what he can pick up, whilst she thinks there is more to life, and is considering leaving him. They are having an argument when Nick discovers that Franco is asleep in the skip. Hungover and disorientated, Franco is an aspiring comedian who has recently been dumped by his girlfriend, Julie, who left him for her colleague, David. She has chucked Franco out of his flat, so he's decided to live in the skip until he can win her back. As the action develops, Nick persuades Franco to teach him to be funny so that Liz won't leave him, and Franco plots to kidnap David. In the final scene of the play, the tension reaches a climax, when Franco's plan to warn David off gets out of hand, and he tries to stab David with a used hypodermic needle.

Franco

Character A man in his mid-twenties.

Location An Irish city, 1998.

Accent Northern Irish or any Irish accent.

Scene The speech comes at the end of the play. Up until now, Franco has seemed slightly unhinged but otherwise harmless. In this scene, however, we see a different side to Franco, as he kidnaps David and tries to force him to 'stick' himself with a used needle. Franco also describes the moment he got dumped; he tells the story of how he found himself in the skip one morning, destitute, and how his ex-girlfriend dumped all of his belongings on top of him.

Who is he talking to? David, his ex-girlfriend's new partner.

Where? On an exposed, desolate wasteland.

What does he want? Franco wants David to feel the pain that he has caused. He tells the story of how Julie dumped him as if it's a weird, fantastical joke, but really he is seething with anger and resentment. Franco wants to justify why he has kidnapped David, and why he's forcing him to stab himself. He thinks that David is the cause of all the pain in his life, and that he deserves to die.

Things to think about Even though Franco is telling the story as if it's a joke, the moment where he had his stuff dumped on him actually happened, so make sure you have a sense of his humiliation when recalls the incident now.

Franco is so revved up that he wants to infect David with a dirty needle – make sure you balance a commitment to his emotional volatility with vocal clarity.

The stage directions suggest that a spotlight focuses on Franco when he delivers the speech, which suggests a heightened quality. Can you try and combine his 'stand-up' style with the emotional truth of the situation.

Earlier in the scene, David accuses Franco of stealing some of Bill Hicks's material – do some research into Bill Hicks. What does Franco's idolisation of him tell us about his character?

■ **Where to find the play** This play can be read on the NYT website (www.nyt.org.uk/monologues, password: nytspeeches).

Franco

Take it. Look, David, I'd really rather you did this of your own accord. I don't want to have to break your arms to make you. Just take the needle.

(*David takes it. Franco sets the cushion down on David's knees.*)

Now of course the needle may not be infected.

But it probably is.

Now. On you go. It's time for your act. Stick yourself.

Stick yourself!

Do I have to do it for you? One last act? You've never seen my act, have you, David? Have you? Do you wanna hear my act? Do you, you humourless twat? Okay, David. I'll do my act for you. I'll fucking well make you laugh.

A man wakes up in a skip. A yellow metal rubbish skip. And he feels like shit. Fucking serious heavy hangover. And he's wondering what happened. He realises he must have been smashed. I don't mean pissed, David, I mean really smashed, because he's lying there in pieces all through the skip. Arms, legs everywhere. Smashed to pieces. So he's sitting there wondering how to put himself back together, wondering if he can put himself back together.

And he's wondering how the hell he ended up like this, waking up in a skip. And he's wondering how he got to the skip and where he was before he got to the skip and he's wondering who the hell he is and how he got to be that way.

And then he sees this woman coming over towards him. And she's carrying a bag of rubbish. A bin bag. And she comes over to him and he thinks she's about to talk to him, but no. She just empties out her rubbish all over him. And he sees that all the stuff in her bin bag is his stuff. And she goes away and leaves him there, just sitting there in pieces, surrounded by his own rubbish.

There that's the punchline. Isn't that funny?

You aren't laughing, David.

Laugh.

Laugh.

Fucking laugh!

Eating Ice Cream on Gaza Beach

Shelley Silas

Eating Ice Cream on Gaza Beach was written by Shelley Silas and was performed at Soho Theatre alongside James Graham's *Tory Boyz*. Exploring the complex political situation on the West Bank, *Eating Ice Cream...* contains a cast of characters, all of whom have different perspectives on the conflict; as the climax of the play approaches, the characters are forced to ask big questions about where their loyalties lie.

Eating Ice Cream on Gaza Beach follows multiple characters and their struggles as they try to deal with life in the Israeli-occupied territories. The majority of the action happens on Gaza Beach, a place that represents different things to different characters in the play: for Maryam it is the place where her son died; for Adrian it is a place to sit in the sun whilst he figures out what to do. The play begins with a discussion about a new wall that is to be built on the West Bank, which sets in motion a series of events that will have tragic consequences. The character in this speech, Rami, is a central figure in the play: his ice-cream van is a place where lots of the other characters meet to talk about politics, life and the past. You will need to read the play carefully to piece together Rami's history, and see what lies beneath his calm exterior.

Rami

■ **Character** A young man who runs an ice-cream van.

■ **Location** The Israeli-occupied Palestinian Territory on the West Bank.

■ **Accent** Palestinian.

■ **Scene** In this speech Rami is talking about how his life revolves around the beach – it is a place where he works and sometimes sleeps. He talks reflectively about all of the problems of where he lives, but also about his feeling of connection to this place.

■ **Who is he talking to?** You could decide that this is a speech to the audience, but in the play Rami is talking to Adrian, a young British backpacker who has come to Gaza on his gap year. (The speech has been put together from a conversation that has been split over two scenes, specially edited together by the playwright, Shelley Silas).

■ **Where?** Gaza Beach.

■ **What does he want?** In this speech Rami wants several things. In the first part he wants to open Adrian's eyes to what going through a checkpoint is like for a Palestinian; in the middle part he wants to spark Adrian into seeing the beauty and importance of the beach; and in the last part he could be trying to open Adrian's eyes to the complexities of the whole situation.

■ **Things to think about** The conflict over Gaza is a complex historical issue, so if you are going to perform this speech make sure you know a little about the context; for example, make sure you know who the muezzin is.

Gaza Beach is a real place, so you may want to research some pictures to get a sense of what it is like, and remember that it's hot!

Rami is an ice-cream seller who believes in horoscopes. What other facts can you find out about him?

Rami occupies a difficult position in Gaza – he is a Christian Palestinian; how does this affect his outlook on life?

This speech has been put together from several conversations, so use the scenes to help you understand the character, but make sure that you link the thoughts in the speech together.

▨ **Where to find the play** This play can be read on the NYT website (www.nyt.org.uk/monologues, password: nytspeeches).

Rami

It's a choice I make. To do nothing. It's a choice. My choice. Living here, you can't always do what you say you will. You can't always arrive when you want to. Things get in the way. People get in the way. Bombs, dead bodies, barbed wire. We're at war. Sometimes a simple journey takes hours. I had a pass to go see my brother in the West Bank. I waited for seven hours at the checkpoint. Seven hours. I could have flown to London and had tea with the queen in that time. Eventually they let me in. We have a saying. Too long or too short a piece of string is never the right size. They make you crazy, these young guys, with their army arrogance, teasing you with the tip of their guns. They make you crazy. A woman beside me pissed herself she'd been waiting so long. We need strong bladders. And a lifetime of patience to get us through just sixty minutes. I wait for the day I can send my patience away. (*Pause.*) The beach is my second home. I have a tent. Nothing fancy. And I stay with my parents, in one of the camps. But I like it here, in the open by the water. We come here to be together, to meet, to talk, away from the craters their bombs have made. Away from the smoke and fumes and buildings that were. Here we can look across the sea and into a new future. (*Pause.*) This is not about war. This is about land and history, religion and fundamentalist nutcases on both sides. The extremists who believe the land is theirs and theirs alone. Other countries interfering. Or not interfering. We're not asking for much, you know. (*Pause.*) People will start coming soon. After work, after school. Or just because they can. Like ants crawling out of the ground, they'll come. Then they'll dip their toes in the water and walk along the sand, smoking and eating burned corn. And drinking sweet mint tea. Soon the muezzin will call them to pray. And some will go and some will remain. Some will sleep on this beach because it's the only place they feel safe. And some will gradually make their way home. (*Beat.*) Sounds idyllic, doesn't it?

Electricity

Miriam Battye

Electricity was first performed in 2015 at the Arcola Theatre in London. Written specially for the NYT Playing Up company, it tells the story of four young people whose lives are sent into a spin when a young man has a heart attack on the London Tube. Each character is somehow implicated in the young man's recovery, which prompts them to question the paths they have followed, and whether they are making the most of their lives.

Electricity is a fast-paced, free-wheeling play. It isn't split into separate scenes, and moments will often blend into one another with characters in different locations inhabiting the same stage. The lives of the four main protagonists are interlinked around an incident on the Tube when a young man called Joe has a heart attack. Mel has had a fling with Joe – he has just left her flat moments before it happens; India is a fantasist who is daydreaming about falling in love with a stranger – when Joe happens to walk past; Abe is Joe's estranged brother; and Gus is a hypochondriac who happens to see Joe being admitted to hospital.

Gus

Character A nineteen-year-old man.

Location London, 2015.

Accent Your own.

Scene This speech has been put together from the first scene of the play. Although in the play Gus's lines have been intermingled with other characters', they are all responding to the question: 'So. Tell me. How do you feel?' Gus answers this question in one stream of consciousness by talking about a heart condition that he has, and how he is worried that he is dying.

Who is he talking to? A doctor. Although you could decide to address the speech to someone else if you like.

Where? The physical space isn't specified, but he could be in a doctor's surgery.

What does he want? Gus is clearly an anxious person. He thinks that he has a serious problem and he wants to convince the doctor that he is not making it up. He wants to be taken seriously about his condition and encourage the doctor to see things from his point of view.

Things to think about Later in the play Gus has a conversation with the doctor – what does the doctor tell him about his heart? And what does he tell him to go and do? This scene gives us an insight into what Gus is like.

Look at how short all of the sentences in this scene are. Gus clearly has lots of different thoughts in a short space of time; try playing with how quickly Gus thinks during this speech.

Gus appears in several different scenes throughout the play, use those scenes to discover more about what Gus is like.

There is obviously a comedic element to the speech – in fact, Gus supplies light relief throughout the play. Think about how you can make sure that you both play the comedic rhythm as well as keeping it truthful.

Where to find the play This play can be read on the NYT website (www.nyt.org.uk/monologues, password: nytspeeches).

Gus

Sweaty. Really really sweaty. I'm so sweaty. And I think I'm dying. Not dying dying, but like. Definitely dying. I don't think I'm working. Do you? Do you think I'm working? Working? Healthy? Normal? I don't feel normal. Can you help me? Can you make me feel normal? I think there's something really wrong with me. (*He pauses briefly.*) Not wrong, not wrong but like, not working, I don't think I'm working. (*He gestures to his chest.*) In this area. Something's a bit. Not working. (*He holds up a fist.*) This is your heart. Every day, it beats about a hundred thousand times, sending two thousand gallons of blood surging through seven hundred trillion cells in your body. That. (*Indicates fist.*) Does all that. That. (*Indicates fist.*) Is terrifying. Have you ever noticed when someone starts talking about the heart you start to feel it? When someone talks about the blood pumping through your veins, putting pressure on your artery walls, blood cells surging out to the ends of your fingertips, you can sort of feel it? You kind of feel it at the centre, become aware of your heartbeat. No? I do. I can't explain it but like I can feel fucking, everything. I was born with a heart defect. A bicuspid aortic valve. I was nearly over before I began. Doctors gave me six weeks. Until my heart would shut up shop. And I'd be another depressing story. But nineteen years later. Nineteen years in and out the revolving doors of South Ealing Hospital. I'm here. I'm standing. I'm working. Still waiting for that flatline.

(*Pause.*)

This. (*Indicates fist.*) Is terrifying. I spend quite a lot of time on the internet. WebMD, NHS Direct, Patient.co.uk, there are some things you can do. To keep your heart working. Dark chocolate every day. Quitting smoking. Exercising. Avoiding stressful situations. Having mind vacations. Having sex.

(*Pause.*)

I spend quite a lot of time on the internet.

India

Character An eighteen-year-old woman.

Location London, 2015.

Accent Your own.

Scene This speech has been put together from India's lines in the first scene of the play. India is responding to the question: 'So. Tell me. How do you feel?' She starts talking about the daydreams she has and how she falls in love *all the time*. Even though she talks about how generally disappointing life has turned out to be, she still manages to find hope and optimism in her imagination. Later on in the play she pretends to be the girlfriend of Joe (the man who has had a heart attack), and while sitting by his bedside constructs a whole rom com-style backstory for their imaginary relationship.

Who is she talking to? All the characters in this scene are talking to a doctor, although you could decide to address the speech to someone else if you like.

Where? The physical space isn't specified, but she could be in a doctor's surgery.

What does she want? India is confiding in her audience at this point, she is bringing them into her world. She wants to conjure for them the image of what it's like to be inside her mind. But she also doesn't want to embarrass herself either, so she wants whoever she is talking to to take her seriously.

Things to think about At first this speech could seem a bit downbeat and depressing, but throughout the rest of play, India is a really fun character – an eccentric free spirit with a vivid imagination. Make sure you don't take the speech at face value, and use the rest of the play to develop her character.

Think carefully about who she is talking to – if she is talking to a doctor, the speech might take on a very different tone to one it might have if you were to imagine she is talking to someone she is on a date with, or even 'the audience'.

India is quite similar to Leah in *DNA* (see page 126) in that she also thinks really quickly and jumps from one thought to another. Make sure you find variety in all these different thoughts.

Where to find the play This play can be read on the NYT website (www.nyt.org.uk/monologues, password: nytspeeches).

India

I fall in Love with Everyone I ever meet.
Every Man, every Woman.
Everyone, I...
I meet someone
I see a Future before we've even started
An End before a Beginning
I see the Fatal Collapse before the first spark.

I do this thing in my head where I sort of
Talk to myself.
I narrate my life.
Like I narrate everything that happens in my head as it's happening, and immediately after it's happened.

It's weird:
Here – (*She points at her mouth.*) nothing
Here – (*She points at her head.*) it's chaos.

I can sometimes get a bit
Carried away.
Sort of like I'm in a movie.
Do you ever feel like that?
Of course you do.
We all do, sometimes.
An epic soundtrack, flattering lighting, impossibly tousled hair
I
am in a movie.
Constantly.

I'm not mental, by the way   I'm know that's not the most reassuring sentence but   I'm not an actual wack job.   I'm not one of those mad fuckers people don't wanna make eye contact with on public transport.
I'm not mental.
I just
I kind of
Make stuff up.

There's something no one told me when I was growing up.
In my formative years
No one ever told me
That life is kind of
Disappointing

Kind of dull
Kind of… less bouncy than you might want it to be
No one ever tells you
You're not Jessica Alba
Or Ingrid Bergman
You're a bit flatter
A bit less shiny
A bit less interesting
But you get given a brain
Endless space
Limitless possibility
It's kind of unfair really
Out there you've got reality. Terrorism and UKIP and cystic acne.
But you've been given infinity right here in your skull.

The Fall

James Fritz

James Fritz's *The Fall* was commissioned for NYT's sixtieth anniversary year, and was performed at the Finborough Theatre, and then revived at Southwark Playhouse in 2018. It is a piece exploring ideas around ageing, death and dying. Made up of three scenes, *The Fall* has an elusive, mercurial quality in which place and time are elastic, and there are no 'named' characters. Despite being open to interpretation, Fritz's play is unflinching in the way it deals examines the pressures that an ageing population puts on society and personal relationships.

In the first scene of *The Fall* we meet Girl and Boy in a flat late at night. The flat, which Girl cleans every week, is owned by a ninety-two-year-old man, and she has snuck round (because she has been told that the old man will be away) so that she and Boy can be alone. Just as things are getting romantic, however, they discover the old man – naked and barely alive – lying beside his bed. They think about calling an ambulance, but then Girl wonders whether he would rather die than be resuscitated. The scene ends as they consider how it would feel to be ninety-two. The second scene plays with time, as we are taken through a couple's life in fast-forward. We follow the characters, One and Two, from the beginning of their relationship through to marriage, children, financial difficulties and eventually having to care for One's elderly mother, Jean. Just as the burden of bills and rent are becoming too much, Jean dies, leaving her flat to the couple. It quickly becomes apparent, however, that Two helped Jean to die by suffocating her; but we are unsure if Jean asked for this or if Two murdered her to inherit her money. The theme of euthanasia continues in the third scene in which we see a group of old people in a dystopian future world, crammed into a nursing home being pressured to take up assisted suicide.

Two

■ **Character** Age and gender unspecified.

■ **Location** Present day.

■ **Accent** Your own.

■ **Scene** The speech is taken from the second scene. One and Two have been going through a difficult time: after their honeymoon period (in which they had their son, Liam), they are now struggling to afford the rent, pay for school trips and deal with mounting credit card bills. Added to this, after a fall, One's mother, Jean, now needs round-the-clock care, which One and Two also can't afford, and the couple are told that she doesn't qualify for any government help because her house is worth too much. Then one afternoon, Two calls One at work to say that Jean has died in her sleep. It seems that their problems have been solved and they can move into Jean's flat, but it becomes clear that Jean may not have died of natural causes. When confronted about it, Two admits that she helped Jean to die.

■ **Who are they talking to?** Their partner, One.

■ **Where?** It's up to you.

■ **What do they want?** Two wants to convince One of two things; firstly, that Jean – One's mother, asked for help to die, and secondly, that Two has done the right thing by agreeing. Two goes about this by reminding One of the constant pain that Jean was in, and how she was worried about having to sell her house to pay for care. Two wants to remind One of Jean's dire situation, whilst also assuring One that when it happened, Jean didn't suffer.

■ **Things to think about** Later in the scene, One mentions a conversation that they had with Jean which casts some doubt on whether Two is telling the truth about what happened. Look at what One says, and think about whether Two is telling the whole truth.

If Two *is* lying, how does this change the way you perform the speech? It is unlikely that Two is a cold-blooded murderer, but how desperate must Two have been to kill their mother-in-law, and if Two was *that* desperate, how much turmoil must they be going through when they describe the moment that it happened?

Like the rest of the scene, the speech is written in short statements. Think about the gaps in between each statement, and all the things that the character *isn't* saying in these moments. This will help you to find the subtext in the speech.

The playwright has not specified a gender for this character.

Where to find the play This play is published by Nick Hern Books (www.nickhernbooks.co.uk).

Two

She asked me. To help her.
We were talking.
She didn't want to.
Move
And
Since her fall
The pain
And
Our situation
Her flat
Those sharks
She knew
That this was best
So she asked me.
I'm sorry.
I love you.
For us.
For Liam.
Her flat.
It's meant for you.
Always.
That's what she said.
She asked me.
I'm tired she said.
I'm ready.
I said no
But
She kept asking
And.
I love you.

Pills.
And I put a pillow
Resting on her.
I love you.

She didn't fight.
It was gentle.
I promise.
She knew.
Every year in that home
Would've been
Worse for her.
Worse for us.
Worse for Liam.
Worse for Liam.
I love you.
So.
Since her fall.
So much pain
And.
She said.

Eskimos.

When Eskimos get old they walk out into the
snow and die.
Choose their time.
And I thought.
If I was her.
What would I want?

Flood

Rory Mullarkey

Flood was performed as an open-air piece on the Salford Quays in 2012. Involving over two hundred members, it completed NYT's environmental trilogy of plays (including *S'warm* and *Slick*) which used large-scale ensembles to explore some of the most pressing issues of the age. *Flood* is written in a semi-rhyming, free-verse form and imagines a modern-day Biblical-style flood. It is a muscular and bold piece of writing from Rory Mullarkey, which combines spoken-word-style monologues with sections of narration and dialogue and asks: what would happen if the world was submerged in water and there were only a handful of survivors left?

Flood presents a world in chaos: a huge deluge has consumed the earth and many people have died. The action of the play features a group of characters who survived the flood and have been drawn towards a flashing light in the distance. They find themselves at the foot of a lighthouse, and waiting for them there is Nat, a kind of Noah figure, or maybe even a Christ-like woman who tells them she has dreamt that she is destined to lead them towards salvation. But should they follow her?

Nat

Character Age and gender unspecified.

Location The future.

Accent Your own.

Scene A chorus of narrators have just told the story of what happened when the flood started, and in this scene we get to know more about the characters who survived. Nat is the first person to speak; she tells everyone present about a recurring and prophetic dream she had about the flood, and how she dreamt that a group of people would gather at her door – just as they have done now. But the dream didn't end there – she also had a vision of a boat, and a voice said to her, 'This is what you must find.' By the end of the speech she announces that, although she doesn't know how, she is going to follow her dream and lead them to this vessel and then to dry land.

Who is she talking to? A group of people that she has never met before, who have gathered at her door.

Where? On a clifftop, which is surrounded by water as far as the eye can see.

What does she want? Nat wants the people to follow her. She wants them to buy into her dream and be persuaded that it means something. She wants them to trust her; the trouble is, she doesn't know exactly what it means herself, and so as well as trying to convince them, she is also trying to convince herself.

Things to think about Think about your own dreams – how difficult is it to describe them? Is Nat's dream difficult to describe? Are any sections of her dream crystal clear? If so, make sure you can see them in your mind's eye.

Is Nat convinced by her dream? Does she have any doubt? Is she more convinced of her story by the end of the speech than she was at the beginning?

Think about how high the stakes are – this is the biggest natural disaster the world has ever seen. Even though the speech is written in a heightened style, the emotions and feelings should feel real.

Think about how you are going to tackle the poetic style of the speech: are you going to make it sound very natural, or will you play up the poetry of the language?

There are other speeches in the play that you might also like to look at.

■ **Where to find the play** This play can be read on the NYT website (www.nyt.org.uk/monologues, password: nytspeeches).

Nat

Hello.
My name is Nat.
It was my light that
You saw gleaming in the night
Me who waved to you across the waves.
I'll tell you who I am.
Since words mean more from people that you know.
My name is Nat.
I've said that.
Erm.
I live here.
And my parents did before.
And before that my grandparents.
It was them who built this lighthouse
As soon as they saw
This spot
This high-up cliff top looking at the sea
They thought it was the perfect place to place
A lighthouse
So that it could face
The water
And guide the fishing ships away from rocks
And warn them in the fog.
So I was born here.
And this is where I've lived my whole life.
In this high tower next to the sea.
And that is who I am
The whole of me.
But anyway
What I really need to say
Others have said before
I had a dream.
I never used to have them
But they started months ago
And they were always the same:

I dreamt the sky cracked open when the clouds rolled in
I dreamt the water fell so hard it bruised my skin
I dreamt the buildings drowned and that the mountains sank
I dreamt the plains were sodden and the deserts dank
I dreamt I climbed my house and I turned on the light
I dreamt I waited and waited through the sunken night
And I dreamt people came
And I dreamt I saw them
Gathered at my door
I dreamt I gathered them
And that I led them
And that they were scared
But that I led them, then,
To some place prepared
Past sunken lands
And through the sunken world
Past waterfalls
And places where the whirlpools twirled
To a calmer place
To where the rapids lulled
And in the distance
There
Afloat
Some kind of craft
A sailing ship
A boat
To carry us somewhere where the flood had fallen away
Where we could look upon dry land
Someday
And a voice in my head
Loud and proud
Said
'This is what you must find.'
And as soon as it spoke
I awoke.
And you
The people
Came.

And now I ask that you all come with me
To find this ship
To go across the sea
And find somewhere where we can all be free.
And though
I don't know
How to go
Or how to start
This quest
I know I feel it in my heart
That we must go
And I know
I have little to offer you
Only my word.
But when all else has been taken from us
What does anyone have left to offer
But their word?

▦ **Character** Age and gender unspecified.

▦ **Location** The future.

▦ **Accent** Your own.

▦ **Scene** Nat has just told the group she has dreamt that she will lead them to safety, but it is clear that not everyone trusts her. A disagreement follows about which path to take. Jaf wants to make mayhem – now that there are no more authority figures she wants to take advantage and create anarchy. Mini pipes up to say that he is scared; he thinks there has been too much destruction already and maybe there is a reason why they were all led to Nat's lighthouse. Roil is unsure about whether Nat is to be trusted and loudly voices his scepticism in front of the whole group.

▦ **Who is he talking to?** Nat, but he is also speaking for the benefit of everyone else.

▦ **Where?** On a clifftop which is surrounded by water as far as the eye can see.

▦ **What does he want?** Roil is in a state of emotional flux. His world has been turned upside down; he swam through the night to get here, his home has been destroyed and he finds himself listening to someone who says they are basically the new Messiah. He wants to vent his anger at the situation, and make it clear that he won't be taken advantage of.

▦ **Things to think about** How might Roil change through the speech? It seems that he is determined not to listen to Nat, but are there any moments where he might feel tempted by Nat's promise of hope?

Make sure you consider the high stakes of the situation; imagine all the things that might have preceded this moment – losing his home, perhaps even his family, and swimming through the night to reach the lighthouse. It might be worth researching some modern-day refugee stories.

As with Nat's speech, think about how you are going to tackle the poetic style of the writing. Try to make the speech flow, whilst also playing with the line endings.

There are other speeches in the play that you might also like to look at.

■ **Where to find the play** This play can be read on the NYT website (www.nyt.org.uk/monologues, password: nytspeeches).

Roil

My name is Roil and I came here
From the city
I swam across a sheer
Sheet of water
Through the night
Towards this place where I could see a light
And when I get here all I seem
To find
Is some mad lighthouse keeper
Who's had a crazy dream.
You had a dream, Nat?
Oh wow.
Oh well done you.
Coz I've had dreams
And I'm sure some others too
Amongst the people here
Have had some dreams
But that doesn't mean
That I or they
Should immediately appoint themselves the master
Of all the rest of us
In the wake of the biggest fucking
Natural disaster
The world has ever seen.
So okay so
I had a crazy dream once I could fly
But that doesn't make me king of the fucking sky
In real life
I had a dream once I could walk
On water
But that doesn't mean I can talk
As if I'm the bloody authority
On maritime navigation technology.
You had a dream?
We all dream

It's not special
It's a standard human trait
So you'll forgive me if I'm slightly cynical about this
If I want to wait a minute
Before I decide you're the new Messiah
And strap myself in for the ride
To some distant imaginary boat
You may or may not have seen a few times
In your sleep
I'm sorry okay I'm just gonna keep
Relatively sceptical
At this juncture
Coz I feel
That where we're at now
This nightmare
This is real
So forgive me if I'm not
Immediately gonna throw in my lot
With some weirdo who's a bit twisted in the head
And has probably been eating a bit too much cheese before
they go to bed.
And so
Thanks so much for your offer
But I don't really want to go
On some wild boat chase with you
Sorry mate
But no.

Fluffy Rabbit

Paul Charlton

Fluffy Rabbit was performed as part of a season of short plays at the Lyric Hammersmith in 2004. It was written by former NYT member Paul Charlton, and explores the world of a young boy living with domestic violence.

The play is set in Boy's bedroom. The stage directions tell us that the walls should be covered with posters of *Star Wars* and footballers, and early on in the piece, Boy tells us that he is eight years old. We gradually learn through the speech that Boy takes refuge in his bedroom from the arguments his parents are having, and he creates imaginary worlds as a way of coping. Throughout the play the sound of these arguments bleed through the walls, and the audience experiences the traumatic circumstances that Boy is living in. The situation gets worse and worse, with Boy creating more and more imaginary ways to try and prevent his parents from arguing, until the play culminates in tragedy.

Boy

■ **Character** An eight-year-old boy.

■ **Location** Present-day Britain.

■ **Accent** Your own.

■ **Scene** This excerpt comes midway through the play. In it, Boy describes a specific argument that his parents are having, and the variety of ways he tries to stop them. He imagines that his actions in his bedroom might have an effect on his parent's behaviour: he tries staying very still, then holding his breath, then using his 'special brain power' to make his dad stop shouting.

■ **Who is he talking to?** Boy talks to the audience, but throughout the play he also reports things that his father has said.

■ **Where?** Boy is in his bedroom; a place where he hides when his parents start shouting. It is also a place where he can create imaginative worlds that shield him from reality.

■ **What does he want?** In this speech, he desperately wants his parents to stop arguing.

■ **Things to think about** Think about the physical space of the bedroom: where is the bed? What other furniture is there? You don't need to build this space when you perform the speech, but having a sense of what the room looks and feels like will help.

We are told that Boy is eight years old. Think about how you might play this age: do you have any brothers or sisters of this age that you could base him on? How are they physically and vocally different to you?

Make a decision about how to do 'Dad's voice': do you want to become the father in that moment, or do you want to be Boy doing an impression of his dad?

Be specific about where the parents' voices are coming from – it will help the audience imagine too.

How does the speech build? As he tries different tactics to get them to stop arguing, how does he feel when these work? How does he feel when they don't?

The whole play is a monologue, and so you may wish to find a different section to perform.

■ **Where to find the play** This play can be read on the NYT website (www.nyt.org.uk/monologues, password: nytspeeches).

Boy

I've been to bed for ages. It was a good night tonight. They laughed. Loud! No bad talking. Til the smash. (*Beat.*) I jumped. It was my fault. I held my breath for ages and I only breathed under the duvet. And only a little bit as well. I stayed really still and hoped that they'd stop. I fort that maybe my mind might be able to make them stop, like Dad said. And it worked. They stopped talking bad to each other. And it felt good cos I could help stop it. Then I breathed proplee and just after that they started again. So I stopped again. But it wouldn't work any more.

Mam was screaming louder than ever, I'd never heard it that bad. I couldn't hear the words they were saying so I went into the spare room to hear better. (*In Dad's voice.*) 'If you leave I'll fucking kill you.' He said a bad word. He never says bad words. Maybe the devil had got him. Or a Sandman or monster. Or all of them together. It must be. They must be making him say it. If they could make him say bad words then they might make him hurt Mam.

God wasn't helping and I didn't think my light sabre would work against all of them and holding my breath had stopped working so I was stuck. I had to use my special brain power in another way. I had to!

I picked up one of my dad's weights that he uses and I held it out in front of me. I thought with all my brain for him to stop. If I could just hold it out and not drop it, he might stop. The monsters might leave him alone. My arms were killing me, they were really heavy. But if I could just stop being so horrible and think about my mam and dad, not me. Think about saving my mam and not being scared. And it was working. It'd gone quiet. But I knew if I let them down it would be like the breathing thing. He would start again. Except this time I wouldn't have a mam afterwards.

I started to shake. I was trying to hold on. Honest. But it just dropped. Smash to the floor. Noise on the stairs. The monster's coming for me! My dad coming to get me! But it was my mam. I'd saved her.

Prasanna Puwanarajah

Treat your audition like a rehearsal – you're going in to do your work, collaborate and make your offer, rather than like you're going in to be judged.

Paul Charlton was a member of NYT from 1998 to 2004. He appeared in *A Midsummer Night's Dream* and *West Side Story* as well as being the first ever assistant director on a course (Junior Course, 2000). He works as a writer, actor and sometime director – winning two Fringe First awards for his plays and co-writing and starring in his own comedy series, *The Ginge, the Geordie and the Geek* (BBC).

What advice would you give a young actor playing this part?

Concentrate on playing the emotional truth and *not* on playing a young child. I audition hundreds of young people for NYT each year and the most successful monologues about young characters are done by actors who concentrate on telling the story with clarity and subtlety and don't just try to do a good impression of a small child.

If you could give one piece of advice about auditions, what would it be?

Concentrate on finding the emotional truth behind the story and live that truth rather than showing the auditioner that you can play that emotion. The former creates nuanced detailed believable acting while the latter creates 'state acting' and rarely feels authentic. An actor should be like a referee in a football match – that is to say, you should never notice them until the end and if you have been caught up in the game/the characters' story then you know the ref/actor has had a good game.

What is your abiding memory of NYT?

Wearing nothing but a little skirt and glitter and hanging from a tree for weeks while playing a fairy in *A Midsummer Night's Dream*. I didn't say a word in that show, but I still loved the experience so much and I think that really says a lot about NYT. It's not about the individual, it's about the ensemble.

How did NYT affect your future life and career?

I met some of my closest friends and had some of my most treasured experiences during my NYT years. It also opened my mind to different ways of thinking and I think I actually grew three inches in height from the positivity and enthusiasm of other NYT members and staff. And I needed those three inches as I'm only a small lad!

Harm's Way

Zawe Ashton

Harm's Way was first produced at the Lowry Theatre, Salford, in 2007. Written by NYT alumna Zawe Ashton, it is an intensely dark comedy that delves into the chaotic lives of three truant teenagers. Whilst some moments in the play are shockingly funny, it also tackles serious issues like rape, violence and domestic abuse. This speech deals with extremely adult themes.

There are three characters in the play: Dawn, Troy and Sam. At the beginning, we see Dawn with a bloodstained wok in her hand standing over a body which is covered with a sheet. This is Dawn's mum, whom Dawn has hit over the head with the wok, and is now dead. Dawn's boyfriend, Troy, comes round with his friend Sam, and as the three of them start to drink alcohol and take drugs, we begin to understand that these are three extremely deprived young people living on the edge. Their behaviour becomes more unpredictable and warped until, at the end of the play in a make-believe game of 'Mummies and Daddies', Troy stabs Dawn.

Dawn

■ **Character** A thirteen-year-old girl.

■ **Location** London, 2007.

■ **Accent** Your own.

■ **Scene** This is Dawn's final speech and it explores her relationship with her mum. We learn throughout the play that Dawn's mum was a prostitute and a heroin addict, and although Dawn was embarrassed by her mum, she defends her when Troy is rude about her. In this final speech, Dawn's complex feelings about her mum begin to surface.

■ **Who is she talking to?** Her dead mother's body.

■ **Where?** In their living room.

■ **What does she want?** In this speech, Dawn talks about the poverty-stricken life she has led. She tells of how she was raped by one of her mum's clients, and how she dreamed of killing her mum afterwards. She also describes some of their life together: from dancing to begging and sleeping without a blanket. Maybe Dawn is trying to forgive her mum for everything she did wrong. Or perhaps she wants her mum to hear how awful some of her life has been. It is clear from the rest of the play that as well as being angry, Dawn also loves her mum and does have happy memories of her. It is up to you whether you wish to explore her anger or her forgiveness, or whether you think the speech contains a mixture of both.

■ **Things to think about** Prior to this speech, Dawn has been stabbed by Troy, and the stage directions say she is *'hurt but alive'* – think about how much you want to explore this in the speech. Be careful not to make the fact that she has been stabbed overwhelm the text. If you like, you could choose to ignore the stabbing, and just have her talk to her mum.

Think carefully about what Dawn would like her mother to feel: would she like her mum to say sorry? Would she like her mum to be soothed by her speech? Or perhaps something else?

Make sure that you have fully imagined Dawn's life. You could start by imagining what the living room looks like, and then begin to picture the rest of the flat. What might an average day in Dawn's life have entailed before she killed her mum?

Where to find the play This play can be read on the NYT website (www.nyt.org.uk/monologues, password: nytspeeches).

Dawn

(*Holding a blood stained wok.*) Mum… Mama… Mama, wake up now, yeah?

You alright, you want a tea or something?

Beat.

Thought the light under the door was you.

Thought it was you with milk and honey, calm the sting, help me sleep.

Fingers through my hair smelt like yours.

Clammy.

Soft.

But you were downstairs.

Whiskey breath.

Missing tooth.

Lost all my milk teeth after that.

Sleepin on that stained sheet made me dream about takin your life away.

When you danced, I danced.

When you begged, I begged.

I slept without a blanket.

Pierced my ears so you'd see me as pretty.

Y'know, *I'm* wrapped in that sheet I'm lit up by a spotlight

I'm visible

I'm runnin to you

I'm in a one cold side bed with a little arm stretched out

I'm bleedin in a place I can't touch

It's okay.

I'm not afraid to die.

Feel the air squeezed out of me anyway.

I'm glad we finally got to talk

(*Beat.*)

(*Looks at the wok.*) What is that thing anyway? (*Giggle turns to laughter.*)

(*Stillness. Birds sing.*)

(*The day dawns.*)

The Holyland

Daragh Carville

The Holyland was performed at Pleasance during the Edinburgh Festival Fringe before transferring to the Lyric Hammersmith in 2001. Written by Daragh Carville, the action is set in the Holyland district of Belfast and gives a snapshot into the lives of the people that live there. Largely focusing on the murky underworld of drugs, Carville's play embraces moments of comedy as well as tragedy as it explores the tensions and struggles of a diverse community of people and asks questions about identity, home and belonging.

The play takes place over the course of one day – New Year's Eve – in The Holyland, a student area of Belfast, so called because of the names of the surrounding streets (e.g. Jerusalem St.). The Holyland of Carville's play is home to a wide variety of people: from Chris, a *Big Issue* seller, to a dysfunctional Velvet Underground tribute band, to Terry, a small-time drug dealer who has got himself into some trouble. The play dips into the lives of many characters, but it is Terry's story which forms the backbone of the play. When we first see Terry he is wide-eyed and agitated – clearly in some distress. Gradually we learn that his friend has died in a drugs-related incident, and he feels in some way responsible. He begins to question whether he has made good life choices and whether or not to continue on this path. Removing himself from the network of dealers and users, however, is harder than it seems, and Rob and Sean – fellow dealers – are keen to keep him in the fold.

Rob

■ **Character** A man in his twenties.

■ **Location** Belfast, at the turn of the millennium.

■ **Accent** Northern Irish.

■ **Scene** Terry, Rob and Sean have just been to the funeral of a friend who has died in mysterious circumstances. In this scene we meet Rob for the first time, who, along with Sean, pressures Terry into snorting some of the dead man's ashes in order to show solidarity with him. Terry doesn't want to take part in the ritual, but Rob insists, questioning Terry's loyalty. At the end of the scene, it looks as if Terry is going to yield to Rob's demand, but the scene finishes just before we can be sure.

■ **Who is he talking to?** Terry, his friend and colleague.

■ **Where?** The front room of Terry's house.

■ **What does he want?** On the surface, Rob just wants Terry to join them in snorting some ashes. He says that he wants to honour their dead friend's memory and make sure they never forget him. Ultimately, however, Rob wants to control the situation and control Terry; he can see that the death and funeral have shaken Terry, and he wants to keep Terry onside and make sure he will continue to be a dealer. Rob tries to make Terry think that they are all part of the same family, and that by snorting the dead man's ashes they will be together forever, unable to escape each other.

■ **Things to think about** Rob wants power and control over Terry – think about the different tactics he might use to achieve this, i.e. sympathy, anger, kindness.

This scene is very much focused on persuading Terry to do what Rob wants him to do. Make sure you are really clear where Terry is, and what he is doing. When Rob is speaking, imagine how he reacts to all the tactics that Rob employs.

Try and imagine what happened to the dead man. In the play it is unclear exactly how he died, but it will be helpful to you to have a clear idea of the previous circumstances to this scene. Was it Rob's fault? Or Terry's fault? How did they come to have control of the ashes?

■ Where to find the play This play is published by Methuen Drama, an imprint of Bloomsbury Publishing Plc (www.bloomsbury.com).

Rob

I'm gonna ask you a question now, Terry. Alright?

(*Pause.*)

What do you think HE would think of you, if he could see you now? Standin there snivelling. Huh? What would he think of you? What do you think he'd say to you, Terry?

(*Terry shakes his head.*)

He'd tell you to buck up your ideas, wouldn't he? He'd tell you to catch yourself on, don't let the side down. Wouldn't he?

(*Terry sobs, nods.*)

Well then. That's what you're gonna have to do then, isn't it? Huh? Isn't it?

(*Terry nods.*)

Now come on now, big lad. You saw the way those people looked at us, didn't you, Terry? Back there, at Roselawn.

(*Terry nods.*)

Lookin down their noses at us. JUDGIN us. They blame us for what happened. You know that, don't you? They think it was our fault. You could see it in their eyes. We're nothing but scum to them people, Terry. And that's what they thought of him as well. Their own son. Their own flesh and blood. Do you think he'd wanna be with them? Do you? Do you think they ever gave a shit about him? WE'RE his fuckin family, Terry. We're his real family, not them 'uns. He belongs here, with us. In the Holyland. This is where he belongs. It's okay, mate, it's okay. You're upset. We're all upset. It's perfectly understandable. We've lost our mate. But we're never gonna forget him, are we, Terry? This way we make sure of it.

(*Sean leans back from the table, his work done. He looks round at Rob. Rob nods and comes forward. Sean moves out of the way, stands back. Rob kneels in at the table. He looks down at the ash. And then he leans forward, presses one nostril closed, and inhales a long line. A moment, and he brings his head up again.)*

It's what he would have wanted.

(Rob stands up from the table, wiping his nose. He moves back, and Sean steps in at the table. Adopts the position.)

Reece Ritchie

Breathe. If there's one thing I've learnt auditioning in high-pressure situations it's that you start to breathe shallower and faster. The adrenaline pumps and lines you know can vanish. Breathing in through the nose, and out through the mouth gives the brain the oxygen it needs and it will help settle you. Sounds daft but trust me, it works.

Inside

Philip Osment

Inside was developed with NYT in 2008 and was presented at Cookham Wood Young Offenders Institution and Soho Theatre under the title *Fathers Inside* (but was later published under the title *Inside*). Based on research conducted in Rochester prison, *Inside* explores the lives of a group of male prisoners and their relationships both with their children and their own fathers.

The play is framed around a series of drama workshops run by Tim and his assistant Dom, which aim to explore what it is to be a father and what a child needs. The seven young prisoners that take part are initially sceptical about the classes – back in their cells, they joke about games like 'Zip, Zap, Boing!' Gradually, they begin to open up about how they feel and start to think not only about how their behaviour might affect their children, but also about how their own relationships with their fathers might have affected them. As the play progresses, the tensions and power struggles between the prisoners begin to creep into the rehearsal room, and the drama of their own lives begins to dominate the workshops.

Aswan

Character A nineteen-year-old man.

Location In a prison.

Accent Your own.

Scene We join this scene midway through, when Aswan is telling his friend Damien what has just happened when he was visited by his ex-girlfriend, Sadie (who is pregnant with Aswan's child). Sadie has revealed to Aswan that she has a new boyfriend and that she is thinking of going to live in Spain with him. She says that she thinks her new boyfriend will be able to provide for their son in a way that Aswan can't, and asks Aswan to see that this is the best thing for their baby. On hearing this news, Aswan goes into a rage and begins to attack Sadie, at which point he is restrained and taken back to his cell.

Who is he talking to? One of his closest friends, Damien.

Where? In his cell.

What does he want? Aswan is full of frustration and confusion. Ultimately, he wants to be a good father to his son. He wants to be able to provide and care for him and be a loving husband, but because he is in prison he feels helpless. He also wants to be a better father than his own father was, but he already feels like he is failing at that. Does he want Damien to sympathise with him, or console him? Perhaps he wants Damien help him resolve the situation, or maybe he wants Damien to leave him alone?

Things to think about Think about how long after Sadie's visit this scene takes place. Is it many hours after or has it just happened? Is Aswan still feeling anger, or has he calmed down?

What does the letter that Aswan reads to his unborn baby in Scene Five tell us about him? How does Aswan's behaviour in this scene contrast to the way he treats Sadie, the mother of his child, in Scene Eight? What does this tell us about Aswan?

Knowing what we know about Aswan's feelings for his unborn son, how do you think he feels when Sadie rejects him?

Think about what Aswan feels like when recounting the incident to Damien, and maybe try exploring his shame and embarrassment as well as the pain and hurt he feels.

Look at the other 'workshop' scenes, where Aswan speaks about his relationships with family members outside of prison to piece together what he is like as a person. Try and come up with three words that you could use to describe Aswan.

▨ **Where to find the play** This play is published by Oberon Books (www.oberonbooks.co.uk).

Aswan

She's sitting there and she's got my kid inside her and she's saying to me that she's going to let some other man be his father and there ain't nothing I can do about it because I'm in here and there's fucking guards all around us, you know? And she's got this fucking lovebite on her neck and she hasn't even tried to hide it, and all I can think of is this guy sucking on her neck and fucking her with my baby inside her. That ain't right. It just ain't right. It's fucking obscene. And she tells me she's going to move to Malaga with this Ramon guy, innit? That's fucking Spain, I tell her. And she even asks me to see that it's for the best for the kid because Ramon is going to provide for him in a way that I won't never be able to. And I ask her if Ramon is a fucking vampire and I'm looking at the thing on her neck, and she says that the trouble with me is that I always bring it down to shit like that. And I says shit like what? And she says stuff about who's shagging who? And I tell her I don't see why my kid should have to put up with Ramon's dick coming in there when he's trying to get ready to be born. And she calls me a fucking dickhead and I call her a fucking ho and she gets up to go, which is when I grab her round the throat. And the screws come up and twist my arm up my fucking back and the last thing I see is her waddling out the door with my baby and she don't even look back when I tell her that I fucking love her and I want to see my kid. And I beg her not to do this to me. It's like I'm not fucking there. I'm just a piece of shit. I'm nothing.

Brownie

■ **Character** A twenty-year-old man.

■ **Location** In a prison.

■ **Accent** Your own.

■ **Scene** Brownie is a disruptive presence; throughout the drama workshops he constantly comments on other people's situations and questions the authority of the workshop leaders. He often disrespects the other prisoners by suggesting that he has slept with all of their wives and girlfriends, and taunts them with racist language. He hates almost everyone in the prison – the governor, the chaplain, the 'screws' and the other prisoners, and they don't like him either. Despite his unpopularity, Brownie has struck up a friendship with Tommy, who is teaching him about philosophy. In this speech, Brownie is dictating a letter to Tommy containing all the things he would like to say to his father – he is opening up about how he feels in a rare moment of vulnerability.

■ **Who is he talking to?** In the letter he is talking to his father, but within the context of the scene, he is dictating these words to Tommy.

■ **Where?** In his cell.

■ **What does he want?** Deep down, Brownie wants his father to care about him, but he also wants his father to know how his absence affected him as a child. Perhaps a small part of him wants to apologise for never wanting to come and see him in prison, but mainly Brownie wants to let his father know how angry he is that he deserted him – both by being in prison, and for committing suicide.

■ **Things to think about** Even though Brownie might seem like a mindless tough-guy at first, he has hidden depths – be careful not to judge Brownie. Imagine him as a fully rounded person with hopes, dreams and aspirations.

Brownie skips in order to 'be in the moment' – what does this tell us about Brownie? Perhaps that he has a busy mind, and that he is constantly thinking about his life and raking over his past.

Brownie can't read – what might this reveal about his past?

In Scene Five, even though Brownie starts the scene displaying negativity, how does his behaviour change? Does he support some of the other inmates? What might this tell us?

In Scene Eleven, after a fight almost breaks out, Tim asks him what he wants from the sessions – what does Brownie say? What does this tell us about him?

■ **Where to find the play** This play is published by Oberon Books (www.oberonbooks.co.uk).

Brownie

I never understood why you were always pissing off and leaving us. I remember all them times Mum took me to see you in those places – going through them big gates and the guards searching Mum, running their fucking hands all over her. Searching my fucking buggy. And I remember the smell of fucking metal and concrete in that place. And sweat. And piss and shit. Then we'd go into this room and there'd be all these other men sitting there with their women and their kids. And Mum would tell me to go and sit on your lap and give you a kiss. And you'd push me away and tell me to put my fists up. And we'd pretend to fucking box. And you'd make me cry because you always ended up punching me too hard. And then when it was time to leave I never understood why you weren't coming with us. And the men in suits would rattle their chains and take you away. Later when I did understand, there was always a fucking row on visiting days because I never wanted to go and see you. And Mum tried to make me. But I hated going there. I hated you for being there. I didn't want to be in that place. Which is fucking laughable seeing as how I've ended up in here with the smell of piss and shit and metal and fucking concrete. But I ain't you. I ain't gonna end up like you because you were a fucking loser.

Standing in the rain with Mum at your grave. I didn't feel nothing. Fucking nothing. The fucking priest talked about you returning to the arms of our Lord and I remember thinking that you'd probably headbutt the fucking Lord if he tried to put his arms round you. He talked about how sometimes it seems like life is too hard to bear and how sometimes we don't feel strong enough to carry on but how the Lord is fucking testing us. Well you failed the fucking test you loser. All you could do was tie your fucking sheet in a noose and put it round your neck. I'd say you got fucking nought out of ten for that answer.

Jekyll & Hyde

Evan Placey

Jekyll & Hyde was first performed in 2017 by the NYT REP company at the Ambassadors Theatre in the West End. Evan Placey's play takes the themes and ideas from R. L. Stevenson's gothic classic, *Strange Case of Dr Jekyll and Mr Hyde*, and reimagines it for the twenty-first century. Like a set of Russian dolls, Placey's *Jekyll & Hyde* contains stories within stories within stories, and explores multiple themes including female agency, repression, the Internet and personal responsibility.

Stevenson's novel is the bedrock for the play, which picks up in the aftermath of Dr Henry Jekyll's death in 1886. To begin with, we follow the story of his bereaved wife, Hattie Jekyll, making it seem at first that the play will be an exploration of what it was like for women in Victorian times. When Hattie follows in her late husband's footsteps and transforms into Lady Flossie Hyde, it's like we are watching a female version of Stevenson's original – exploring similar themes but from the perspective of a woman. Halfway through, however, another layer is introduced as we discover that we are actually watching fan-fiction written by a young woman, Florence, in the twenty-first century, and it seems that her stories online have been encouraging people around the world to commit crimes in the name of combatting violence against women and bringing down the patriarchy. As both the Victorian and contemporary stories unfold, the play begins to explore the alter-egos we create both in real life and online, and questions whether violence is ever an option when trying to bring about social change.

■ **Character** A school-age girl in her teens.

■ **Location** Present-day Britain.

■ **Accent** Your own.

■ **Scene** The speech comes from the first scene of the second act of the play. We are in the modern day and Florence, the author of the 'fan fiction' which has been brought to life in the first act, has been arrested on suspicion of the murder of Police Constable Michael Rose. Constable Rose had previously been accused of sexually harassing a young woman who was in custody, but after settling out of court, was never charged. The young woman's name got leaked, however, and she was subject to a great deal of abuse – especially online. Hearing about this, Florence then took to social media calling for the police officer's name to be hacked and released to '*Give him a taste of his own medicine,*' also saying, '*I wish someone would make him see what it feels like.*' As well as this, she also wrote a chapter of fan-fiction in which a character called Michael Rose gets murdered. Florence denies committing or encouraging the murder, and maintains that she is not responsible, despite what she has written.

■ **Who is she talking to?** DCI Renford and DC Williams.

■ **Where?** In an interrogation room.

■ **What does she want?** Primarily, Florence wants the police officers to believe that she is innocent (even though we find out later in the play that she is much more involved in violence than she first admits). She also wants DCI Renford to recognise his own hypocrisy: just prior to this speech, Florence brings up the fact that she has received a great deal of online abuse for standing up to misogyny in her school, but when she reported it, she was told to ignore it. She is now indignant that she is accused of being complicit in the police officer's murder – because she wrote a story about it – whereas direct threats against her were considered to be empty.

■ **Things to think about** Read the rest of the play, and think carefully about what Florence *doesn't* reveal at this point. What is she hiding?

To what extent are her tears halfway through the speech play-acting, and how much are they fuelled by real emotion?

Remember that she desperately wants the police officers to believe her so that she can carry out her plan – she has to be convincing.

Think about how it feels for Florence to have been arrested and now interrogated by the police. Does she feel worried or frightened? Or does she feel like she is being given the chance to stand up for what she believes in?

In his introduction to the play, Evan Placey writes: '*Sometimes sentences are broken across multiple lines of text; this is to help break up a chunk of text and give it a rhythm, but it's not about stopping or pausing between lines, especially when there's no punctuation at the end of a line – the rule above still applies, the next line comes right in. The spacing is to help push the pace and drive the shift in intentions within a hefty bit of dialogue.*'

■ **Where to find the play** This play is published by Nick Hern Books (www.nickhernbooks.co.uk).

Florence

I just write a little blog with some thoughts and fan fiction that no one even reads.
I don't kill people.
I just…
post stuff.

It's not a crime to post my feelings.

It's not a crime to post my desires.
To express my desires –
I'm not enacting the crime,
and before you say it, if this is what you're going to say, if this is what this is about,
I'm not *inciting violence*.
Because I never told someone to do it.
I never encouraged someone to do it.
I just expressed my desire, a fantasy you might say.

(*She's gotten herself worked up, grabs some tissue for her tears. And then a shift.*)

Because it's actually really a case of language, grammar.
Because if I'd said
'Please someone go kill this police officer, assault him' well yeah totally, but I didn't.
I said *I wish*.
Which is like
Which is like someone saying, um, say
'I wish someone would rape her and glue her slutty mouth shut'
Because when I showed you messages I was receiving, like
'I wish someone would rape her and glue her slutty mouth shut'
You said it wasn't a threat, you couldn't really do anything because –
he wasn't saying someone should do it.
He was saying 'I wish'

And we can't be arresting people for fantasies in their head,
however deranged.
And they were just words, just a...
'post' you said.
And maybe I should just ignore it.
Maybe I should just come offline.
So.
Can I go home now?

Kes

Barry Hines
adapted for the stage by Lawrence Till

Kes was presented by NYT on the main stage of the Lyric Hammersmith in 2003. Based on the book *A Kestrel for a Knave* by Barry Hines, *Kes* was already well known through Ken Loach's critically acclaimed film adaptation, which was released in 1969. *Kes* tells the story Billy Casper, a young boy who lives with his mother and half-brother on an estate in Yorkshire. One day, Billy finds a young kestrel on a nearby farm and decides to train it up, offering a glimmer of hope in his otherwise bleak life.

Depicting one day in Billy Casper's life, *Kes* is a portrait of a young boy who is struggling at school and has a difficult home life too. He lives with his half-brother, Jud – a heavy-handed bully – and his neglectful mother who is more interested in her new boyfriend than looking after Billy. Billy's school life is even worse: picked on by other pupils, he finds it difficult to concentrate. Furthermore, his prospects of finding work when he leaves school are slim. Then one day, he finds a kestrel on a nearby farm, and after stealing a book on falconry from the library, he begins to train Kes (the kestrel), an experience that gives Billy a feeling of purpose and value. This is all threatened, however, when he forgets to place a bet for his brother, and in retaliation, Jud takes the kestrel.

Billy

Character A fifteen-year-old boy.

Location Yorkshire in the 1960s.

Accent Yorkshire.

Scene In this scene Billy is talking to Mr Farthing, the only character in the play who appears to take any interest in Billy. After being caught up in a playground fight, Billy starts to tell Mr Farthing that he has fallen out with some of his old gang because his time is now being taken up with caring for Kes. Mr Farthing then asks if he can come and see the kestrel. As they both watch Kes flying, Billy begins to tell the story of the time he first let Kes fly free, and in doing so reveals some of the deeper reasons he feels so attached to the bird.

Who is he talking to? Mr Farthing, a teacher from Billy's school.

Where? In the fields behind Billy's house.

What does he want? Billy is telling the story of a special moment in his life. He wants to communicate the tension and exhilaration of this moment to Mr Farthing. Billy also enjoys the opportunity to educate his teacher – usually someone who tells *him* what to do. Billy is generally seen as a bit of a down-and-out at school, but he's proud of his achievement with Kes so wants to celebrate his accomplishment and maybe even prove that he is not a loser.

Things to think about At the beginning of the scene, Billy talks about how he used to raise animals with his dad. Does caring for Kes remind him of the memory of his father? How might this make him feel?

How does Billy feel talking to one of his teachers *outside* of school?

Throughout the play we see Billy disappear into comic-book style daydreams, but in this scene he has something real to be excited by – try and explore the full range of Billy's emotions around the memory of letting Kes fly free.

There are several words like 'creance' and 'jesses' in the speech which are specific to training a wild bird – make sure you know what they mean.

Try watching Ken Loach's film to get an idea of the world that Billy lives in.

■ Where to find the play This play is published by Nick Hern Books (www.nickhernbooks.co.uk).

Billy

The most exciting time was when I let her fly free for t' first time. I'd been flying Kes on t'creance for about a week, and she was coming to me owt up to thirty, forty yards, and it says in t' books that when it's coming this far, straight away, it's ready to fly loose. I daren't though, sir. I kept saying to myself, I'll just use t'creance today to make sure, then I'll fly her free tomorrow. But when tomorrow came I did the same thing again. Tomorrow. Tomorrow. I did this for about a week than I got right mad with myself cos I knew I'd have to do it some day. So on t' last night I didn't feed her up, just to make sure that she'd be sharp set next morning. I hardly went to sleep that night, I was thinking about it that much.

I wake up and I think right, if she flies off, and it can't be helped. I go down to t' shed. She's dead keen an all, walking about on her shelf behind t' bars, and screaming out when she sees me coming. I take her out in t' field and try her on creance first time, and she comes first time, an' she comes like a rocket. I think, right this time. I unclip creance, take swivel off an let her hop on to t' fence post. There is nowt stopping her now. She just stands there with her jesses on. She can take off and there is nowt I can do about it. I am terrified. I think, she's forced to go, she's forced to, she'll just fly off and that'll be it. But she doesn't. She just sits there looking around while I back off into t' field. I go right into t' middle, then hold my glove up and shout her.

Come on Kes! Come on then!

Nowt happened at first. Then, just as I go walk back to her, she comes. You ought to have seen her. Straight as a die, about a yard off t' floor. And t' speed! she comes twice as fast as when she had creance on, cos it used to drag in t' grass and slow her down. She comes like lightning, head dead still, and her wings never make a sound, then wham! Straight up onto my glove, claws out grabbing for t' meat. I am that pleased I don't know what to do with myself. Well, that's it. I've done it. I'd trained her. I trained her.

Shane Zaza played Billy Casper in the 2003 production of *Kes* at the Lyric Hammersmith. He has worked on many theatre shows at the National Theatre, Royal Court and Globe. On screen he has appeared in *Happy Valley* (BBC); *Black Mirror* (Netflix) and *The Da Vinci Code* (Columbia Pictures).

How did you prepare for this part?

To prepare for Billy, I re-read the novel *A Kestrel for a Knave*, which the play is based on, read the entire play and watched the wonderful movie directed by Ken Loach. And like a detective, I tried to extract any clues whilst still making it my own and bring out my own character within it.

What advice would you give a young actor playing this part?

Be truthful. Try not to embellish, and trust the words on the page. Allow the audience to see what you see, feel what you feel.

If you could give one piece of advice about auditions, what would it be?

Tell a story and engage the audience. Just as if you were telling a friend or partner something interesting. Excite and intrigue.

What is your abiding memory of NYT?

Family.

How did NYT affect your future life and career?

NYT gave me confidence and insight – not just into the industry – and also helped develop my social skills and ability to adapt to a multitude of environments. Forever grateful.

Killing Time

Barrie Keeffe

Killing Time was first performed by NYT in 1977 at the Soho Poly Theatre Club (now Soho Theatre). It was written by Barrie Keeffe, who was previously an actor with NYT before going on to be a highly successful playwright. *Killing Time* is a one-act play and forms part of a bigger piece called *Barbarians*, which follows the fortunes of three young men, Paul, Jan and Louis, as they try to give sense and meaning to their lives in a world of unemployment and limited horizons. In 2006, Barrie Keeffe wrote a companion piece for NYT called *Still Killing Time*, which was also performed at Soho Theatre.

Killing Time is set on the streets of Lewisham in the Jubilee year of 1977, just after a worldwide recession when unemployment for young people was rife. In the opening scene we see Paul and Jan kicking around the streets of Lewisham talking about the job centre, and their families, and contemplating what happens to you when you die in a car crash. The young men also complain about going through education and training and still ending up on the dole. Paul then says that his cousin has offered to pay him to find a Rover 3500 on the streets of London so that he can steal it and sell it in France. The pair decide to find their mate Louis, and go on a search for the car together. As the play progresses the three find themselves getting into deeper and deeper trouble; smashing up phone boxes, stealing from unsuspecting couples who are making love in the park and wading about in a pond searching for car keys, until they spot a Rover 3500 in the distance – but are they too late...

Paul

Character A sixteen- or seventeen-year-old boy.

Location Lewisham, 1977.

Accent South London or your own.

Scene The three lads – Jan, Louis and Paul – are all on the look out for a car to steal, when Jan tells Louis that Paul's mum is pregnant again. Paul turns to the audience and begins to recount the story of how his mum got pregnant again, and how everyone in his family is struggling for work. He talks about when the careers officer at school told him that he needed to set himself apart from all the other school leavers, and how, despite his best efforts he still couldn't earn more money than he did when he used to have a milk round when he was at school.

Who is he talking to? The audience.

Where? On the streets in Lewisham.

What does he want? It would be easy to think that the characters in *Killing Time* don't want anything it all; they seem directionless and apathetic, but they are products of a situation that has given them little hope. Paul wants the audience to see how pointless life is. He wants them to understand that his joblessness isn't his fault, and in fact, the adults in his life are deluded. Perhaps he also wants to confide in someone – to drop the bravado and banter that he has with his friends, let his guard down and be vulnerable for a moment.

Things to think about Who might the audience be for Paul? Could they be like a counsellor who is listening to his problems? Or could they be a theatre audience, who Paul thinks haven't got a clue what it's like to be young and jobless? Or someone else of your choosing?

How does Paul feel about having a baby brother? Is he excited? Resentful? Could he even be worried for his future brother, given how hard life is proving for him?

Think carefully about how Paul's tone changes through the speech – make sure that he goes on a journey as he's telling the story about buying the suit, and the optimism he felt.

You might want to do some research into the period and find out how different it was for young people at the end of the seventies – you may also find some similarities.

■ **Where to find the play** This play is published by Methuen Drama, an imprint of Bloomsbury Publishing Plc (www.bloomsbury.com).

Paul

I think he did it deliberate, like giving her another one to tie her down. They was cutting back and they stuffed him on the night shift, like. On the night shift at his age. He didn't fancy it, but they was cutting back, see. Thought he'd keep her out of mischief so give her another one. Gonna seem funny, calling a bleeding baby a brother. He tried to get me in there, but they was cutting back. It's all been a waste of bleeding time… I can't remember when it weren't a waste of bleeding time. Everything was boring. This careers bloke kept rubbing it in, he kept saying he did, future is in your hands, he said. Yeah, yeah… like trying to catch a fucking frisbee in the wind. He was right panicked all the time. Tell you the truth, I felt sorry for the bloke I did. Dashing about trying to fit people up and he knew, and we knew and *he knew we knew* that it was all fucking hopeless, but it's hard to imagine. He said once, he said… look here, he said, imagine Wembley, Cup Final… all them people, hundred thousand he said. Right, imagine that. He said that's how many school leavers have been on the dole for more than a year. So he says, you've got to make yourself presentable ain't you, make yourself presentable, get in there, get stuck in. Tell yourself you ain't gonna be one of them. So what did I do, I bought a suit didn't I. Fucking suit. For the interviews. Traipsing round London, all keen at first, so's I wouldn't be one of them and… I give it to me brother when he got married. Eight quid seventy, a week. I was better off when I did the milk round at school. I was buying records then, I bought an album most weeks. Spot the motor for me cousin, be few quid… no trouble, at Tiffany's.

The Kitchen

Arnold Wesker

Arnold Wesker's *The Kitchen* was first written and presented in 1959 at the Royal Court, and then revived by NYT thirty years later in 1989 at the Bloomsbury Theatre. Set in a busy kitchen serving the Tivoli restaurant, the play takes place over one day and gives a snapshot of the working life of the staff there. With thirty characters bringing *The Kitchen* to life, Wesker's play imagines cooking on an almost industrial scale, and poses philosophical and political questions about 'work' and the way it functions in our lives, and whether it liberates or enslaves us.

The play's events begins at 7 a.m. on a Friday morning in the summer. As various chefs enter, they greet Magi, the Night Porter, as he lights the ovens ready for the day's work. Gradually, the stage becomes inhabited with numerous chefs and waitresses of different nationalities, and as they work, we start to learn about the relationships between them; for example Peter (who is having an affair with Monique) had a fight with Gaston the previous night, whilst Paul has recently split up from his wife. A complex web of interactions builds as each character happens upon another, just as it might in a normal day's work, but as the play reaches its explosive climax, we witness how the pressurised conditions of a busy kitchen can lead to physical and mental collapse.

Paul

Character A man in his twenties.

Location The kitchen of the Tivoli restaurant, London, 1959.

Accent London or your own.

Scene The first half of the play presents the manic lunchtime service, which builds to a rhythmical climax at the interval. This speech occurs in the post-lunch lull, where various chefs are waiting around for the evening's onslaught to begin. Peter, the slightly unhinged pastry chef, is inviting some of the other chefs to dream about what they would do if they didn't work there. He asks Paul, a young Jewish pastry chef, what he dreams about, and Paul reflects on friendship, solidarity and how disconnected society can feel. He tells a story about a conversation he had with a local bus driver, in which the bus driver showed no solidarity with a peace march that recently happened.

Who is he talking to? Peter, and several other chefs in the kitchen.

Where? In the kitchen, between services.

What does he want? Paul is a thoughtful young man and in this speech he considers how to reconcile himself with people that he may not immediately agree with – like Peter, who he finds confrontational. Through telling this story, he tries to work out how, in a world that is becoming more and more industrialised and impersonal, he can find friendship and solidarity. He wants Peter to consider his story and become less argumentative.

Things to think about Through a conversation with fellow pastry chef Raymond, we discover in the first scene that

Paul has recently broken up with his wife. What does he say about their break-up and what does this tell us about him?

See if you can find out what life was like for Jewish people in post-war London. How is Paul's life different from your own?

Although this seems like a reasonably inconsequential speech, it has obviously had a profound affect on Paul. Later in the scene, he suggests that he didn't even know why he told the story; what do you think prompted him to recount the event?

Make sure you have fully imagined the meeting with the bus driver – how did Paul feel when he saw the hatred in his eyes?

■ **Where to find the play** This play is published by Oberon Books (www.oberonbooks.co.uk).

Paul

Listen, I'll tell you a story. Next door to me, next door where I live in Hackney is a bus driver. Comes from Hoxton. He's my age, married, got two kids. He says good morning to me, I ask him how he is, I give his children sweets. That's our relationship. Somehow he seems frightened to say too much, you know? God forbid I might ask him for something. So we make no demands on each other.

Then one day the busmen go on strike. He's out for five weeks. Every morning I say to him 'Keep going, mate, you'll win!' Every morning I give him words of encouragement, I say I understand his cause. I've got to get up earlier to get to work but I don't mind – we're neighbours – we're workers together – he's pleased.

Then one Sunday there's a peace march. I don't believe they do much good but I go, because in this world a man's got to show he can have his say. The next morning he comes up to me and he says, now listen to this, he says 'Did you go on that peace march yesterday?' So I says, yes, I did go on that peace march yesterday. So then he turns round to me and he says, 'You know what? A bomb should have been dropped on the lot of them! It's a pity,' he says, 'that they had children with them cos a bomb should have been dropped on the lot!' And you know what was upsetting him? The march was holding up the traffic, the buses couldn't move so fast!

Now, I don't want him to say I'm right. I don't want him to agree with what I did – but what terrifies me is that he didn't stop to think that this man helped me in my cause so maybe, only *maybe*, there's something in *his* cause – I'll talk about it. No! The buses were held up so drop a bomb, he says, on the lot! And you should have seen the hate in his eyes, as if I'd murdered his child.

And the horror is this – that there's a wall, a big wall between me and millions of people like him. And I think – where will it end? What do you do about it? And I look around me, at the kitchen, at the factories, at the enormous bloody buildings going up with all those offices and all those people in them, and I think – Christ! I think, Christ, Christ, Christ!

The Life and Adventures of Nicholas Nickleby

Charles Dickens
adapted for the stage by David Edgar

NYT first staged *Nicholas Nickleby* at the Lyric Hammersmith in 2001 and then toured to The Lowry, Salford, a year later in 2002. Based on the novel by Charles Dickens, *Nicholas Nickleby* was first produced by the RSC in 1981, and quickly became a landmark in British theatre for the size and scale of its ambition along with the strength of its ensemble performance. In 2001, David Edgar produced an edited script for NYT (that ran to six hours, over two parts), which depicts the adventures of Nicholas Nickleby who, after the death of his father, has to make his own way in the world and so, along with his family, he travels to London.

The play of *Nicholas Nickleby* takes its story from the epic 800-page novel, and as such, has a plot that features over 120 characters and ninety-five scenes. Written for a cast of twenty-three, the play uses all of the actors to narrate the action as well as playing multiple characters. The action begins with Nicholas, along with his mother and sister, moving to London to find their uncle following the death of his father. Nicholas's uncle, Ralph Nickleby, is a mean and heartless businessman who has no desire to help his relatives, and he especially dislikes his nephew Nicholas, because he reminds him of his late brother. So whilst supporting his mother and sister in slum housing in London, Ralph sends Nicholas off to work at Dotheboys Hall school, which is run by the brutish Wackford Squeers. From there Nicholas's adventures begin, and a story of love, greed and honour unfolds over the course of the two parts.

Narrator

■ **Character** Age and gender unspecified.

■ **Location** London, 1800s.

■ **Accent** Your own.

■ **Scene** This is the first piece of narration from the play. In the NYT production the lines were shared amongst the whole ensemble, but on its own, this speech sets the scene for the coming action. It describes how, after Nicholas's father lost all his money when playing the financial markets, he took to his bed and lost his mind before swiftly dying. The speech evokes themes of greed and familial loyalty in the face of poverty, which the play then goes on to explore in great depth.

■ **Who are they talking to?** The audience.

■ **Where?** In an imaginary space.

■ **What do they want?** It is up to you to decide who the Narrator is. In the original production the narration was split up and delivered by every actor in the company (regardless of their part) as if they were telling the audience about what happened. You need to think about how the Narrator wants to entice the audience, and draw them into the story. Who do they want the audience to sympathise with? Do they also want to excite the audience about the story that will follow – how might they achieve that?

■ **Things to think about** NYT's large ensemble shows often feature direct address to the audience, so think about how you can hold the stage with your presence and the simplicity of your storytelling.

This might be a good choice of speech for a young actor who doesn't feel comfortable with the idea of transforming into another character, but do think about how you can start to create the world of the play in the audience's imagination.

How might the pace of your delivery throughout the speech change? Will some sections benefit from a burst of energy, whilst others may benefit from more time and attention?

This is a long speech, so you may need to edit it down to fit within the time allowance.

There are several other short speeches in the plays which you may like to look at.

■ **Where to find the play** This play is published by Methuen Drama, an imprint of Bloomsbury Publishing Plc (www.bloomsbury.com).

Narrator

There once lived in a sequestered part of the county of Devonshire, one Mr Godfrey Nickleby, who, rather late in life, took it into his head to get married. And in due course, when Mrs Nickleby had presented her husband with two sons, he found himself in a situation of distinctly shortened means, which were only relieved when, one fine morning, there arrived a black-bordered letter, informing him that his uncle was dead and had left him the bulk of his property, amounting in all to £5,000. And with a portion of this property, Mr Godfrey Nickleby purchased a small farm near Dawlish, and on his death some fifteen years later, he was able to leave to his eldest son £3,000 in cash, and to his youngest, one thousand and the farm.

The younger boy was of a timid and retiring disposition, keen only to attach himself to the quiet routine of country life. The eldest son, however, resolved to make much use of his father's inheritance. For young Ralph Nickleby had commenced usury on a limited scale even at school, putting out at interest a small capital of slate pencils and marbles, and had now in adulthood resolved to live his life by the simple motto that there was nothing in the world so good as money.

And while Ralph prospered in the mercantile way in London, the young brother lived still on the farm, and took himself a wife, who gave birth to a boy and a girl, and by the time they were both nearing the age of twenty, he found his expenses much increased and his capital still more depleted.

Speculate. His wife advised him.

Think of your brother, Mr Nickleby, and speculate. And Mr Nickleby did speculate, but a mania prevailed, a bubble burst, four stockbrokers took villa residences at Florence, four hundred nobodies were ruined, and one of them was Mr Nickleby.

And Mr Nickleby took to his bed, apparently resolved to keep that, at all events. Cheer up, Sir! said the apothecary. You mustn't let yourself be cast down, sir, said the nurse. Such things happen every day, remarked the lawyer, and it is very sinful to rebel against them, whispered the clergyman, and what no man with a family ought to do, added the neighbours. But Mr Nickleby shook his head, and he motioned them all out of the room and shortly afterwards his reason went astray, and he babbled of the goodness of his brother and the merry times they'd had at school, and one day he turned upon his face, observing that he thought that he could fall asleep. And so, with no one in the world to help them but Ralph Nickleby, the widow, and her children, journeyed forth to – LONDON!

Kwami Odoom

Our goals and dreams can be so much closer than we think. That's why it's always worth giving something a shot even if you aren't confident of success – you just never know!

Liminal

Rebecca Manley

Liminal was performed at the Arcola Theatre in 2014 as part of a double bill with Simon Vinnicombe's *Swipe*, and both plays look at the increasing influence that technology has on our lives. *Liminal* confronts the ways in which online activities have started to affect our real-life existence, but also how the Internet allows us to connect with people and explore issues around gender, sexuality and identity.

Depicting the relationships between a group of people both in real life and an online world called 'Otherness', *Liminal* presents many different forms of interaction on stage: text messages, dream sequences, a virtual world and also real-life conversations. In the first scene of the play, we see a text conversation between George and Alex, who are girlfriends. The conversation is unexpectedly cut short, however, and we soon learn that, whilst sending the final text, Alex has been run over and killed. The play then examines George's grieving process, which is further complicated by her exploration into the online existence that Alex led in Otherness. As the play progresses, George starts to come to terms with Alex's online persona, Dante, and accepts the positive ways that it influenced her life. When she enters Otherness and meets Alex's online community, including her friend Simon, she also starts to learn about herself, and begins a journey towards acceptance.

Lorna

■ **Character** An eighteen-year-old woman.

■ **Location** Present-day Britain.

■ **Accent** Your own.

■ **Scene** Lorna is one of Alex's friends from Otherness, whose avatar is named 'Shayla Snakeankle'. The first time we meet Lorna is through her avatar in Otherness, when she welcomes George into the virtual world after Alex's death. We then meet Lorna both on- and offline, and in this scene she is talking to a therapist who is trying to address whether Lorna spends too much time in an alternate existence. Lorna gets angry with the therapist and begins to argue that Otherness provides a positive space where she can grow in confidence.

■ **Who is she talking to?** A therapist.

■ **Where?** In a small office in North London.

■ **What does she want?** Lorna wants the therapist to acknowledge the positive impacts that Otherness has on her life. She wants to break free of the language and ideas about her online life being 'unhealthy', which she says have been forced upon her by her parents. She also wants the therapist to acknowledge the hypocrisy of her parents, who spend just as much time online but in different ways. Lorna is passionate about Otherness and the relationships she has formed in there, and she wants these connections to be valued by other people.

■ **Things to think about** Think about how long Lorna has already spent in this office, and how many therapy sessions she has been through. This speech is an eruption of emotions which have been building up over a long time.

Later in the play, Lorna says she has had things happen to her that made it difficult to imagine kissing someone in real life, and that Dante helped her explore this side of herself by doing it in Otherness. What do you think she is referring to? And how might this have affected Lorna?

Lorna says that she is holding a remembrance service for Dante (Alex) next week – how much might her outburst be fuelled by grief? And how does she feel when she talks about Dante's death?

■ **Where to find the play** This play can be read on the NYT website (www.nyt.org.uk/monologues, password: nytspeeches).

Lorna

Unhealthy? Unstable boundaries? Does that sound like something I came up with myself, or an idea people like you and my parents farted out enough times to make me believe it. You're all such hypocrites. Unhealthy? What and it's not unhealthy that she's got a iPhone practically stuck to her hand 24 fucking 7, checking work email whilst she's 'talking' to me, he's texting his mates whilst he's 'listening' to me, they're both obsessively tandem tweeting about some really important political issues of the moment? I suppose that's all healthy, that constant emailing, texting, tweeting, checking, chattering? Because it's with *real* people, yeah? Well I tell you what, the connections I make in Otherness are way more thoughtful, more honest, more real than all of that.

We're having a remembrance service next week for someone in Otherness. She died in real life, hit by a car, but the service is for her character, Dante. And I'll be there because he meant something to me. Something real. And her friends will be there and her girlfriend, who's never been in Otherness before wants to come. And she's going to do that as her girlfriend's character, as Dante. What's not human about that?

And you're wrong that these sessions, these nod-orgies only happen here, in your reality. There's counsellors there you know, in Otherness. There's therapists, priests, rabbis, prostitutes, shamen… you know whoever you want to talk to you, to listen to you.

Except there you can do it beside a technicoloured waterfall or in an infinity pool looking out across the ocean, or on a big fluffy pink cloud. Not in a pokey, elephant-phlegm-painted back bedroom in Kilburn.

Simon

■ **Character** A young man of unspecified age.

■ **Location** Present-day Britain.

■ **Accent** Your own.

■ **Scene** Simon's speech comes in the final scene of the play, which takes place in the virtual world of Otherness, where her friends are holding an online remembrance service for Dante, Alex's avatar. During this scene, all of the real characters talk about the way in which Dante/Alex had helped them. Simon talks about how Dante allowed him to feel 'cool', and how Otherness has helped him in many ways.

■ **Who is he talking to?** Initially it seems that Simon is talking to Lorna and George, but as the speech progresses he also begins to think about Alex too, and thanks her at the end of the speech.

■ **Where?** At a remembrance service in the virtual world of Otherness.

■ **What does he want?** Simon wants to pay tribute to Dante for all the ways he has helped him grow in confidence; he especially wants George to hear how her girlfriend affected his life. Simon also wants to celebrate Dante's existence as well as celebrating the existence of Otherness as a safe place for him to grow. Finally, as this is a remembrance service, Simon is also trying to say goodbye to Dante.

■ **Things to think about** Keep in mind that although set in Otherness, the purpose of this scene is remembrance, so you could choose to perform it as if Simon is at a real-life service.

At first this scene seems complicated, with various avatars speaking on behalf of real people. Try just playing Simon and imagine that he is speaking from his heart, rather than being his avatar character.

In the character description Simon is described as a young man who has Asperger syndrome (this explains why he says he doesn't usually use metaphors). Research what Asperger syndrome is and decide if this aspect of his personality will be noticeable in your performance.

Even though Simon's avatar is a woman, at the end of the play we get a sense that he may be starting a relationship in the real world with Lorna. Think carefully about how you might play Simon and be careful not to stereotype your characterisation.

■ **Where to find the play** This play can be read on the NYT website (www.nyt.org.uk/monologues, password: nytspeeches).

Simon

Otherness has changed my life. I know that sounds stupid. But it isn't. And Dante was a massive part of that especially at the beginning. I love it here. I feel like I can be myself. By being Beatrix.

Once you learn how to be in Otherness, it's easier to progress. There's a limited range of expressions. Dante said it makes everyone a bit more like me. Instead of me trying to be more like everyone else.

It was Dante who suggested I bring my brother to Otherness. My brother is really cool in real life. But he wasn't cool in Otherness.

He was rubbish with the commands. He poured coffee over his head rather than his mouth because he couldn't get the hang of the controls. He met Shayla once. She's beautiful. With her big breasts that seem to be bursting out of the top of her clothes. Even though she has lots of outfits, this is a common design feature. Me and Dante talked about that a lot. Shayla laughed at my brother with the coffee on his head and the sleeping when she was talking to him about her new beach house. It was because he was so busy talking to me about her breasts that he forgot to keep manipulating his char. Shayla thinks I am cooler than my brother. She said so. That would never happen in real.

Dante and me used to talk about how annoying it is when people call Otherness a game. It's a whole world, a life. Which is funny because often for me, real life feels like a game where I never quite learn the rules. I guess that's a metaphor. Which usually I don't use to explain things so maybe that's something else it's helped with. Being cool and using metaphors.

Goodbye Dante. Thank you.

Little Malcolm and His Struggle Against the Eunuchs

David Halliwell

Little Malcolm and His Struggles Against the Eunuchs was written by David Halliwell in 1965 and first directed by Mike Leigh in Liverpool. It was then produced in 1966 by NYT at the Royal Court and was later restaged in the West End and on Broadway starring John Hurt, before being made into a film in 1974. Set in Huddersfield, it tells the story of Scrawdyke, an art-school bohemian, and his two sidekicks Wick and Ingham, who have aspirations to take over the world. The play starts as a comedy about these three incompetent drop-outs, but gradually becomes an examination of how political delusion and male arrogance can result in violent misogyny.

Malcolm Scrawdyke has been expelled from art school for smoking outside the principle, Mr Allard's, door. We quickly learn that this isn't an isolated incident and that Scrawdyke is a rebel who regularly flouts the rules. In the opening scene of the play, his two friends, Ingham and Wick, come to tell Scrawdyke that they've been banned from seeing him – if they do, they too will be expelled, and so Scrawdyke convinces them to drop out and start a new political movement called 'The Party of Dynamic Erection'. Amongst their many aims, the group plans to kidnap Mr Allard and destroy his career by blackmailing him. Despite his outward confidence, Scrawdyke is racked with insecurity when alone – especially with regards to Ann, a girl he fancies. As the group gets more involved in their plan, their fantasies of world domination become more outrageous and gradually more sinister. Firstly they threaten to kill a friend for a crime they know he hasn't committed, and then, when Ann comes to challenge Scrawdyke, she is met with an unpleasant confrontation.

Ann

Character A young woman of university age.

Location Huddersfield, 1965.

Accent Yorkshire.

Scene Throughout the play, in several monologues, we hear Scrawdyke torturing himself about how to woo Ann, and then on the day of the planned kidnapping, she turns up uninvited. When she first arrives she confidently surveys his room before propositioning him. Perhaps for the first time in the play, Scrawdyke is on the back foot, and cannot cope with having a woman speak to him in this way. To begin with, Ann just says that she knows he's not as experienced with women as he claims to be, but when he pretends he was never interested in her, she really lets rip.

Who is she talking to? Scrawdyke.

Where? In Scrawdyke's room.

What does she want? Ann has already worked out that Scrawdyke's not as experienced as he thinks he is, and she has come to his flat to test him once and for all. She says that she initially came here to help him, but by this point she wants to expose him, to undermine him and make him feel like the 'little man' she says he is. She wants to defend Allard, and in doing so, stand up for women who are made to feel like lesser beings by people like Scrawdyke.

Things to think about How does it feel to be in Scrawdyke's room challenging him this way? Does she feel empowered? Nervous? Angry?

How is she different at the end of the speech to the beginning? Did she know that she would say all this before she arrived, or did Scrawdyke say something to provoke her?

Look at what Scrawdyke says about Ann in his monologues – what sense of Ann do we get from what Scrawdyke says about her?

Even when Ann is exposing Scrawdyke as a spineless fraud – how does she feel about him: does she hate him? Does she still have some sympathy for him?

How do you think Scrawdyke reacts while Ann is speaking? Try and imagine what he is doing, and how this might give her the impulse to keep on speaking.

■ **Where to find the play** This play is published by Samuel French (www.samuelfrench.co.uk).

Ann

Never mind what A can't see. Let me tell y' what A can. I see three timid little men. One 'oo leads the other two along becos 'e's got a louder voice that's all an' fills 'em up wi' big ideas of 'emselves. One 'oos very quick at ev'rything but standi' up for 'imself. 'E's another great lover. I once caught cold waiting for 'im t' make a move on a freezin' yard. And a third – well, 'e's only ever anywhere becos 'e's not somewhere else. A see y' recognise these descriptions. Well these three supermen are goin' t' pinch a paintin' from a completely unguarded art gallery, they're goin' t' sneak up be'ind a completely unsuspectin' 'eadmaster an' clout 'im over the 'ead. Then they're goin' t' blackmail 'im by threatenin' t' expose the fact that 'e kissed a girl student under t' mistletoe at a Chris'mas party unless 'e's prepared t' smash up the paintin' they've pinched. Then they're goin' t' break their promise to 'im an' tell ev'rybody what a rotter he is. Then ev'rybody'll see what great big 'eroes they all are. This's the great scheme these three giant brains 'ave been buildin' up over the last week. But Allard's worth ten of 'em.

Character A young man of university age.

Location Huddersfield, 1965.

Accent Yorkshire.

Scene On a whim, Scrawdyke has decided that Nipple, a wannabe writer who is tagging along with the group, is not to be trusted. In Scene Seven, Scrawdyke, Wick and Ingham act out an elaborate improvisation where they imagine Nipple collaborating with Mr Allard at the top of a church tower. In this scene, despite the fact that this story is completely made up, Scrawdyke, Wick and Ingham put Nipple on trial and find him guilty of being a traitor. Ingham is called upon as the chief witness to describe something he never saw, and struggles to put together a convincing story.

Who is he talking to? Scrawdyke (who is pretending to be a judge), Wick (who is acting as chief prosecutor) and Nipple, the defendant.

Where? In Scrawdyke's room.

What does he want? Throughout the play, Ingham wants to impress Scrawdyke. He isn't at all sure what he should say (because everyone knows this never happened) but he also doesn't want to let the side down. He is caught between wanting to enter into the game and be a 'credible witness', whilst also struggling to get the story out because he's trying to remember the details of the story that they made up together.

Things to think about There very few full-stops in this speech, which tells us that Ingham is constantly having new thoughts and ideas. You will have to work out where to breathe, while also maintaining the relentless rhythm of his speech. If you pause too much it will take forever!

Does Ingham expect to be called to take part in the proceedings? Is he surprised (and so on the back foot), or is it nervousness that makes him stutter his way through? Or both? Think about how you might maintain Ingham's nervous energy through the speech.

In the final scene, Ann describes Ingham as someone who's 'only ever anywhere becos 'e's not somewhere else'. What might she mean by this? Think about how it might affect your characterisation.

Look at Scene Seven to give you the details of the made-up story that Ingham is describing in the speech.

■ **Where to find the play** This play is published by Samuel French (www.samuelfrench.co.uk).

Ingham

Oh – aye – well – Well – I er – A mean they were up – an' um, an' 'e said er – what it was like, an' y' see I'd been walkin', A mean A was walkin', just by there, an' as A was walkin' A saw like 'em, y' know, like goin' in, like goin' into it. Well I didn't know – A mean I didn't know – then, y' know, er – Well, A mean, A wondered. So, like, as A say, they went – A mean they went in, an' then, well, A suppose they went up. Well one at a time – like – A mean that's what – And anyway, as A say, one went up, one of 'em, then – then the other like and er – And anyway when they'd – when they'd gone up, gone in, y' know, an' they'd well, they'd got there, got up there, to the top of – y' know, where it er – was – Well – they met A suppose. A mean like they did like – Then, then when they were – this – well they er – A mean they er – to each. A mean when they went in, when they first went in, when one went in an' then the other, 'e went in, well then I went, I went in an' then the other, 'e went in, well then I went, I went in, y' know because it just seemed a bit – Anyway, so, as A say, went – I followed, A suppose y' might say, that, an' A saw 'em go, through this – an' then go up – an' I – an' when I, A mean when I got – they were er – y' know, An' when they'd finished well, they came, they came down. They came down an' went out, an' then I came down an' I went out. A mean after they'd come down, come out, gone down, come out, I'd gone, A mean come, A mean out – I'd, well, y'know – An' so really that's er – what I c'n, y' know, that's just er – that is what, well, y'know – that's it.

Scrawdyke

■ **Character** A young man of university age.

■ **Location** Huddersfield, 1965.

■ **Accent** Yorkshire.

■ **Scene** Scrawdyke has been torturing himself earlier in the play about how to get Ann in his room, and then on the day of the planned kidnapping, she turns up uninvited. Ann offers Scrawdyke sex, but as she suspects, he is a virgin and so doesn't know how to respond. After outing him for being a fraud, she tries to leave just as Wick and Ingham arrive. The scene quickly turns nasty when Scrawdyke tells his friends that she is a spy, and in a frenzy, the three men brutally attack her. She manages to escape, and in this speech, Scrawdyke attempts to justify what the young men have done.

■ **Who is he talking to?** Wick and Ingham.

■ **Where?** In Scrawdyke's room.

■ **What does he want?** To begin with, Scrawdyke pretends that Ann was faking it and wasn't hurt, he then tries to justify the act of violence that he, Wick and Ingham have just committed, saying that they weren't hard enough. He wants to convince them (and himself), that what they just did was right – that it was all part of the struggle.

■ **Things to think about** Think carefully about what has just happened – Scrawdyke's heart would be beating fast, pumping adrenaline all through his body. How will this affect the speech? Does he get more pumped as he goes on, or does reality slowly start to dawn on him?

Look carefully at what Ann says about Scrawdyke before they attack her – is she right about him? How might he feel having these truths exposed?

This is the dramatic climax of the play, and the moment everything begins to unravel for Scrawdyke. Play around with how he attempts to reassure his friends even though he knows what he has done is wrong.

In Scene Two he admits that if he can succeed in wooing Ann, he'll forget about his new political movement – so he clearly feels strongly about her. Think about the rage he feels when she humiliates him, and how this fuels the speech.

Where to find the play This play is published by Samuel French (www.samuelfrench.co.uk).

Scrawdyke

Tergiversator!* The whole thing was feigned. The whole thing was nothing but another trick! We ought to 'ave been more thorough. She ought to 'ave been dead. She deserved it. You seemed abashed, you seemed disconsolate. We mustn't be abashed by things like this. We must steel ourselves. It's them or us. Remember that. It's those 'oo strike first. Do you think she'd 'ave 'esitated for a minute, for a second, if she'd been the stronger? Oh no! I know 'ow y' felt, lads, the first time. We're too humane that's our trouble, it does us credit. I had a suspicion all along that she was feigning. But I didn't let on. Do you know why? I'll tell you why. There's a streak of weakness, of sentimentality, in all of us. It's got to be recognised, it's got to be wrestled with. It's got to be brought out into the open. It needs the right incident to entice it out. I used this incident. I let it come out. I gave it full play. I let it suffuse me. So that once and for all time, with utter finality, I could reject it. That's the way to handle temptations. Every saint knew that, let 'em roll then smack 'em down. Well I smacked mine down. I was just on the verge of giving mine the chop when she shoved off. Another second and I was goin t'say: 'Hack up the body.' Never mind, there'll be other opportunities. What we've just done makes the putsch even more urgent. If we don't act decisively now our destruction of her threat will have been in vain. We shall have done it all for nothing. Have we been through so much, suffered such privations, been goaded to such extremities for nothing? We most certainly have not. We are about to leap from our corner at the throat of the world! And then we shall see who cries for mercy, and then we shall see who begs for it, and then we shall see who gets it! We are the Arbiters of the Future!

---

* 'Tergiversator' is a term used a lot by Scrawdyke in *Little Malcolm and His Struggle Against the Eunuchs*, and means someone who is disloyal, or shifty – someone not to be trusted, who doesn't believe in the cause.

Murder in the Cathedral

T. S. Eliot

Murder in the Cathedral was performed five times by NYT between 1982 and 2003. Each time it was directed by the company's then Artistic Director Ed Wilson, and in 2003, the role of Thomas Becket was played by Matt Smith. Telling the true story of the assassination of the Archbishop of Canterbury, Thomas Becket, T. S. Eliot's tragedy, first performed in 1935, is a complex and challenging piece of theatre that mixes theatrical forms and asks big questions about theology, politics and individual responsibility.

The play tells the story of Thomas Becket, the twelfth-century Archbishop of Canterbury, who was exiled to France by King Henry II after challenging his authority. Seven years pass, and then, early one December, news reaches the priests at Canterbury Cathedral that Thomas has landed on the Kent coast. His return is greeted with joy by many in England as he travels home, although there are others – including Thomas himself, who fear that his homecoming will bring chaos. After arriving at Canterbury Cathedral, Thomas begins to ponder the way forward, as several 'tempters' try to persuade him away from his moral duty. By the end of the first act, however, he has resigned himself to submitting to God's will – he will become a martyr. In the second act, he is visited by four knights on behalf of the king and, when he refuses to comply with their demands, he meets a grisly end on the Cathedral altar.

Thomas Becket

■ **Character** A man in his fifties.

■ **Location** Canterbury, 1170 AD.

■ **Accent** Your own.

■ **Scene** The speech comes right at the end of Act One. Thomas has returned from exile in France and knows that his life is in danger. He has been visited by four 'tempters' who try to lure him towards four different courses of action, the last of which is seeking a path to martyrdom. It is this final temptation that grabs him, but he is wary of his pride, and does not want to die for the sake of glory. In this speech he tells the women of Canterbury and his priests what he has decided to do: he will give himself freely and openly to God, and if that means death, then so be it.

■ **Who is he talking to?** The women of Canterbury and three priests.

■ **Where?** The Archbishop's Hall

■ **What does he want?** Thomas Becket has to balance his moral duty to his religious beliefs with his fear of what might happen if he acts upon them – his death. He has to make the most momentous decision of his life: whether to choose the easy path, or to martyr himself. He wants to explain and justify to everyone how he reached his decision, and perhaps to impart to them the same sense of resolution or peace that he now feels.

■ **Things to think about** By the end of the speech he has decided to martyr himself – he has clearly found this decision difficult. Is there still an internal struggle within him, or has he found peace?

What is his emotional journey through the speech? Make sure you are clear on how he changes as his argument progresses.

The stakes are very high for Thomas – so it's important you don't get lulled by the poetry of the speech.

This is a complicated and poetic speech, make sure you know the meaning of words like 'venial', 'tiltyard' and 'sacrilege'.

Thomas Becket really existed; research his life. Try and make sense of how he describes his behaviour *before* he became the Archbishop.

■ **Where to find the play** This play is published by Faber & Faber (www.faber.co.uk).

Thomas Becket

Now is my way clear, now is the meaning plain:
Temptation shall not come in this kind again.
The last temptation is the greatest treason:
To do the right deed for the wrong reason.
The natural vigour in the venial sin
Is the way in which our lives begin.
Thirty years ago, I searched all the ways
That lead to pleasure, advancement and praise.
Delight in sense, in learning and in thought,
Music and philosophy, curiosity,
The purple bullfinch in the lilac tree,
The tiltyard skill, the strategy of chess,
Love in the garden, singing to the instrument,
Were all things equally desirable.
Ambition comes when early force is spent
And when we find no longer all things possible.
Ambition comes behind and unobservable.
Sin grows with doing good. When I imposed the Kings' law
In England, and waged war with him against Toulouse,
I beat the barons at their own game. I
Could then despise the men who thought me most
     contemptible,
The raw nobility, whose manners matched their fingernails.
While I ate out of the King's dish
To become servant of God was never my wish.
Servant of God has chance of greatest sin
And sorrow, than the man who serves a king.
For those who serve the greater cause may make that cause
     serve them,
Still doing right: and striving with political men
May make that cause political, not by what they do
But by what they are. I know
What yet remains to show you of my history
Will seem to most of you at best futility,
Senseless self-slaughter of a lunatic,

Arrogant passion of a fanatic.
I know that history at all times draws
The strangest consequence from remotest cause.
But for every evil, every sacrilege,
Crime, wrong, oppression and the axe's edge,
Indifference, exploitation, you, and you,
And you, must all be punished. So must you.
I shall no longer act or suffer, to the sword's end.
Now my good Angel, whom God appoints
To be my guardian, hover over the swords' points.

Women of Canterbury

■ **Character** A chorus of women of unspecified ages.

■ **Location** Canterbury, 1170 AD.

■ **Accent** Your own.

■ **Scene** This speech occurs towards the end of Act One and was written for a chorus of women. Like a Greek chorus, the women challenge Thomas and voice the concerns of the wider community about his actions. Early in the play the women say that his presence in England will bring doom and that they want Thomas to return to France. Despite being told off by the priests and called 'foolish, immodest and babbling women', they are still worried by Thomas's presence and ask him one last time to save himself by leaving – and in doing so, save them too.

■ **Who are they talking to?** Thomas Becket, Archbishop of Canterbury.

■ **Where?** The Archbishop's Hall.

■ **What do they want?** They want Thomas to listen to them, to take their fears seriously and for him to return to France. In the first half of the speech they acknowledge that in their twelfth-century society women are not highly respected, but they want to prove that they are worldly. In the second half of the speech their language becomes more poetic and they passionately want to persuade Thomas that his actions will bring ruin to them all.

■ **Things to think about** Think about the status relationship between the women and Thomas; whilst the women are clearly of a lower social standing, they still speak with passion and eloquence – try to explore how their status conflicts with their desire to persuade Thomas, and think about how hard it is for them to speak up at this point and how they have been driven to do so by their deeply held beliefs.

Even though this speech was written for a group of women, you will have to deliver this speech by yourself in an audition; who is *your* woman? What circumstances does she live in?

The play explores the tension between satisfying one's moral conscience and behaving in a way that is politically acceptable – make sure you explore this internal struggle in your performance.

■ **Where to find the play** This play is published by Faber & Faber (www.faber.co.uk).

Women of Canterbury

We have not been happy, my Lord, we have not been too
    happy.
We are not ignorant women, we know what we must expect
    and not expect.
We know of oppression and torture,
We know of extortion and violence,
Destitution, disease,
The old without fire in winter,
The child without milk in summer,
Our labour taken away from us,
Our sins made heavier upon us.
We have seen the young man mutilated,
The torn girl trembling by the mill-stream.
And meanwhile we have gone on living,
Living and partly living,
Picking together the pieces,
Gathering faggots at nightfall,
Building a partial shelter,
For sleeping, and eating and drinking and laughter.

God gave us always some reason, some hope; but now a
    new terror has soiled us, which none can avert, none can
    avoid, flowing under our feet and over the sky;
Under doors and down chimneys, flowing in at the ear and
    the mouth and the eye.
God is leaving us, God is leaving us, more pang, more pain
    than birth or death.
Sweet and cloying through the dark air
Falls the stifling scent of despair;
The forms take shape in the dark air:
Puss-purr of leopard, footfall of padding bear,
Palm-pat of nodding ape, square hyaena waiting
For laughter, laughter, laughter. The Lords of Hell are here.
They curl round you, lie at your feet, swing and wing
    through the dark air.
O Thomas Archbishop, save us, save us, save yourself that
    we may be saved;
Destroy yourself and we are destroyed.

Oedipus the King

Sophocles
translated by Don Taylor

NYT first presented *Oedipus the King* at the Bloomsbury Theatre in 1998. Translated by Don Taylor, the play was originally written almost 2,500 years ago; it is thus one of the earliest plays in Western literature. Often spoken of as the archetypal tragedy, it tells the story of Oedipus, a man who becomes the King of Thebes after saving the city from the Sphinx. When the city falls into famine, Oedipus's attempts to find out the cause of the suffering lead him down a path to his own destruction.

The play begins with the City of Thebes in chaos; there are plagues, drought and famine and no one knows why. Oedipus has sent his brother-in-law, Creon, to the Oracle for advice. When Creon returns he brings the message that in order to stop the suffering, they must find the man who murdered Laius (the previous king of Thebes before Oedipus). Creon then recounts to Oedipus the story of how Laius was murdered before Oedipus came to Thebes, reminding him that no one ever found out who killed him. Oedipus takes it upon himself to find the murderer, decreeing that when the man who killed Laius is found, he will be banished from the Thebes. As the story progresses, however, Oedipus comes to see that he is more involved in Laius's death than he realised; as the full facts become clear, the play hurtles towards a tragic conclusion.

Oedipus

▪ **Character** The king, unspecified age.

▪ **Location** Ancient Greece.

▪ **Accent** Your own.

▪ **Scene** At the beginning of the play, Oedipus has sent for Teiresias, an old, blind prophet, for help. From the moment Teiresias arrives, he says that he has bad news, and that he shouldn't have come in the first place. Oedipus, however, insists that Teiresias should tell him everything he knows, and so Teiresias accuses Oedipus of being a traitor and having murdered Laius. Oedipus assumes that Teiresias is either mad or has ulterior motives, and begins to suspect that Creon has set the whole thing up. In this speech, Oedipus rails against Teiresias and tries to prove that he is loyal to the city.

▪ **Who is he talking to?** Teiresias and the Chorus.

▪ **Where?** In Oedipus's palace.

▪ **What does he want?** Oedipus desperately wants to make sense of the situation as he feels he is being plotted against. He has just been accused of murdering the previous king, and so he wants to defend his honour. He wants to convince the Chorus that Teiresias is lying, so he tries to undermine Teiresias's character. He also wants to prove that he is not a traitor as he fought hard from the city, saving it from destruction.

▪ **Things to think about** Think carefully about when Oedipus is talking to Teiresias and when he's talking to the Chorus, and then think about what relationship he has with each: he wants to belittle Teiresias, and he wants to convince the Chorus of his innocence.

Is the Chorus one person, or is it made up of several people?

245

Oedipus's anger has ignited in this speech, but think carefully about how he changes through the speech and how it might ebb and flow. When is Oedipus in control of what he's saying, and when does he let rip?

Plays like this are widely studied in school and college – but be careful not to be overawed by the history of the text. Make sure you think of Oedipus as a real person, with a backstory and fully rounded emotions.

■ Where to find the play This play is published by Methuen Drama, an imprint of Bloomsbury Publishing Plc (www.bloomsbury.com).

Oedipus

Political rank, wealth and power,
And men's ambitions clawing at each other,
Till life becomes a battleground,
And envy everyone's motive!
Creon is, and has been my friend.
I've trusted him completely. This crown
Was given to me, freely, by the people,
I didn't ask for it. And this man,
My friend, is secretly plotting to overthrow me
With a spiritual quack, a charlatan,
A paranormal stuntman, whose eyes
Are stone blind when it comes to prophecy,
But where money's concerned, very sharp,
Wide open then! Astrology,
Fortune-telling, forecasting the future,
Where was all that when we need it?
There was a monster here – do you remember?
I'm sure you do – with the face of a woman
And the body of a dog, who terrorised this city.
Where were you then? What was your advice
To save this country? She set a riddle
Which no ordinary man could answer. Someone special
Was required. What else are prophets for?
But you hadn't a clue, had you!
Not a word, not the slightest suggestion!
And then I came along, a young man,
Quite ignorant, knowing nothing, with only the wit
My mother gave me. But I stopped her mouth.
I did it, Oedipus! I guessed her riddle,
Without any gobbledygook about birds!
And I, Oedipus, I am the man
You hope to depose, you and Creon,
So that he will be king, and you his guru.
Well. You will regret it. You will both regret
This attempt to turn me into a scapegoat.
If you weren't an old man, punishment would teach you
The difference between prophecy and sedition.

Our Days of Rage

Written and devised by and for the NYT Company

Our Days of Rage was performed in 2011 at the Old Vic Tunnels. Directed by NYT Artistic Director Paul Roseby, the show took place in a labyrinth of subterranean tunnels under London and featured a large ensemble cast. It was written by a team of NYT Write to Shine writers, with this speech written by writer and performer Deanna Rodger. *Our Days of Rage* tells the complex story of four decades of struggle in Libya, and asked probing questions about the West's complicity in the unrest that took place.

Like *Whose Shoes* (page 363) and *Slick* (page 326), *Our Days of Rage* was a large-scale piece of promenade theatre, which took the audience on a journey through the disused railway tunnels under London's Waterloo station. The story focuses on Hana, a young woman born in Libya to a British mother and Libyan father, who moves to the UK after her sister commits suicide in the wake of being raped by a group of soldiers. As Hana grows up and gets a job in a big, corporate organisation, she starts to question her own lifestyle choices, and towards the end of the play, is given the opportunity to make a stand by blowing herself up at an art exhibition called 'The Art of Protest'. By interweaving Libya's complex history with Hana's personal story, *Our Days of Rage* poses questions about violence against women, capitalism and the power of protest.

Dee

■ **Character** A young woman of unspecified age.

■ **Location** The tunnels under Waterloo Station.

■ **Accent** Your own.

■ **Scene** This speech is taken from the final scene of the play, and is delivered by Dee – a spoken word artist – as part of the 'Art of Protest' exhibition, which Hana has helped to organise. As part of a corporate social responsibility scheme at the company she works for, Hana has decided to put on an evening of art which responds to all the protests going on around the world; Dee has been chosen from the local Lambeth community to present her poem at the event. The speech explores the idea of voting and the ambivalence that many people feel about the power of their vote. Whilst Dee only appears in this scene and does not take part in Hana's story, the speech encapsulates many of the themes and ideas that *Our Days of Rage* explores.

■ **Who is she talking to?** The audience.

■ **Where?** At an art exhibition.

■ **What does she want?** Dee wants the audience to sit up and listen. She has been plucked from a local community centre as part of a scheme run by big business, and is surrounded by corporate types who are dressed in suits, sipping wine, so this is a chance for a young woman to speak to a room full of rich, powerful people. She wants them to understand how disenfranchised and hopeless some people feel, to bring home the reality of many people's lives.

■ **Things to think about** The speech has a fluid, mercurial sense of logic, so make sure you have fully understood all of the imagery in the speech, even when metaphors are smashed together – you need to be certain that you own every word.

249

Like lots of spoken word, this speech has a rhythm and energy that is undeniable, so enjoy the flow of the speech, but be careful not get caught up in a rhythm at the expense of exploring the language and ideas. Try to vary the pace and intensity throughout – just like any other speech, the character has to go on a journey.

Even though this is a poem, these thoughts and ideas are rooted in real life; try and imagine the world that Dee comes from, and what has inspired her to write the poem; for example, who are the 'victims' of credit schemes? Does Dee know them personally?

Think about where Dee is when she is reciting the poem; you may want to remove it from the context of the play and decide that she is speaking in a more intimate environment, or you may want to imagine her at the exhibition, speaking to hundreds of people. Whatever you decide, be clear about exactly who the audience is, try to imagine them listening, and think about the effect Dee wants to have on them.

Where to find the play This play can be read on the NYT website (www.nyt.org.uk/monologues, password: nytspeeches).

Dee

Who cares about voting nowadays?
Nowadays voters wait and watch locked outside as elections count without them so who cares about politicians nowadays?
Nowadays, they just perch in their taxpayers-paid-for whatever they conned out the system and bitch and moan about benefits who lead the country into deficit by taking and not giving back
So who cares about promises nowadays?
Nowadays manifestos are written in jargon by people detached from the mass
Swallowed in parliament and removed from common language so big words confuse and diffuse, cos no one's got time to read headnote to foot- and take notes to contrast and compare,
No one stares until they see between the lines the lies that hide inside smiles that style campaigns
So who cares about truth nowadays?
Nowadays credit cards are deceiving victims believing they're needing to live to repay
So each breath feeds debt,
And their souls become slaves to the pound
So who cares about protest nowadays?
Nowadays tents are removed from the root and destroyed like weeds
Cos the silence is soiled if the stem breaks free and dreams left to bloom for ideas to pollinate

Who cares about stories nowadays?
Stories that reveal human nature at its peak and expose where we're weak but courageous,
Stories of the past before the world spun fast and left day to artificial light.

Nowadays life is a competition where youth is a trophy that should be protected from age

Cos change of any kind is feared.

So, who cares about voting nowadays?

Those whose energy is spent trying to outbid odds that are
built around them in capitalism and greed,
Those who educate minds outside of a structure which is
designed to dictate destinies with narrow paths in concrete
labyrinths.

Freedom is often mistaken for the sight of light at the end of
a tunnel.
It's the sense that we are free that keeps us trapped.
But who cares about that?

Matt Lucas

It actually doesn't matter too much if you forget a line. If you do,
just start again. It's far more important that you perform well.

Out of Me

Jane Bodie

Out of Me was part of the 2008 season at Soho Theatre. Written by Jane Bodie, it is a multi-narrative piece that follows the lives of four newly pregnant young women, all of whom are considering having an abortion. With wit and warmth, *Out of Me* delves into the lives of each character, exploring the variety of circumstances that influence this momentous decision.

The opening scene of the play features four intercut monologues from our main protagonists explaining the circumstances by which they each became pregnant – from a chance encounter at a university open day to an affair in the back room of a florist's. None of these pregnancies have been planned, and the action that follows explores the effect that unexpected pregnancies can have on young women's lives. Through the course of the play, we watch each character navigate their way towards the final decision of whether or not to continue their pregnancy, and how this decision might affect both them and the people around them.

Billie

■ **Character** A twenty-four-year-old woman.

■ **Location** Present-day Britain.

■ **Accent** Your own.

■ **Scene** By this time, the audience has met Billie a few times – often in the gym. In a previous monologue she has been talking to the audience whilst on an exercise bike, gossiping about her office job, her boyfriend, Jay, and her life with him in their new one-bedroomed flat. In this speech, Billie has recently found out that she is pregnant and she is back at the gym doing some sit-ups. Finding out that she is pregnant has not been easy for Billie, and in this speech she begins to reflect on her relationship with Jay. Not only is she unsure whether she wants a baby right now, she also doesn't know if she ever wants to have children with Jay.

■ **Who is she talking to?** The audience.

■ **Where?** In the gym, doing sit-ups.

■ **What does she want?** Billie wants to decide whether to tell Jay about the baby, and whether she wants to keep it or not. She is doing sit-ups in an attempt to hide the fact that she is pregnant, so it is clear that she isn't yet ready to make a decision about what to do, but through the speech she wants to clarify what her feelings are, and what she should do next.

■ **Things to think about** The stage directions suggest that she is doing sit-ups during the speech; think about whether you want to follow this suggestion, or whether you want to stage the speech differently. If you do decide to do the sit-ups, be careful that they don't break the flow of the speech too much.

Billie is trying to work out what she thinks and feels. Try and think about what she *doesn't* say in the speech as well as what she does say. This will help you to understand the subtext.

This is a really big decision for Billie, so even though she is flippant at points, make sure you've fully considered how conflicted she feels about what course of action to take.

At the end of the speech, she says that she has decided to tell Jay about the baby, but is she being honest with herself? Look at what happens at the end of the play.

■ **Where to find the play** This play can be read on the NYT website (www.nyt.org.uk/monologues, password: nytspeeches).

Billie

I haven't told Jay yet, he's upset enough about the credit crisis, without… He's an accountant, which makes him sound boring, but he just likes to map things out. Preferably on Excel. With Jay, there's never a… grey area.

(*She leans back, does another sit-up, stops.*)

Everyone keeps saying how well I look. Yesterday, Keeley in finance comes up and says – *you look good*. And then she says *have you put on some weight?* I wanted to say, no, I haven't actually, and I notice you still haven't put a clean shirt on either. But I didn't. It's just my hormones, going mental.

I know what Jay'll say. He'll say that we can do this, we're a winning team. He'll see it as the next logical step, to where we should be heading. On his map. He loves me. He does. I'm his world. But I don't… burn for him. But then that stuff makes you mad, makes you lose control.

(*She does another sit-up, hard, stops.*)

I've never had a boyfriend that could cook. Adrian, my last boyfriend, he couldn't boil an egg. But when I was with him I still put on a lot of weight. Adrian wasn't dad material. Jay's gonna be a great father.

(*She does a few manic sits-up, then stops.*)

I haven't got any energy, but I've been eating like a horse. Last night Jay tried it on, in front of the TV. And when I tensed up, he said 'What, now you're up for this promotion, you gone off me, is that it?' I could see he was hurt. I said no, Jay, that isn't it.

He said, what is it then? I said, 'I've got a yeast infection and they've said I have to give the ointment a couple of weeks.'

(*She lies back, and then can hardly sit back up.*)

I've got this, line of hair, on my stomach, and it's getting darker, it's. It's like this arrow pointing, to…

Sometimes, it's like there's this… this gap.

I can't see it, but I know it's there. I can feel it, in between my body and, what I could be, my... potential. There's this big empty space, a *void*.

I am going to tell him, I just want it to be the right time. And, last night was the final episode of *The Apprentice*, so that wasn't going to work.

You know, when you type the word 'kid' into your phone, it comes up as Lie.

Does that mean a lie's more important, or just more useful?

Sasha

■ **Character** An eighteen-year-old woman.

■ **Location** Present-day Britain.

■ **Accent** Your own.

■ **Scene** This is the first and only time in the play we meet Sasha. At first the audience thinks that she is just another random customer in the florist's that Alice works in. That is until Sasha announces that she is Alan's daughter. Up to this point, the audience knows that Alice is pregnant and they suspect that Alan is the father, but they don't know anything about Alan except that he runs the florist's. When Sasha confronts Alice, we see these two young women start to realise that Alan has betrayed them both.

■ **Who is she talking to?** Alice.

■ **Where?** In the florist's.

■ **What does she want?** Sasha initially comes into the shop to see who works there. She doesn't know for sure that her dad is having an affair with his colleague, but when she discovers that Alice has been working there for a year, she works it out. Sasha has to think on her feet throughout this speech: she feels betrayed by her father and is furious with Alice – maybe she wants an apology, maybe she wants to know the truth, or maybe she just wants to humiliate Alice.

■ **Things to think about** Think about being in the shop, and all the memories this brings back for Sasha. How does she feel talking about her past and her family to Alice when she suspects that Alice is having an affair with her father?

Why does she tell Alice the story of the text message? Is she trying to read Alice's face and see her guilt? Or is it to make Alice feel bad?

How does Sasha change from the beginning to the end of the speech? Does she feel better for having confronted Alice, or is she more upset than when she first started speaking?

Sasha is dealing with a lot: not only is she furious with her dad, she will also have to decide whether to tell her mum. As a result, the stakes are very high in this speech, despite Sasha's calm demeanour.

■ **Where to find the play** This play can be read on the NYT website (www.nyt.org.uk/monologues, password: nytspeeches).

Sasha

We used to come in the shop when we were little. I don't really remember it. And he always used to come home, in the evening, smelling of the place. Mum wouldn't let him take a bath until he'd let us all have a good sniff of him, the whole family. She said it was the smell of life. Now he comes home later, and he always goes straight up and has a bath, before he lets any of us near him.

(*Beat.*)

He texted me the other day. He doesn't do that, wasn't even sure he knew how to. *My lovely*, that's how it started, the text. He's never called me that before. Then it said… he wasn't going to make it back, and that he'd make it up to me.

And I thought it was a bit… a bit serious, you know, from Dad. But I went downstairs, and he was there. He was sitting at the kitchen table, I was going to say something to him about it, but then I looked at him, he was smiling and I knew the text wasn't for me. He'd meant to send it to somebody else. His lovely. It was my birthday.

(*Beat.*)

Do you fuck him? Or, does he fuck you? Don't know why I want to know that. But I do. I want to know.

(*Beat.*)

You've gone red, redder than anything in the shop.

(*Alice looks at the floor.*)

Do you use something? Are you on the pill?

(*Sasha looks disgusted.*)

Oh *god*, does he wear a condom. Does my dad… If you're not. He better fucking wear a condom.

He still loves her, my mum. I don't know what he's said to you.

They've been together for twenty-two years.

Sometimes on the weekend, they don't come out of their room for hours. It's embarrassing at their age. I stand outside their door, and they'll be laughing in there, in their bedroom. And he still brings her home flowers, every night. Tulips, those are her favourites. I think it's disgusting. A man of his age, a married. I hope he pays you properly, at least. No, I don't. I expected you to look different. And it stinks in here. It's too much all in the one room. Dunno how you stand it.

Outright Terror Bold and Brilliant

Dan Rebellato

Outright Terror Bold and Brilliant was written shortly after the London 7/7 bombings, and presented as part of the 'Young at War' season of short plays at Soho Theatre in 2005. Performed only two months after the attack, the play takes its title from the review of the movie *The Descent*, visible in a poster on the side of the Number 30 bus that was bombed on 7 July 2005.

The play is split into four parts, all of which shed some light on the effect of the terrorist attack: the first features text taken directly from a message board on the pop band Blue's website. These are the words of real people responding to the attacks on 7 July, and worrying about whether Blue will be able to perform at Wembley that evening. The second section involves a group of theme-park designers thinking about how they can create the most fear-inducing ride ever. The third then depicts a girl gang – named the 307s – telling the story of how they once toppled a bus. The final section is a monologue from Simone – also a member of the 307s, talking about her life on the day of the attack.

Character A school-age girl in her teens.

Location London, 2005.

Accent Your own.

Scene This is a standalone speech in the play, but it is still linked to the other scenes. It is most closely connected to the 'Travel Sweets' section, as Simone tells us that she is part of the 307 gang. At first this speech seems very simple – a girl talking us through the details of her daily routine, her friends, her likes and dislikes. But gradually small details creep in that locate the speech on 7 July. As Simone leaves to go to work, we aren't sure whether she might be getting on one of the Tubes that were attacked. Suddenly the bombings are presented in the context of real people's lives and the audience begins to understand the personal effect that this act of terrorism had. I have included second half of the speech in which Simone talks about the morning of 7 July, but you may like to look at the first part and perform that instead.

Who is she talking to? The audience.

Where? The play doesn't specify where she is: might she be in her bedroom? In her house somewhere? Getting ready to go out?

What does she want? As with any speech, whether the character is talking to another character or the audience, you need to think about how they are trying to change or affect the person or people they are talking to. Why is she telling them about her routine? Maybe she wants to confide in the audience and open up to them about her private life. Or perhaps at times she is showing off to the audience about how mature she is. Maybe she wants to invite the audience to share her excitement about what the future holds. The speech is full of understated detail, so make sure you have thought about what prompts her to speak to the audience in each moment.

■ **Things to think about** Look at the first part of the speech in the playtext where Simone tells us about her likes and dislikes: what do these details tell us about her? Can you describe her in three words?

Think about how Simone reports other people's speech: does she do an impression of them or does she speak their words in her own voice?

Look at the scene called 'Travel Sweets'. Even though Simone doesn't appear in this scene, these are her friends and she is part of this gang. What clues does this scene give you about Simone?

At first, the speech could seem quite plain and undramatic. In the context of the play it is given dramatic tension because the audience gradually understands that Simone is talking on the date of the bombings, and we begin to worry that she might be caught up in the attack. See if you can focus on creating a really truthful sense of character to make your performance as engaging as possible.

■ **Where to find the play** This play can be read on the NYT website (www.nyt.org.uk/monologues, password: nytspeeches).

Simone

Yesterday I'm at home and I hear my dad calling me. I go in to the front room and he's watching TV going, 'It's London, it's London.' And I'm like, yeah whatever, but my dad is like crying – like *physical* tears – and he's going, 'I don't believe it, I don't believe it.' And I can't work out what's happening on the TV. Loads of people shouting. Commotion, stuff. And I calm him down, and he goes, 'I don't believe it, look: we got the Olympics.' And I'm like, 'What? What don't you believe?' And he goes to me, 'Nothing like this ever happens to London.' And I go to him, 'That is so wrong, Dad, cos everything happens to London, that is the brilliant thing, everything happens to London.'

I'm seeing a movie with Kelly and Lauren after work. I seen a poster on the side of the Number 30 for that new one; it's about these girls what go pot-holing and there's something down there, something in the dark. On the poster some paper reckons it 'Outright Terror, Bold and Brilliant'. That's my kind of movie. I tried to tell Kelly about it and she starts being crude about 'pot-holing' and I'm like *'gross* girl', ring *off.*

I got a mirror in my room. It's been there since before we moved in and it's too high on the wall. I got to stand on a chair to see what I look like. I don't know who ever could have seen themselves in it. A giant maybe. Most times it looks like an empty picture frame up there.

My job is just for the summer. Three days a week. I don't know what I want to do after that. My mum says I'm lucky. (*Accent.*) 'It's not often when you can stop for a breath in the middle of everywhere. You can go where you like, or you can stay where you are. But whatever you do, take some time to look around you.' These are the good days, she says.

To get to work I catch the Piccadilly line at Southgate. Just before the station at Southgate Circus it turns cold. I think about going back to get my jacket but it's a clear sky, so I swipe my Oystercard and I go down to the trains.

Pigeon English

Stephen Kelman, adapted for the stage by Gbolahan Obisesan

Pigeon English was adapted by NYT alumnus Gbolahan Obisesan and first performed in 2013 at Bristol Old Vic and the Edinburgh Fringe. It was then restaged as part of the 2016 REP season in the West End. The main character is Harri Opoku, an eleven-year-old who has recently emigrated from Ghana. When the play begins, the fictional Dell Farm estate is reeling from a fatal stabbing in which a young boy has been murdered. Seen through Harri's eyes, as the story unfolds we encounter a world in which gang violence collides with ideas of family, loyalty and community, as Harri and his friend Dean take it upon themselves to investigate the murder. In the REP production, Harri was played by Seraphina Beh.

In the opening scene of the play Harri and his friend Dean are standing behind some police tape looking at the flowers and tributes to the dead young man on their estate. Harri is an innocent but enthusiastic boy who lives with his mum and sister on the ninth floor of a tower block; his dad and little sister are still back in Ghana. As the story of the dead young boy unfolds through the play, Harri also introduces the audience to a variety of characters from his community – from Terry Takeaway and his dog Asbo; to his neighbour Jordan, who got excluded from school for kicking a teacher; to Kylie Barnes, a girl his year who says she saw the boy getting stabbed when she drove past her brother's car. As the story picks up pace, Harri and Dean get more and more embroiled in the events around the murder and, when Harri is found in possession of the dead young man's wallet by X-Fire – the leader of the gang responsible – the gang fears that Harri knows too much. On the last day of term, when Harri is running home, he becomes their next victim, getting stabbed in the stairwell of his own tower block.

Harri

■ **Character** An eleven-year-old boy.

■ **Location** The Dell Farm Estate, London, present day.

■ **Accent** Ghanaian/London or your own.

■ **Scene** Harri and Dean have just decided to try and find out who killed the boy, when Killa and the Dell Farm Crew accost them in the corridor. The gang talk about what it feels like to stab someone, and then they try and persuade Harri to do a mysterious job for them, but he refuses. In contrast to the underlying violence of the scene in the corridor, this speech, which comes immediately afterwards, shows Harri's innocent infatuation with his classmate Poppy in art class, and how her blonde hair becomes an inspiration for his 'mood picture'.

■ **Who is he talking to?** The audience.

■ **Where?** In art class.

■ **What does he want?** Harri wants to tell the audience about an important moment in his life – when Poppy sat next to him in art. He obviously felt feelings that he has never felt before, and he wants to share his observations with the audience, and make them realise how special Poppy Morgan is.

■ **Things to think about** Think about who might the audience be for Harri and how he feels letting them into his private thoughts about Poppy.

Later in the play Harri says that Poppy fills him with yellow – what does he mean by this? Could you try filling this speech with yellow?

If Harri is infatuated with Poppy Morgan, how does he feel about Tanya Sturridge? Try and give as much detail to moments like this as you can.

Even though Harri is telling the story in the past tense, make sure you have fully imagined how he feels at every moment in the speech – for example, when Poppy sits next to him, how may he have reacted?

■ **Where to find the play** This play is published by Methuen Drama, an imprint of Bloomsbury Publishing Plc (www.bloomsbury.com).

Harri

In art Tanya Sturridge was absent and Poppy sat in her chair instead. Then Poppy was almost right next to me. She stayed there for the whole lesson, she didn't even move away. It made me go all hot. I couldn't concentrate because I wanted to see what Poppy was doing. She was painting her fingernails. She actually used the paint for pictures to paint her fingernails with. I watched her the whole time. I couldn't even help it. She painted one fingernail pink and the next fingernail green, and then the next one pink again, in a pattern. It took a very long time. She was very careful, she didn't make a single mistake. It was very relaxing. It made me feel sleepy just watching it. Mrs Fraser says inspiration for your mood picture can come from anywhere, from the world or inside you. I got my inspiration from Poppy Morgan's hair. I used Poppy's hair for my yellow. I only didn't tell her for if it ruined it.

Harri

■ **Character** An eleven-year-old boy.

■ **Location** The Dell Farm Estate, London, present day.

■ **Accent** Ghanaian/London or your own.

■ **Scene** This speech comes from the final moments of the play. It is the last day of term, and Harri has decided that they have enough evidence to go to the police the following morning and reveal who killed the young man from the beginning of the play. When he leaves school for the summer holidays he is kissed by Poppy, the girl he has fancied for months, and runs home feeling the happiest he's ever felt. Racing against his best ever time to get from school to home, he doesn't notice when a shadowy figure approaches and stabs him. As he lies bleeding to death in a stairwell, his mind goes towards his little sister, Agnes, whom he hasn't seen since he came to England.

■ **Who is he talking to?** The audience.

■ **Where?** Running from school to home.

■ **What does he want?** To begin with, Harri wants to celebrate the fact that he has been kissed by Poppy. He wants to run home as fast as he can and as he's doing so, make the audience see how brilliant the world can be. When he gets stabbed towards the end of the speech, he wants to try and stay alive, but also for the audience and his family to have happy memories of him if he dies.

■ **Things to think about** In the speech, Harri is running home. How are you going to stage this? Do you want to physically exert yourself by running? Or will you let the audience imagine it? Make sure you don't let the physical action upstage your vocal clarity or your emotional connection to the text.

Make sure you explore the journey Harri goes on, from exuberant joy at the beginning of the speech to the pain and confusion at the end of the speech.

Harri changes a great deal over the course of the speech – at the beginning he is joyous, in the middle he gets stabbed, and at the end he is considering his death. Make sure you don't play the ending at the beginning of the speech.

Make sure you have clearly imagined the physical journey Harri goes on; for example, when he sees pigeons or his block of flats, be specific about where they are and how he feels about them – that way the audience will also be able to imagine them clearly.

Where to find the play This play is published by Methuen Drama, an imprint of Bloomsbury Publishing Plc (www.bloomsbury.com).

Harri

Poppy just kissed me – right on the lips… (*Privately whispers to the audience.*) It felt lovely – She's my girlfriend now –

(*Harri celebrates with a dance.*)

(*Harri takes in a big breath and gets himself into a running start position.*)

I was going to count how long it takes to get home.

(*Harri starts to move his arms as if warming up.*)

I could feel my blood getting stronger. I started running. I ran fast. I ran down the hill and through the tunnel.

(*Harri shouts.*)

Poppy I love you –

I ran past the real church.

I ran past the jubilee centre.

I ran past the CCTV camera.

I let it snap me for luck.

I ran past the pigeons and pretended they said hello to me.

Pigeons I love you.

I ran past the playground and the dead climbing frame.

(*Harri runs even faster.*)

I was running super fast.

I ran so fast my feet were just a blur.

I was going to break the world record.

My lips still tickled from where Poppy's kiss had been.

I ran past a tree in a cage.

Tree I love you –

I could see the flats.

The stair would be safe.

I ran through the tunnel.

My breath was nearly gone, I couldn't get the words out any more.

Aaaaaaaaaaaaahhhhhhhhhhhhhhhhhhh!

Asweh, It was the best echo ever.

(*Harri breathes heavily.*)

The sweat was itching on my face.

It felt less than seven minutes, it felt like only five. I did it.

(*A hooded figure approaches Harri and stabs him swiftly.*)

I didn't see him. He came out of nowhere.

I couldn't get out of the way, he was too fast.

I should have seen him but I wasn't paying attention. You need eyes in the back of your head.

I've never been chooked before –

(*Harri falls to the bottom of the stairs holding his belly.*)

I could smell the piss... I didn't want to die.

(*Struggles for voice.*) Mamma

Mamma was at work. Papa was too far away he'd never hear it.

I would tell the police I only saw the handle for one second, It could have be green or brown.

(*Harri closes his eyes.*)

I wanted to laugh but it hurt too much.

(*Harri opens his eyes.*)

It could be a dream except – (*Looks down at his stomach.*) there was a bigger puddle and it wasn't piss it was me.

My blood is darker than I thought.

I hope Lydia tells Agnes my story, the one about the man on the plane with the fake leg.

She'll love that one.

I can see your face Agnes and your tiny fingers.

All babies look the same.

Seraphina Beh became a NYT member in 2015. She still works as an actor and has performed in theatres including the Bush, Albany, Ovalhouse and Lyric Hammersmith. Screen roles include *Live at the Electric* (BBC3), *Casualty* (BBC1) and Madison Drake in *EastEnders* (BBC1).

What advice would you give a young actor playing this part?

Have fun! I certainly did. The joy of Harri is he's young, curious, and impulsive at times. I strongly advise any young actor or actress playing this part to find their own version of Harri's fun, find their inner child and the rest will follow.

If you could give one piece of advice about auditions, what would it be?

Find the layers in your piece. It's easy with the pressures of auditions to panic and make the mistake of playing everything on one note – even after you've been given direction (trust me, I've done it before). For me, the best way to do this is to play about with different emotions when I'm rehearsing the speech – even if they're against the tone of the piece. It's a fun way to keep it fresh, alive and full of colour so that you don't get too stuck in your ways!

What is your abiding memory of NYT?

The Sixtieth Gala was a special moment. Up to that point most of the interaction I had with other NYT members was through my experience on Playing Up, then my two-week intake course and then the REP company 2016; in all of these, it was more like small little families that I loved and adored but seeing and being a part of this big daddy of families, filled with such wicked talent on and off stage was a bonus! Paul Roseby summed it up perfectly at the end when, with arms wide to the audience, he said 'This Is NYT! We are an ENSEMBLE!' Words I'm not forgetting anytime soon.

How did NYT affect your future life and career?

It's honestly changed my life. It made me fearless, confident, and so much more sensitive to the needs of others (and myself). NYT has allowed me to learn life lessons I definitely would have failed at on my own; I've been given more of a sense of endurance, responsibility, longevity and knowing when I do need help and knowing I can make opportunities for myself – all principles I plan to keep within my life. NYT has been a huge part of my life for the last two years and this is just the start.

Prince of Denmark

Michael Lesslie

Prince of Denmark was first performed in 2010 as part of the National Theatre's Discover programme, with a cast of NYT actors, and later produced alongside *Tory Boyz* and *Romeo and Juliet* in the 2013 REP season. Written by Michael Lesslie, *Prince of Denmark* is a prequel to *Hamlet*, and imagines the circumstances that lead up to the events of Shakespeare's play. If you don't know the story of *Hamlet*, it is easy to enjoy *Prince of Denmark* as a study of power struggles, ambition and unrequited love; however, if you are familiar with Shakespeare's play, *Prince of Denmark* also offers an enlightening perspective on characters you'll know well.

Prince of Denmark begins with a furious Laertes, who is outraged to discover that Prince Hamlet has been sending love poems to his sister, Ophelia. Laertes and Ophelia are new to court, arriving with their father Polonius who has become a servant to Hamlet's uncle, Claudius (the king's brother). Laertes warns Ophelia not to go anywhere near Hamlet, saying that she is jeopardising the family name. Ophelia maintains that she is in love with Hamlet, but Laertes thinks he is not to be trusted, and certainly not fit to be king. As the play progresses, Laertes's dislike turns into jealousy and hatred; he becomes focused on not only protecting his sister, but bringing about Hamlet's downfall. Laertes conspires with several other characters to lure Hamlet to a secluded place and murder him, although when the time comes to commit the act, not everything goes to plan.

Laertes

■ **Character** A boy in his late teens.

■ **Location** Elsinore, in medieval Denmark.

■ **Accent** Your own.

■ **Scene** Laertes has sent his friend Reynaldo to spy on Hamlet, and find out what his intentions are towards Ophelia. Reynaldo tells Laertes of Hamlet's plan to swap clothes with one of the players who will perform that evening after the performance, so that he can escape the castle in disguise and go and meet Ophelia on the cliffs. Laertes is insulted that Hamlet does not want to be openly seen with his sister, and begins to rake over everything he dislikes about Hamlet. As the speech progresses, Laertes starts to think about how much of a better king *he* would make than Hamlet, until he decides that the only course of action is to kill him.

■ **Who is he talking to?** This speech is a soliloquy, and so it is up to you whether he is talking to the audience, himself or a mixture of both.

■ **Where?** On the battlements of the castle, at night.

■ **What does he want?** Ultimately, Laertes wants respect. He is aware of his lowly position in court and he does not like being at the bottom. He also doesn't believe that Hamlet has honourable intentions towards his sister and perhaps subconsciously sees that as an insult to his family – and subsequently to himself. He wants everyone to be able to see what he sees – that Hamlet is self-involved and not fit to be king. Laertes is also ambitious, and wants power. The system, as he currently sees it, is loaded against him, and so his decision to try and get rid of Hamlet is part of his attempt to change the world for the better.

■ Things to think about Laertes constantly says that Ophelia is only a girl, and is therefore less capable – what might this tell us about him? Is he protective of his sister? Is he a misogynist? Try and mine the complexities of his character.

Chart how much he changes through the speech. At the beginning he is described in the stage directions as 'seething'; how might you describe him at the end of the speech?

It might be easy to think of Laertes as a macho, misogynist young man (which at times he is), but try and think about the pressure he puts on himself. Can you locate his vulnerabilities in the speech?

There is also a speech towards the beginning of Scene Two by Hamlet, which you might consider performing.

■ Where to find the play This play can be read on the NYT website (www.nyt.org.uk/monologues, password: nytspeeches).

Laertes

Disguised as a player, he says? So, not content with debasing my sister, with ruining my family and stealing from me the only being precious enough to sustain a belief in the gods, this lecher lord is yet so embarrassed by his lust that he must carry out our humiliation in disguise! As a tawdry player! God's blood, his shame confirms his base intentions! This is no prince, this is a tyrant, one who views his subjects as fairground rides for venal entertainment! If he knew the nobility of soul my mother contained he would weep before he dared whisper to her youthful image, let alone board it, and yet this whore-maker will be king! Taken by the whole nation as the measure of a man! What then will happen to Denmark? I have seen him in court, glowering and mumbling to himself as though his troubles would defy the comprehension of mortal men, and we imitate our monarchs as pets their masters. Thus will Denmark be reduced to a nation of cowards, brooding solipsists so paralysed by soliloquy as to be blind to their social duty. And all for nothing. For convention. Why must this player be king? Why Hamlet and not another? My natural capacities are as strong as his. Stronger, my friends might say. Is it man's duty to accept the future handed down to him, or to arm himself against the will of fate and carve out his own fortune? What would happen, say, if Hamlet were removed from Denmark? If he were to fall from the cliffs this very night? Then the direct succession would be interrupted, and the King's brother would become heir. Claudius, my father's lord. And sure, I have seen that when the presumed line is thus disturbed, men's minds are opened to the true possibility of their limitless election. A meritocracy may be born. Then, who is to say that a peasant could not be king? Who is to say not Laertes? And would Denmark be better off? All for a push! I must act. Hamlet, make your peace. Your audience tonight will pay you handsomely for your player's costume. (*Glancing offstage.*) But hold, my tongue, for here comes a weapon in my plan.

Private Peaceful

Michael Morpurgo
adapted for the stage by Simon Reade

Private Peaceful was staged at the Ambassadors Theatre in the 2014 REP season. Performed in the centenary year of the start of the First World War, Michael Morpurgo's story is not a typical wartime tale of heroism against the odds. Instead it gives new insight into the horror and futility of war by examining what happened to soldiers that were accused of cowardice and desertion, telling the little-known story of how they were unjustly executed by their own side.

Told from the perspective of Private Tommo Peaceful, the play operates through a dual timeframe; some scenes are set in the middle of the night in 1916, when Tommo is by himself waiting for dawn (we only find out what he is waiting for at the end of the play), and the other scenes are recreations of Tommo's past, as he remembers his life until this moment. In the scenes from Tommo's memory, we are transported back to an idyllic life in rural Devon where he lived with his mother and two brothers Charlie and Big Joe. Tommo and Charlie are great friends, but as they grow older things become complicated when they both fall in love with a local girl called Molly. Much to Tommo's disappointment, Molly ends up marrying Charlie, and having his baby. Then, when the war begins, both Charlie and Tommo leave the family behind and volunteer for the Army out of a sense of duty. Life in the trenches is gruelling, and when Tommo is wounded in battle, Charlie promises to stay with him against the orders of a superior officer, a decision that has fatal consequences.

Charlie

■ **Character** A school-age boy in his teens.

■ **Location** The frontline during the First World War.

■ **Accent** West Country,* or your own.

■ **Scene** This scene is the dramatic climax of the play, where we discover that Charlie has been court-martialled and found guilty of mutiny. He is to be executed by a firing squad at 6 a.m. and Tommo has been permitted to see him before he dies. Charlie is explaining to Tommo what happened in the court martial, and why he feels he was not given a fair trial.

■ **Who is he talking to?** His brother, Tommo.

■ **Where?** Waiting for the firing squad.

■ **What does he want?** The stakes for Charlie are incredibly high – he is going to die shortly, but before he does he wants Tommo to know the truth. Although Charlie has been accused of mutiny, he is a man of honour and loyalty so it is essential to him that Tommo is able to tell everyone what *really* happened to him. He also says in the speech that he doesn't want to cry, so he is holding back his emotions, even though they are bubbling under the surface.

■ **Things to think about** Think about where the two characters are when they have this exchange: are they in a prison cell? Or a hospital ward? Is it public with people listening, or in private?

Does Charlie feel he can talk at leisure, or is he also keen to make sure he says everything he needs to say – might he be taken away at any moment?

* 'West Country' denotes an area of the South West of England which can include Cornwall, Devon, Dorset and Somerset.

Use the rest of the play to inform the decisions you make about Charlie's character: think about his relationship with his brother, the injustice he is facing, the woeful situation in the trenches and the family he is leaving behind.

Why does he say he wants 'no tears' from Tommo? Is it because he's a 'stiff-upper-lip' Englishman, or is it because he's trying to hold back his own emotions? Or a mixture of the two?

■ **Where to find the play** This play is published by Oberon Books (www.oberonbooks.co.uk).

Charlie

I want no tears, Tommo. This is going to be difficult enough without tears. Understand? You'll tell Mother and Molly how it really was, won't you, Tommo? It's all I care about now. I don't want them thinking I was a coward. I don't want that. I want them to know the truth…

I tried, I tried my very best. They had their one witness, Sergeant Hanley, and he was all they needed. It wasn't a trial, Tommo. They'd made up their minds I was guilty before they even sat down. I had three of them, a brigadier and two captains looking down their noses at me. I told them everything, Tommo, just like it happened. I had nothing to be ashamed of, did I? I wasn't going to hide anything.

Yes, I did disobey the Sergeant's order because the order was stupid, suicidal. A dozen or more got wiped out in the attack; no one even got as far as the German wire. And I had to stay behind to look after my brother, Tommo.

I asked for you, Tommo, but they wouldn't accept you because you were my brother. I asked for Pete, but then they told me Pete was missing. So they heard it all from Sergeant Hanley, and they swallowed everything he told them, like it was a gospel truth. I think there's a big push coming and they wanted to make an example of someone, Tommo. And I was the Charlie. (*Laughs.*) A right Charlie…

The whole court martial took less than an hour, Tommo. That's all they gave me. One hour for a man's life.

Tommo. Look on the bright side. It's no more than we face every day in the trenches. It'll be over very quick. It's all over and done with, or it will be soon anyway.

We won't talk of Big Joe or Mother or Moll, because I'll cry if I do, and I promised myself I wouldn't.

You've still got the watch. Keep it ticking for me, and when the time comes, give it to Little Tommo, so he'll have something from me. I'd like that. You'll make him a good father, like Father was to us.

Molly

■ **Character** A school-age girl in her teens.

■ **Location** Devon, prior to the First World War.

■ **Accent** West Country, or your own.

■ **Scene** This scene is one of Tommo's flashbacks, and marks the moment when the relationship between his brother Charlie and their friend Molly begins to change. All three have been best friends for several years, until Molly's parents decide that Charlie is a bad influence after he is accused of stealing, and they prohibit Molly from seeing him. Tommo agrees to deliver secret letters between Charlie and Molly, even though he is in love with her himself. In this scene Tommo has gone to deliver a letter, but he and Molly are caught in a rain shower, so they hide in a haystack to wait it out. Molly begins to talk about the war, but little does she know how it will affect her future.

■ **Who is she talking to?** Her friend, Tommo.

■ **Where?** In a haystack.

■ **What does she want?** Molly doesn't go on a big emotional journey in the speech. She is talking to an old friend, with whom she feels very comfortable. She is confiding in him about what she's heard, and maybe she wants to prove that she is mature by talking about current affairs. Or perhaps she wants to be reassured by Tommo because she's worried. In the latter part of the speech she begins to talk about the Wolfwoman (also known as Grandma Wolf – Tommo and Charlie's great-aunt, who is the Colonel's live-in housekeeper), and she wants to make Tommo laugh about her.

■ **Things to think about** What does Molly think of Tommo? Does she know that Tommo is secretly in love with him? How might this affect the way she talks to him?

They are sheltering from the rain sitting on some haystacks; how might this situation affect your delivery of the speech.

Did Molly put salt in the Wolfwoman's tea? If so, what might this tell us about her character?

■ **Where to find the play** This play is published by Oberon Books (www.oberonbooks.co.uk).

Molly

Do you know what they're all talking about up at the Big House? All the talk these days is of war with Germany.

Everyone thinks it will happen sooner rather than later. I've read about it myself in the newspaper so it must be true.

It's my job, every morning to iron the Colonel's *Times* before I take it to him in his study. He insists 'the newspaper should be crisp and dry, so that the ink doesn't come off on my fingers while I am reading it'.

I'll admit I don't really understand what the war is all about, but some archduke – whatever that is – has been shot in a place called Sarajevo – wherever that is – and Germany and France are very angry with each other about it. They're gathering their armies to fight with each other and, if they do, then we'll be in it soon because we have to fight on the French side against the Germans.

The Colonel is in a terrible mood about it all. Everyone up at the Big House is much more frightened of his moods than they are about the war! Although he's as gentle as a lamb compared to the Wolfwoman –

Grandma Wolf – everyone calls her the Wolfwoman nowadays, not just us. Someone put salt in her tea instead of sugar and she swears it was on purpose – which it probably was! She's been ranting and raving about it ever since, telling everyone she'll find out who it was. Meanwhile she treats us all as if we're guilty…

Ayten Manyera was part of the NYT REP company production of *Private Peaceful* in 2014, when she played the part of Molly alongside other roles including Jade in *Selfie* and a witch in *Macbeth*. She currently works as an actor on both stage and screen.

What advice would you give a young actor playing Molly?

Hold on tightly, let go lightly. If you make mistakes, it's fine, you are supported throughout with an ensemble, and because Molly is a young girl, she would realistically make mistakes in life – she has fun and acts like a child would. The best part about playing a child is you can act like a child, relive memories with friends and enjoy being in the moment.

If you could give one piece advice about auditions, what would it be?

Breathe. I know it may seem obvious, but breathe before you start, throughout and after. We get so caught up about impressing the panel, we forget that they want us to do well! Know the lines, breathe, take your time, and everything will flow.

How did NYT affect your future life and career?

You are always looked after there. It is a home away from home. Everyone has a place there. They offer constant opportunities and experiences. I didn't go to drama school, but knew I always wanted to make acting a profession, and over the years NYT has given me constant opportunities to achieve that and get my foot in the professional industry.

Tommo

Character A school-age boy in his teens.

Location Devon prior to the First World War.

Accent West Country, or your own.

Scene This speech comes halfway through the play, just before the brothers volunteer for the war. Tommo has been in love with Molly for a while, but unbeknownst to him, Molly has been secretly meeting with Charlie. In the scene preceding this Molly has turned up at the Peaceful house and revealed that she has been thrown out of home because she is pregnant. In this speech, Tommo recounts what happened when Charlie and Molly got married and how his life changed immediately after.

Who is he talking to? The audience.

Where? In an imaginary space.

What does he want? Tommo can't have what he really wants – to have married Molly himself – so you have to decide what his new objective is. Perhaps he wants to cover up the depths of his feelings for Molly and to convince the audience that he is supportive of his brother's marriage. Given what happens at the end of the play, maybe he also wants to find the joy in the marriage, to remember it as a happy moment. Or perhaps in the middle of the speech he wants to confide in the audience how hard it was to watch them together.

Things to think about There is a great deal of subtext in this speech. You need to ask yourself: how does Tommo feel about the wedding, sleeping in Joe's bed and his relationship with Molly and Charlie? And then ask yourself what he wants the audience to think.

Think about who he is talking to: is it a friendly audience? Is he confiding in them? Is it hard to say this to them? Could you imagine he is speaking to a fellow soldier? Do whatever works best for you and the speech, but make a clear decision for yourself.

Think about the fact that Tommo is waiting for the firing squad at dawn – how does the fact that he is waiting for his brother's execution affect his recollection of this moment?

■ **Where to find the play** This play is published by Oberon Books (www.oberonbooks.co.uk).

Tommo

They were married up in the church a short time later – a very empty church. There was no one there except the vicar and the five of us, and the vicar's wife sitting at the back. Everyone knew about Molly's baby by now, so the vicar agreed to marry them only on certain conditions:

'That no bells are rung, no hymns sung.'

He rushed through the marriage service as if he wanted to be somewhere else. There was no wedding feast afterwards, just a cup of tea and some fruit-cake when we got home.

I moved into Big Joe's room and slept with him in his bed, which wasn't easy because Big Joe was big, and the bed very narrow. He talked loudly to himself in his dreams, and tossed and turned all night long. But, as I lay awake, what troubled me most was that in the next room slept the two people I most loved in all the world who, in finding each other, had deserted me.

At home, I tried never to be alone with Molly – I didn't know what to say to her any more. I tried to avoid Charlie, too.

On the farm, I took every opportunity that came my way to work on my own. Farmer Cox was always sending me off on some errand or other and I always took my time about it. (It was while I was making a delivery to Hatherleigh Market one day that I came face to face with the war for the first time.)

Razia Sultan

Jamila Gavin

Razia Sultan was first performed in 2010 at the Tramway, Glasgow. Set in thirteenth-century India, it tells the story of the real-life figure, Raziya al-Din – the first female Sultan of Delhi. Based on historical accounts of Razia Sultan's life, Jamila Gavin's play explores what it means to be a capable, passionate woman in a society that thinks of women as the lesser sex. It is an epic story of sibling rivalry and political power-wrangling that invites us to think about our attitudes to gender and religion in the modern Western world.

The opening scene presents a country in turmoil as Hindu India has been occupied by Muslim Turkish invaders; civil unrest is breaking out despite the best efforts of the Muslim Sultan, Iltutmish. Things are not much easier in the Sultan's private life either; his two wives are jealous of each other and his sons are a mixture of irresponsible, incompetent and uninterested in the matters of state. The only child who he feels could be his heir is Razia, but she is a woman, and the idea of a female sultan at this time is unheard of. Despite this, when Iltutmish has to go into battle to deal with an uprising, he leaves Razia in charge (against protestations from his noblemen and his family). Razia proves herself to be a capable ruler who is liked by the people – she is sympathetic to the Hindus and institutes a justice system that is fair to everyone. But when her father dies, her ruthless brother Rukn becomes sultan despite the fact that Iltutmish had wanted Razia to succeed him. She believes that she should be in charge and, in her efforts to seize control, challenges the preconceptions around her gender, attempting to prove that a female sultan can be just as good (if not better) than her male rivals.

Razia

■ **Character** A seventeen-year-old girl.

■ **Location** Thirteenth-century Delhi.

■ **Accent** Your own (but be sure you are comfortable pronouncing some of the names).

■ **Scene** This scene happens after the Sultan has died, and Rukn has taken over. Razia has just discovered that her favourite brother, Ghiyas, has been murdered, and she is warned that if she doesn't leave Delhi immediately, she will be next. She is unafraid, however, and instead of fleeing, decides to stay and address the crowds who are protesting against the tyrannical rule of Rukn. Her life depends on this speech, and her ability to convince the crowd that, against convention, she should be Sultan.

■ **Who is she talking to?** A swelling crowd of angry protesters.

■ **Where?** On the steps of the palace.

■ **What does she want?** Razia wants to prove herself in this speech – she believes that she would make a better ruler than Rukn, and she wants to belittle and undermine him. She also wants to convince the people that she is on their side, that she understands them and cares about them. It is important to Razia to honour her father's wishes and be given the chance to continue the work of a man she admired so much, despite the fact that she is a woman.

■ **Things to think about** Early in the play, Razia says she will be 'a slave to no one, not even to my sex'. Think carefully about how Razia views her gender – does it matter to her? How might she communicate strength and certainty to convince the crowd?

Razia's brother has just been murdered and she fears for her life; how might these emotions give power to the speech?

Even though she is making a public speech, make sure that you vary the tone and volume throughout – find moments where you can draw the crowd in.

Make sure you clearly imagine where she is when she delivers the speech and how this will affect your delivery.

She is described in the stage directions as being like a female Alexander the Great, with echoes of Joan of Arc. If you like this speech, you may also want to look at Joan's final speech in Bernard Shaw's *Saint Joan*, which occurs in Scene Six, towards the end of the play.

■ **Where to find the play** This play can be read on the NYT website (www.nyt.org.uk/monologues, password: nytspeeches).

Razia

People of Delhi! I have a grievance! People of Delhi, my brother Prince Ghiyas has been murdered. I too fear for my life. Hear what I have to say. I am Razia, daughter of Iltutmish, your sultan who brought you peace and prosperity; Iltutmish, who brought you justice and stability; I Razia am my father's daughter who believes in these things too. Only I can bring you justice!

(*The guards are frightened by the mob, and back away.*)

Everyone knows Iltutmish wished me to be sultan. (*Points to Turqaan.*) Queen Turqaan knew. My brother Rukn knew. (*Points to Rukn.*) He is unfit to rule. He knows it, you know it – everyone in the kingdom knows it – my father knew it. He loved you too well to want you to be left in the hands of a degenerate. But they have sabotaged his wishes. Too many think a woman can never rule a kingdom and fight her people's enemies. So they ignored my father's wishes, and made my brother Rukn ud-Din Firuz Shah your ruler. And has he ruled you? Has he brought you justice? Are your daughters safe, and your houses secure? And neither am I safe. My sweet brother, Prince Ghiyas is already dead; killed by them – by Rukn ud-Din Firuz Shah and his mother Turqaan Shah, and they want me dead too. Citizens! Citizens! Only you can save me! Do not see me as a woman. I was your regent. You have seen me rule the kingdom, organise the distribution of wheat and rice, administer justice. I am trained in warfare. You know that there is nothing a man can do that I am not capable of doing – especially him! (*Points to Rukn.*)

It was my father's wish that I should be sultan, and carry on his protection of you, his beloved citizens. But you have fallen into the hands of a clown; a degenerate good-for-nothing. He insults your gods – he insults Allah by his behaviour. Citizens of Delhi, fulfil my father's wish. Make me sultan! Give me a chance to prove my worth, and if I fail, and can do no better than your best man, then cut off my head, and dispatch my soul. Citizens – I wear red to show you I'm on your side. I want justice, justice, justice!

Relish

James Graham

James Graham's *Relish* was performed in 2010 at the Tramshed in Shoreditch, London. Inspired by the biography of the same name by Ruth Cowen, *Relish* is a rumbustious, playful look at the life of Britain's first celebrity chef, Alexis Soyer. Starting from the moment he leaves France, the play charts his rise to the top echelons of society and back down again as he attempted to change the face of cooking in Britain forever.

Relish opens after the end of the Napoleonic wars in Paris. Democracy has been established, but things are starting to kick off again with protests growing against the king, so Alexis Soyer decides that it's time to leave and go to London. Starting from low beginnings, Alexis quickly makes a name for himself and becomes the head chef at the brand new Reform Club – a fashionable members club opened to serve the newly empowered middle classes. From there he meets a host of famous figures from history whom the play treats with a playful mischievousness, from Queen Victoria who is played as a Sloane Ranger, to a hard-as-nails Florence Nightingale. Fame begins to go to Alexis's head, however, and despite his efforts to revolutionise the lives of everyone, rich and poor, he begins to take on more than he can handle, leading to tragic consequences in his personal life.

Eddie

■ **Character** A man of unspecified age.

■ **Location** Paris, 1830.

■ **Accent** London.

■ **Scene** As the audience enters, they are entertained by a scene of bustling chaos from the kitchen of a restaurant on the Quai d'Orsay in Paris, full of smoke and clattering pans. Cutting through the mayhem enters Eddie, who is the apprentice to senior chef, Alexis. Originally from London, Eddie is a typical Cockney geezer; he begins to explain the context for the beginning of the action. Initially cheeky and charming, at the start of the play Eddie behaves as a kind of narrator, but as the action progresses he becomes embedded in the action; at the end of the play, we discover a steelier, more ambitious side to his character.

■ **Who is he talking to?** The audience.

■ **Where?** In the kitchen of a restaurant on the Quai d'Orsay, Paris.

■ **What does he want?** This speech explains the situation and context, but it also serves to introduce the audience to the bold and playful tone of the play. Eddie's main aim is to make the audience feel comfortable, whilst also giving them the information they need to understand the following action. He wants to draw them in and put them at ease, whilst also entertaining and sometimes teasing them.

■ **Things to think about** Think about the scene that has preceded Eddie's speech – full of action, movement and noise. See if you can bring a sense of that dynamic into the speech.

Think about what Eddie feels about the audience – does he treat them as an old friend? Perhaps he might see them as a junior chef he is showing ropes to? Or are they just a crowd of people that he wants to entertain.

Go through the play and see if you can find further clues to his character. What happens later in the play when he takes over the Reform Club? What does this tell us about Eddie – how does he change as the play progresses?

■ **Where to find the play** This play can be read on the NYT website (www.nyt.org.uk/monologues, password: nytspeeches).

Eddie

You're probably all wondering what the fuck is going on. No *parlez-vous* the old Français and all that. Don't worry. You'll catch up. This banquet is for the First Minister. Showing off in front of lots of big cheeses in there. *Le grand fromage* – there, you can have that. Now, listen. This is Quai d'Orsay.

Left bank of the river Seine. Big bloody pretty thing from the outside. Gorgeous bloody thing inside. Fucking nightmare in these kitchens, as you can no doubt observe. I've just finished serving up the first course. The *amuse bouche* for those of you *au fait*. French onion soup.

Used to be the food of paupers, you know? People like me and thee. Been made more 'palatable' for people like them in there now. A thick layer of rich Gruyère cheese on top; hiding the more 'humble' ingredients underneath.

I reckon you can tell a lot about a nation by taking a butcher's at its cuisine. Take the onion, *par exemple*, the very symbol of France. Layer upon complicated layer, wrapped tightly around one another, strong and sturdy, yeah? But it only takes a little effort to begin peeling them off, and the whole thing falls about. And that's when the tears start coming…

(*Some banging outside. The kitchen quietens down, as everyone turns to look towards the door.*)

It's 1830, right? Anyone know their history? Revolution's over, so is the Napoleonic Wars. New democracy installed here, okay, things were quietening down, but then this first minister, he's only gone and given some of the royal prerogatives back to the king, ain't he? Which some folk have got a little bit pissy about, know what I mean? After all that blood. But this banquet, right, will be remembered for more than what's about to happen next – ergo, vis à vis, ipso facto, it going properly tits up – just wait. More than because of who is out there, but because of who is in *here*. The kitchen. Monsieur Alexis Soyer. Senior cook. And only twenty years old. Twenty, I know! Culinary star of Paris. (*Noise off.*) That's my cue to leave, I reckon. But don't worry. You'll see me again.

The Reluctant Fundamentalist

Mohsin Hamid, adapted for the stage by Stephanie Street

The Reluctant Fundamentalist was adapted, from Mohsin Hamid's novel of the same name, by Stephanie Street, and staged at the Finborough Theatre in 2016 as part of NYT's sixtieth birthday year. It is told from the perspective of Changez, a young Pakistani man who travels to study in the USA. After graduating from a top university, he lands a job on Wall Street, but gradually becomes disillusioned with the 'American Dream' and begins to question where he fits in in the world. Tackling the themes of Islamophobia and capitalism, *The Reluctant Fundamentalist* is a provocative meditation on identity, memory and belonging.

From the opening of the play, Changez addresses the audience as if they are sitting with him outside his brother's tea shop. He begins to unpack the question 'who am I?', and in doing so, he takes us through his life from the moment he arrived at Princeton University in New Jersey. After graduating with flying colours, he gets a prestigious job as an analyst at a financial institution called Underwood Samson, and begins to live the high-life; unlimited bar tabs, hotels and international travel. Then, on 11 September 2001, when the planes fly into the Twin Towers, his world begins to change; post 9/11, he gets harassed at airport security and people's attitudes toward him begin to shift – for example his colleague April thinks he should condemn the attack more vociferously. Changez even begins to surprise himself – not least because as he watched the World Trade Center collapse, he felt... pleased. From this moment on, everything shifts; he begins to question his involvement in American capitalism, and his search to discover who he is, and what he wants, leads him back to his home city of Lahore.

■ **Character** A young man of working age.

■ **Location** In between a hotel room in Manila, the Philippines, in 2001, and outside a teashop in Lahore, Pakistan, 2007.

■ **Accent** Pakistani-American or your own.

■ **Scene** There is a fluid sense of time in the play where scenes blend into one another between timeframes; just prior to this speech, Changez has been in a scene with his colleagues at Underwood Samson doing business in the Philippines. We come into the present moment (2007), and Changez begins to recall the moment in his hotel in Manila when, as he was packing, he looked at the TV in his room and saw the attack on the World Trade Center. As he talks, he takes the audience through his thoughts and emotions until he reaches a revelation at the end of the speech which changes the course of his life.

■ **Who is he talking to?** The audience.

■ **Where?** Outside the teashop in Lahore in 2007.

■ **What does he want?** Changez wants to transport the audience back to the most important moment in his life – this is the moment he changed. He also wants to explore it again himself, to experience this moment again so that he can understand the effect it had on him.

■ **Things to think about** Think carefully about the complex set of emotions that led to Changez's reaction to 9/11. Why might he feel like this? Does Changez know why he felt pleased that the Twin Towers collapsed? Don't worry if he can't explain it – use that sense of confusion to drive the speech forward.

Who is the audience for Changez? In the original book, he is talking to a specific person – if you want you could read the book and imagine Changez is talking to one person. Alternatively you could make your own decision about who the audience is.

How does Changez feel about opening up to the audience? Does he feel nervous? Ashamed? Mischievous?

Even though Changez is recalling the story from Lahore, he is talking about an incredibly important moment – make sure you have fully imagined the hotel room, the moment that he looked up at the TV and the moment the second plane hit.

■ **Where to find the play** This play can be read on the NYT website (www.nyt.org.uk/monologues, password: nytspeeches).

Changez

At the time I thought it was one of those early-nineties action films. The sound was down after listening to Erica's message, and I was sure Van Damme or, or Mel Gibson was about to burst onto the streets of lower Manhattan. Then I saw the CNN logo… I turned up the volume. And heard the rambling voices, struggling to fill time over this strange image of a sapphire sky and smoke pouring out of Windows on the World… Where we'd been drinking, me, Wainwright and the rest, on our new hire cultivation…

The first thing I thought was all those people up there eating eggs Benedict and drinking mimosas, enveloped in black smoke. Coughing and spluttering into the Hollandaise sauce.

And then it came screaming out of the sky. Faster and braver than anything Van Damme could handle. Like retribution itself, flying in over the Statue of Liberty. In that moment I understood. As the airplane ploughed into the South Tower.

Someone very wise once shared a quote with me: 'Know the true definition of yourself. And when you know it, flee from it.' In that moment I came to know something about myself. Something I hadn't till then been aware of. And when I tell you what it was, as I am about to… it will not… please. In fact, I take a big risk here because chances are… you will like me a great deal less after I say this. And frankly you could do anything out of that… dislike. The world has proven that much…

But I feel we have reached a point of openness and honesty. So… I will tell you that my first response, that night was… to smile.

As I expected. You are shocked. But believe me, I am not pathological; I feel empathy, I feel the pain of others. And I was not the only one to think this way. Many, many people felt a sense of just deserts being served up to your country that morning.

Look, of course I felt sadness for all those burning bodies. But to strike her at her most audacious and bring America crumbling to her knees. Just like those towers, folding in on themselves, shattering into dust. The symbolism was outstanding.

Daisy Lewis

You only lose if you don't try. You need to actively put up a really good fight against the voice of doubt in your head that says 'I'm too northern/southern/tall/short.' Switch that voice off and just give it a go. The key to performing a speech is that it should speak to you. Don't try to put on an accent, don't try and do any clever stuff: what they essentially want is you. Don't think you can't do it and don't think that everyone else who auditions isn't as terrified as you are – because everyone is.

Ripple

Monsay Whitney

Ripple by Monsay Whitney is a dark comedy exploring the rippling effects of one man's suicide bid on the world around him. Performed as part of a double bill at the Arcola Theatre in 2015, *Ripple* combines social commentary with elements of absurdist farce to shine a light on issues around mental health, housing and unemployment.

The play begins in the middle of the night with an agitated young man, Ronnie, standing near the edge of a tower block with no trousers on, preparing to throw himself off. He has accidentally sniffed a line of ketamine and is hallucinating that rats are crawling all over him. As he prepares to jump off he is joined by Yoga Boy, who begins to talk to Ronnie as if nothing unusual is happening. Intent on jumping throughout the play, Ronnie is gradually joined by a cast of weird and wonderful characters including Social Media Girl and Sleep-Deprived Mum who all have an opinion on Ronnie's situation.

Ronnie

■ **Character** A young man in his late teens.

■ **Location** London, 2015.

■ **Accent** London or your own.

■ **Scene** In this speech Ronnie is explaining to Yoga Boy how he got up to the roof of the building that day. After going to his nan's funeral and having an argument with his family, Ronnie was on his way to the job centre when he got chucked off the bus, so he went into Tesco which is when it all started going *really* wrong. Ronnie tells a lively story about people he knows, including missed appointments and drugs, which is both amusing and also enlightening about Ronnie's life.

■ **Who is he talking to?** He is telling the story to Yoga Boy as a way of explaining the series of events that led him to sniff two lines of ketamine and find his way up to the top of the tower block.

■ **Where?** On the roof of a block of flats.

■ **What does he want?** Ronnie wants Yoga Boy to stop what he's doing. He says it's distracting him and does a deal that if he tells Yoga Boy this story then Yoga Boy will give him some peace. Ronnie could also be trying to justify how he got up there to himself, and perhaps make sense of what is going on around him, and his behaviour. Ronnie has clearly had a stressful and emotional day, so he wants to make sense of everything that has happened.

■ **Things to think about** Look through the play at all the things that have happened to Ronnie prior to the speech; for example, how might his nan's funeral have affected him?

How does he want Yoga Boy to feel about his story and the characters in it? Is there a sense that he enjoys telling this story?

Once you have read the whole play, think about whether the characters that Ronnie talks to are real, or are they just figments of his imagination? Whichever you decide will have an impact on how you perform the speech.

The physical setting of this play is very specific – standing on the top of a tower block – so how might it affect the way that you deliver the speech?

■ **Where to find the play** This play can be read on the NYT website (www.nyt.org.uk/monologues, password: nytspeeches).

Ronnie

Look, do you wanna hear the story or not?

Young Nicky's got himself caught up with Claire. Claire's having it with Paul Francis, local hardman. Claire's a bully. So now she's seeing Young Nicky behind Paul Francis' back, she's using it to get him to do what she wants to do, i.e. credit cards. Tobacco and booze. That sort of thing.

All round London.

Young Nicky, there's seven stone of him, suit on, sunglasses, sweating buckets – he's at the kiosk now, with the booze and the fags. Security's eyeing him, he knows it's on top. He makes a dash for the door – security are on him. Just as they pounce on him – *she* comes skidding up – Claire, in a battered old Mini Metro, passenger door open.

Young Nicky manages to struggle free and get to the motor as she takes off, him nearly losing two legs, her streaming with laughter. After the initial elation of getting away, he realises he's fucked. Not only has he left the cards at the checkout – he's been spotted with Claire by Paul Francis.

He's hoping the police catch him first.

Meanwhile, Tesco's has been cordoned off. No one can enter, no one can exit. I was stuck in there half hour, next to some do gooder Community Support Officer, spliff in my pocket, arsehole squeaking.

Quarter past five, they let us go. I splurted up the road. Sprinted straight past a phone box, done a double take. Thought I best call the Job Centre. Try and straighten things out. Darted in. And racked up on the internal fitting; two lines of coke. Fat. Fat lines. This long. Sniffed them in one go. Ten minutes later – I'm walking like this.

I managed to dial the Job Centre, but they had me on hold for ages, by the time I got through I was making – (*Pigeon sounds.*) down the phone. Frothing out the front of my mouth.

Sleep-Deprived Mum

■ **Character** A young mother of unspecified age.

■ **Location** London, 2015.

■ **Accent** London or your own.

■ **Scene** In this speech, Sleep-Deprived Mum explodes into the scene. Her baby is constantly crying and so she doesn't care whether Ronnie jumps or not – she just wants to get rid of everyone from the rooftop. The speech itself is prompted by the Caretaker questioning whether she is doing everything she can to help the baby sleep; in response she manically lists off all of the contradictory advice she has been given, getting more and more stressed the more she talks.

■ **Who is she talking to?** She begins by talking to the Caretaker but could also be addressing the other characters on the roof.

■ **Where?** On the roof of the block of flats where she lives.

■ **What does she want?** Sleep-Deprived Mum wants some sleep. She also wants to ridicule the Caretaker for asking her whether there is a guideline she could follow. In listing all of the different strategies for helping babies to sleep she wants to crush any idea that bringing up a child is easy.

■ **Things to think about** Sleep-Deprived Mum doesn't have a name. This could be because she is meant to represent a 'type' of character, or it could be because she is a figment of Ronnie's imagination.

Try and think about bringing this character to life by thinking about her backstory. For example you could think about what has happened just before she enters the scene. What has made her so angry?

This speech clearly has a comedic element to it – in fact, all of the characters in *Ripple* are larger than life. How might you bring this character fully to life by making her both funny and realistic?

In the speech she lists off many different ways to make a baby sleep – do you think she has tried them all? If so, when you are learning the speech try to imagine what each scene would have looked like, it might help to give energy and impulse to the speech.

How is Sleep-Deprived Mum different throughout the speech? Is she always angry? What other emotions might she be feeling?

This is a long speech to fit within three minutes; you may want to cut some sections out.

Be careful not to play the whole speech with the same energy.

Where to find the play This play can be read on the NYT website (www.nyt.org.uk/monologues, password: nytspeeches).

Sleep-Deprived Mum

Oh yeah. Yeah. Guidelines. Let's see. Okay, so; You should *never ever* sleep train *at all, ever*. In fact, *only* sleep train after one year. Or six months. Or four months. But remember, if you sleep train too late, baby will *never* be able to sleep without you, *ever*. Of course, adults don't need to be nursed, rocked or helped to sleep, so don't worry about any bad habits, however, nursing, rocking singing, swaddling are all bad habits, and should be stopped immediately.

Naps should only be taken in a bed. Never in a swing, a car seat, or a pram because that will damage baby's skull, however, if baby has trouble sleeping, put baby in a swing, car seat or pram.

Put baby in your bed. Co-sleeping is above all, the best way for baby to sleep. Except it can kill baby. So never, ever do it. If baby doesn't die they will still be sleeping in your bed, aged eighteen.

Keep the room warm. But not too warm. Swaddle baby tightly. But not too tightly. Sleep baby on baby's back. But don't leave baby on its back too long or baby will be developmentally delayed.

Give baby a dummy, to reduce cot death. But be careful with dummies, because they will cause jaw deformities and stop baby from sleeping soundly, which reduces the chance of cot death.

Don't let baby sleep too long, except if they are napping too much, then you should wake them, but *never, ever* wake a sleeping baby. Any baby problem can be solved by putting baby to bed earlier, even if the problem is that baby wakes up too early.

You should start a routine and keep track of everything – but don't watch the clock. Put baby on a schedule – scheduling will make your life impossible because baby will constantly be thrown off of schedule and you will become a prisoner in your own home.

Using the 'Cry It Out' method, CIO for short, will make baby think it's been abandoned and will be eaten by a lion shortly. It also causes brain damage. However, not sleeping will cause behaviour and mental problems in baby, so be sure to put baby to sleep by any means necessary, especially CIO, which is the most effective form. CIO is cruel beyond belief and the only thing that really works because parents are a distraction.

Solid foods *will* help baby sleep longer – solid foods shouldn't be given at night because they might wake baby. If you respond too quickly with food and comfort, baby is manipulating you. Babies *can't* manipulate. Babies older than six months *can* manipulate.

Sleep when baby sleeps, *if* baby *ever* sleeps, and *never* worry about baby. Because stress causes baby stress and a stressed baby won't sleep.

Silence

Moira Buffini

Silence was first performed by NYT at Wilton's Music Hall in 2007. Set 1,000 years ago in medieval England, as Vikings are threatening to take over, *Silence* is a bold and funny exploration of gender, religion and power. Ymma, a French princess, has been banished to England by her brother as punishment for challenging his authority. On arrival she is told by King Ethelred that she must marry young Lord Silence of Cumbria, and live with him in the wastelands of the North. Initially furious at this pairing, Ymma soon comes round to the idea when she discovers, on her wedding night, that Silence is actually a woman. The pair resolve to live together in harmony, out of the control of men. Shortly after, however, King Ethelred has an apocalyptic dream where he makes love to Ymma, and decides that he wants to marry his sister himself. Wanting to escape this fate, Ymma and Silence flee to Cumbria, but King Ethelred follows in pursuit.

Ethelred

■ **Character** The king, unspecified age.

■ **Location** Medieval England.

■ **Accent** Your own.

■ **Scene** This speech happens towards the end of the play; Ethelred has reached Cumbria ahead of Ymma and Silence and is waiting in Silence's castle. On his journey he has transformed from the pathetic, 'scrawny' man who couldn't get out of bed to a ruthless killer who has ransacked many villages. When he arrives at Silence's castle it is deserted, except, that is, for Silence's priest (whom Ethelred considers to be a pagan witch). While he waits for Ymma and Silence to arrive, Ethelred decides to explore his new sense of power by torturing the priest to death. This speech recounts the final moments of the priest's life.

■ **Who is he talking to?** The beginning of the speech could be to the audience, but the end of the speech is directed at Silence. It is up to you if you think that Ethelred is talking to Silence throughout.

■ **Where?** In Silence's castle.

■ **What does he want?** Ethelred wants to prove his power over Silence. Even though Ethelred doesn't know that Silence is really a woman, Silence has undermined his authority and challenged his masculinity by marrying the woman that he wants for himself, so he wants to prove that he is ultimately in control.

■ **Things to think about** Ethelred talks at length about the Viking myth for Judgement Day. Why does he do this? Is he trying to ridicule Silence's religion? Perhaps he feels threatened by it, or else maybe he is drawn to it.

In Scene Five, Ethelred talks about how he is trying to 'save England from destruction' by discovering God's will; have a look at this scene and see if it informs your understanding of Ethelred's actions prior to this speech.

Early in the play Ethelred is described as a 'naked, scrawny youth', but in this speech he is trying to project the image of a powerful king. See if you can explore both aspects of his character in your performance.

Try placing all of Ethelred's speeches together to get an idea of his journey up to Cumbria.

This speech is all about power; when you are staging it, think about where you might imagine Silence is on stage. How might Ethelred exert his power over Silence physically?

In Scene Twenty-two, Ethelred has a revelation about power and torture; look at that scene and think about what this revelation tells us about his character.

■ **Where to find the play** This play can be read on the NYT website (www.nyt.org.uk/monologues, password: nytspeeches).

Ethelred

After thirty hours, the witch was nearly dead. I had slept and watched, dreamt and listened in a daze of fascination, as my men expertly broke her. To keep myself amused, I began to tell her what she might expect on the Day of Judgement. But she said: 'This, now, is judgement. This is the winter and every winter is the winter without end.' I questioned her as to what she meant. It appears that in her theology, the end begins when our mother, the sun, is torn out of the sky by a ravenous wolf. The world freezes and we perish in endless dark and cold. Every winter they fear it: an apocalypse of ice. They only know they have escaped it with the first warmth of spring. This wolf, this giant evil, is the very spirit of chaos. I've been meditating on his image; it is indeed powerful. So, as the wolf howls with victory in the darkness, Odin and the hordes of Valhalla meet him for the final battle on the frozen seas. No one wins. All is destroyed, matter, spirit, evil, good, everything, utterly lost. As the witch died, she told me that the last act of Odin, with the jaws of the wolf around his neck, is to fling fire over the world. 'It'll end in flames,' she said. 'Everything will end in flames.' 'And afterwards?' I asked, but she was dead. An eternity of nothing, I suppose. The concept of salvation is too refined for these barbarians. What do you make of it, Lord Silence? There's not a lot of dignity in torture – but your witch impressed us all. I've hung her naked body from your walls, as a sign of our respect. Shall I do the same with you?

Ben Lloyd-Hughes played the part of King Ethelred in the 2007 production of *Silence* at Wilton's Music Hall. He went on to train at the Guildhall School of Music & Drama, graduating in 2011. He works extensively in film, theatre and television.

How did you prepare for the part of King Ethelred?

I don't think I had much time to prepare for this part. My memory is that I had just got back from travelling, and received a call out of the blue from Paul Roseby asking if I could play the part because someone had dropped out. So I read the script. And headed for rehearsals!

What advice would you give a young actor playing this part?

Make it your own. Think about the different aspects of the character, that you can show as an actor. Both his vulnerability and his viciousness. Think about the pace. Think about how you can take whoever you're talking to on this journey using different pace.

If you could give one piece of advice about auditions, what would it be?

Preparation. Preparation. Preparation. When I was younger, I used to think I shouldn't prepare something too much because I would lose the freshness. I now realise that was just an excuse for not working hard enough. If you haven't done your work on the audition beforehand, the nerves and the adrenaline during it could mean you won't do your best stuff in the room. Also: remember you are auditioning them as well. Maybe you won't want to work with them, or go to their drama school. So remember they want you to do well just as much as you do.

What is your abiding memory of NYT?

A fantastic place filled with young people who all loved acting as much as I did. It was the first time I had been around people who also took it as seriously. And I still see people all the time from my course and the productions I was in.

How did NYT affect your future life and career?

It gave me amazing experience of performing in professional theatres. NYT treated you like professionals, requiring you to step up to the level of dedication they expected. The course and the whole ethos also gave me a fundamental idea of ensemble.

Skunk

Zawe Ashton

Skunk was first performed in 2009 at Soho Theatre. Inspired by Kafka's *Metamorphosis*, it tells the story of Otto, a young man who shows great potential – his mum thinks he is 'Cambridge material' whilst his dad wants him to play for Arsenal. What they don't know, is that Otto regularly smokes skunk* and one day, he wakes up to find that he is actually turning into a skunk. Soon after, his teacher, Mr Weiss, arrives to offer Otto a scholarship but is quickly put off by the stench that Otto sprays from his behind. The family cleaner, Janna, then admits that this has happened to her son too – but he now lives in the wild. The story becomes increasingly more absurd when they are visited by a doctor who insists on telling bad jokes. The doctor diagnoses Otto's condition as resulting from smoking skunk and proceeds to perform a gruesome operation to get rid of the smell. Gradually Otto deteriorates and during a dream sequence where he enters a 'magic forest', he has to decide whether to leave his family for good.

* 'Skunk' is a particularly potent type of cannabis, which is grown specifically to be smoked.

Slinky

■ **Character** Age and gender unspecified.

■ **Location** Present-day Britain.

■ **Accent** Your own.

■ **Scene** This is the opening speech of the play, which describes the morning that Otto turned into a skunk. The narration was originally spoken by a house band, who delivered their speech through a mixture of spoken words and music. The lines were divided between the band members, but can be spoken as one speech.

■ **Who are they talking to?** This speech is narration which is addressed directly to the audience, although you could deliver it to someone on stage if you like.

■ **Where?** The play takes place in Otto's home, but the stage directions state that the set should be 'sparse'. This is an absurd, theatrical play, so let your imagination run wild.

■ **What do they want?** Slinky is a narrator and exists outside of the action. But in the speech, when he describes Otto turning into a skunk, he wants to draw the audience in and startle, trouble and excite them.

■ **Things to think about** It is worth considering who Slinky is: what do they look like and how do they dress? How old are they? How do they feel about Otto's situation? Do they also smoke skunk?

In this speech Slinky merely describes what happens, but what is their attitude to Otto smoking skunk, and also how do they feel about him turning into one?

As Slinky tells the story, consider how physical you want your performance to be. If you are choosing to dramatise some of the experiences that you describe, make sure that you physically commit to these moments.

The speech is written in a loose, irregular verse form; paying attention not only to the language but also to the rhythm and internal rhymes will give you a playful sense of dynamic.

Where to find the play This play can be read on the NYT website (www.nyt.org.uk/monologues, password: nytspeeches).

Slinky

When Otto awoke in the morning from uneasy dreams
He found that things weren't quite what they seemed.
Thick black fur sprouted from under the cover
From just downstairs he heard the voice of his mother.
She was rising to wake him, shake him out of his bed

But all he could think of was the hair on his head

On his arms, on his belly

He watched himself like he was watching the telly.

The palm of his hand was raised like dry tar
He asked himself 'I wonder where my hands are?'
In place of his fingers were shiny white claws
They glinted like blades attached to his paw.

All of a sudden, a burning, a shooting-like pain
Went from his lower back and up to his brain
A tingling sensation took over his spine
If only he could move then all would be fine

But all he could do was lie stuck to his bed clothes
Until his shoulders, both at once, suddenly just rose.
An invisible force pushed him to the floor
But he managed to land on his feet

Yes – all four!

He crashed with a bang that rang in his ears
He looked in the mirror and was filled up with fear.
A huge white tail hung up above
It was big, fat and bushy and white as a dove.

Startled with fear and dread and confusion
Otto told himself that this was just an illusion.
He tried to get dressed in his cap and his Nikes
Tried to bite the laces that had come loose in places
But the clothes and the shoes both put up a fight

Dressed in thick fur and starting to sweat
Otto felt tangled, caught up in a net
Of questions, and answers
His feet moved like dancers
Scratching out a beat on the floor of his room
Walking too soon
With his tail over his head he looked up at his bed and
wondered if this was his doom.

"

Joan Iyiola

Never be afraid to ask for help. The truth is we all need a team.
Run your speech with a friend, tell them why you love the play
you've chosen, and share your thoughts on acting. Build and
understand your creativity with the people that you trust.

Kyle Winfield was a member of NYT's Playing Up 2 programme from 2008 to 2009. He played the part of Slinky in *Skunk* at Soho Theatre in 2009 and still works as an actor after having graduated from RADA.

How did you prepare for the part of Slinky?

I was in a pretty unique and fortuitous position as the play had been written particularly for my group of actors. (It was the final piece for our Playing Up 2 year group.) I'm pretty sure Zawe wrote the play to support our strengths, which meant that the characters were similar to how we were in everyday life.

I'd prepare for each performance by cycling from my house in West London to Soho Theatre (where we were performing); I would arrive quite early, and then warm up, relax, and listen to music... I liked to get in the space early and run through lines.

What advice would you give a young actor playing Slinky?

Well... the advice that was given to me was to not do too much with it. The poetry is so beautifully written, you actually just need to enjoy saying the words and know why you are saying them. I found the less I did, the better the performance was, which was very hard for me because I thought in order to be interesting I had to bounce around the stage. But, actually, just standing on stage, and relishing telling the audience a story was more than enough.

If you could give one piece of advice about auditions, what would it be?

The best advice I have is to act because you *want* to act; I've caused myself a lot of misery going into auditions and trying to impress the panel, or trying to give them what I think they want to see. I feel happiest when I go in, and do what I want to do with the part; and fully accept that this may be the only time I explore the role.

What is your abiding memory of NYT?

NYT was one of the first places I felt truly accepted, honoured and respected. I was encouraged, and seemingly loved, because of who I was, and not just because of what I could do. I felt cherished and nurtured. I was able to grow, and learn, and laugh. I laughed so much – so many good memories.

Slick

Ali Taylor

Slick was a large-scale site-specific piece which was performed in Sheffield in 2011 on the Park Hill estate. Against the backdrop of a vast, derelict estate, *Slick* transported the audience to the world of Eutopia – an island made of plastic in the middle of the ocean – and asked questions about our attitudes to recycling and how much we are really willing to give up to save the environment.

Slick is an immersive piece of theatre and so although there are 'scenes' within the piece, the action unfolds in a series of different locations. As they enter the performance, the audience are greeted by employees of Odyssey and are told they are going to travel to Eutopia – a paradise island built out of discarded plastic. We are joined on this journey by several characters including Rachel, who we quickly discover has boarded the ship in order to find her boyfriend, Joe. Joe went to work at Eutopia because he was inspired by the eco-friendly message and the promise of helping the planet, but he hasn't made contact for over a year. Rachel suspects something has happened to Joe, but as she discovers his whereabouts, she is confronted with some difficult decisions.

Joe

■ **Character** A young man of post-school age.

■ **Location** An alternate universe, on an island in the middle of the ocean.

■ **Accent** Your own.

■ **Scene** As the action unfolds, it becomes clear the Eutopia is hardly paradise. There are wards full of malnourished, exploited workers, all of whom cough up plastic because of the polluted fish they have been eating, and Eutopia resembles more of a prison camp than a holiday paradise. Eventually we discover that Joe has become the second-in-command at Odyssey, and has been subjecting the workers to appalling conditions. He seems to have lost his belief that climate change can be reversed and has decided to pursue his own happiness instead.

■ **Who is he talking to?** His girlfriend, Rachel – although he hasn't seen her for over a year.

■ **Where?** In a refugee camp, but out of sight of the other characters.

■ **What does he want?** Joe wants to convince Rachel that the path he has chosen is the right one. Before he came to Eutopia, he was an eco-warrior, but since then he has lost faith that anyone can change the course humanity has chosen, and that the human race is doomed. He wants to persuade Rachel that she is deluded if she thinks she can help, and instead she should join him on the island and enjoy herself whilst she has the chance.

■ **Things to think about** How does Joe feel seeing Rachel for the first time in years? She has clearly changed a great deal since he saw her last; how might he feel standing in front of her now?

Joe admits that the human race is polluting itself into extinction, but he still manages to find hope for his and Rachel's future – how can you show this?

To what extent does he see that Rachel doesn't agree with him – is he in his own world? Or is he really trying to persuade her to see things from his point of view? And when she looks sceptical, might this be why he proposes to her?

Do you agree with Joe? How can you make Joe as persuasive as possible?

■ **Where to find the play** This play can be read on the NYT website (www.nyt.org.uk/monologues, password: nytspeeches).

Joe

There is nothing lost, Rachel, because there was never anything truthful to lose. Do you remember when everyone became green? I remember it like it was yesterday. Suddenly, everyone was worried about the environment. We all bought our bags for life, didn't buy vegetables wrapped in plastic and we separated our rubbish into different bins and boxes. For a year, we didn't take a long haul flight! Do you remember that, Rachel? Do you remember we didn't go to New York because our carbon footprint was too big? But do you remember what happened just twelve months later? The recession hit and we'd completely forgotten all about being green. We went to Sydney, we bought more plastic than ever, we kept on consuming. And that made me think, that we're not really up for recycling. Our hearts aren't in it. I'm not talking about us. I mean other people. They don't care. I don't believe anyone that says they care. If they cared they wouldn't keep using plastic. If they didn't use it, no one would make it. I'll take you to the beach here. There are waves and waves of rubbish. It doesn't matter how hard we work, there is more and more getting washed up. Its pointless. See this is what I've learnt about human beings. We're like mould on an apple. We spread across the apple, spewing out toxins until the apple is black and rotten.

But we're worse than mould because mould has always got somewhere else to spread to. We've got nowhere. We'll keep polluting until everything is dead. So, if we're doomed why not make ourselves happy and rich in the time we have left? Yes, it might not be everything I once believed. But with money, I'll be well fed, with a nice flat and beautiful wife...Yes, Rach, why not?

We can be happy and rich. Eutopia will become rich. Banks are paying to come here. Governments pay us to do the clean-up so they don't have to. These kids'll pay for the privilege of cleaning up the older generation's mess. Everyone gets to feel all virtuous and green.

David Edwards joined NYT in 2008 and then performed in the large-scale ensemble production *S'warm* in 2010, before continuing on to play the part of Joe in *Slick* in Sheffield in 2011. He has worked as an actor on stage and screen, playing Stevie in *Fresh Meat* (Channel 4).

What advice would you give a young actor playing this part?

I envisaged Joe as a modern statesman. His rhetoric and turn of phrase reminded me of a politician, specifically someone like Tony Blair. Joe is completely committed to his role as leader and is so passionate about the project that he's blind to what's really going on. To prepare for the role I watched countless videos of Tony Blair giving speeches, specifically watching his mannerisms. Joe's silky-smooth oratorial skills really reminded me of Blair and I wanted to include that in my performance, almost as if Joe had used Tony Blair as his blueprint for a 'good leader'.

How did NYT affect your future life and career?

Teamwork is at the heart of NYT, it teaches you to work and interact with other people to the best of your ability. Realising your strength as an individual amongst an ensemble is a really great skill to remember. It's a skill that has stayed with me and is useful in all areas of life. I loved my time with NYT, it transformed the way I think about theatre, being an actor and interacting with all different types of people.

Stars Over Kabul

Rebecca Lenkiewicz

Stars Over Kabul was first presented in 2009 at the Tramway in Glasgow. It was Rebecca Lenkiewicz's second play for NYT and presents the world of post-Taliban Afghanistan. Inspired by the true story of Razia, the first female crane-driver in Afghanistan, *Stars Over Kabul* combines facts with fiction to tell the story of Razia's family. The play uses several narrative devices in order to shed light on how Afghanistan's troubled past has influenced the present, and explore what life is like in modern day Kabul.

Although Razia really exists, *Stars Over Kabul* is a fictionalised version of her story. It is a play that takes place in multiple times and places – sometimes simultaneously – giving a sense that Afghanistan is a complex, multifaceted place. The main framing device for the play is the TV show *Afghan Star*; scenes from the programme are staged at many points during the play. By watching the characters' response to contestants in the show, we begin to see the variety of attitudes held towards women in post-Taliban Kabul, and how the echoes of the Taliban's influence still ring out. The main story is that of Razia, whom we see at several points in her life: as a young woman driving a crane – back when women were allowed to work, but also as an older woman (Razia Mother). The older Razia tells of how her husband went missing when the Taliban first came to power and also how her son was killed in a terrorist attack. Her relationship with her daughter, Parastoo, is strained, as Razia tries to navigate her way through living life and grieving for her child and partner.

■ **Character** A woman in her late thirties.

■ **Location** Afghanistan, present day.

■ **Accent** Afghani, or your own.

■ **Scene** Razia's husband, Farzi, went missing years ago, but she never found out what happened to him. In this speech, Razia is imagining that Farzi is there with her, and she's talking to him about the day he disappeared and what she thinks might have happened. In the play the speech is actually divided by a scene in which Parastoo comes to her room to ask about her father, and we then see a flashback of Razia on the day that Farzi disappeared. Here, these two sections are presented together as one single speech.

■ **Who is she talking to?** Her dead husband, Farzi.

■ **Where?** In her bedroom.

■ **What does she want?** Razia desperately wants to know what happened to her husband, and she wants to keep his memory alive by talking about him. Perhaps Razia wants to feel the comfort of returning in her mind to a time when she was with her husband. Maybe Razia feels some kind of guilt, and wants her husband to know that she cared about him.

■ **Things to think about** Razia was the first woman to drive a crane in Afghanistan; what does that tell you about her as a person? Look for clues in the play that tell you more about her attitude to life and work.

Why does Razia start talking in this speech? In the play she has just been rejected by her daughter – is she desperate to talk to someone? Or do you think that she talks to Farzi every night?

The TV show *Afghan Star* really exists; try researching the show to give you an idea of the context of the play.

Make sure you are clear about the details in the play: who were the Taliban and when did they come to power in Afghanistan? What is the political situation like now? What is an oud?

■ **Where to find the play** This play can be read on the NYT website (www.nyt.org.uk/monologues, password: nytspeeches).

Razia Mother

I replay that morning, Farzi. I didn't even see you… you left so early… I just heard you close the front door quietly so as not to wake the children. When we were at university you kept joking that you'd find yourself a woman in the mountains. You'd live in a cave with her if I continued to be so nervous about everything. You'd lead a life of playing the oud and smoke hash and make love with your wild woman. And when you had finished every new story about your gypsy lover we would kiss. You will always be twenty-nine. You stopped there. I grow older but in my mind I am the same age as you. I am two people. One is with you and one is not.

I have imagined your death a thousand times. Prison. Beatings. A wall that you are turned towards as they shoot. A pit. A fast running river with rows of men stood on the wall above it. Every time I hear of a new execution I think perhaps that one might have been yours. They killed a woman just after you disappeared. In the football stadium. Crowds watched. You would have run onto the pitch shouting. You would have died a thousand ways under the Taliban if they had not taken you so early. She fell to the grass, Farzi. And she fell so neatly, quietly, wrapped in her burqa. It seemed so strange that life could be taken so easily, so fast. All that thought and weight. Gone. Men carried her away quickly like ants removing a blue leaf. And all that was left was the grass and thousands of people watching the spot where life had once been. That is all that I can hope for. That your death was swift.

Karla Crome was a member of NYT from 2005 to 2010. She played the part of Razia Mother in *Stars Over Kabul* at the Tramway Theatre in 2010. Karla studied on the BA Acting Course at Italia Conti Academy. She works widely on screen and has performed at the Royal Court and National Theatre.

How did you prepare for the part of Razia Mother?

We were very privileged to have our writer, Rebecca Lenkiewicz, in rehearsals with us as the play was developed. This meant we were able to share some source materials, probably the most memorable of which was a documentary called *Afghan Star*, a film about Afghanistan's version of *The X Factor*. The documentary really opened our eyes to what it was like to be female in Afghanistan. The women in the documentary had the same hopes, dreams and aspirations that we have here in the West – but they lived under the constant threat of religious fundamentalism. As well as watching *Afghan Star*, we researched a real woman called Razia who, before the war, was a crane-driver. In our version of the story, she was forced to quit by the Taliban, who later executed her husband for his liberal ideology.

What advice would you give a young actor playing this part?

This is a very moving speech. Razia Mother relives some dark, disturbing memories. It would be tempting for an actor to play guttural emotion, to show a woman in turmoil and wild anger. I would advise the actor to resist that temptation. Razia Mother plays these moments in her head hour after hour, day after day, year after year. She is vulnerable. She is exhausted. She has little fight left in her – but she is talking to the man she loved, and believing that he can hear her gives her comfort and hope. It is not easy for her to talk about, it is distressing – but it should also be cathartic. Find the balance.

If you could give one piece of advice about auditions, what would it be?

Know your pieces inside out and back to front. Practise the speech as often as you can. A good director or audition panel will want to see how malleable you are as an actor. They may ask you to do the speech completely differently. This is to see if you have the skills to take direction. The better you know your speech, the easier it will be to adapt the delivery. If you are concentrating on remembering your lines, you block yourself from playing with the text.

What is your abiding memory of NYT?

Doing this play introduced me to lifelong friends. We were all at different stages of our lives and careers and we've all gone on to do very different things: acting, directing, journalism, law and business. I just remember meeting this wonderful mix of people and coming together to tell a story that felt important to share. As an actor, sharing stories is always a privilege... but you hit the jackpot when you do it with people you like!

How did NYT affect your future life and career?

I'm a professional actor and writer now, so the skills I learnt were essential in my career. I honed my skills as a writer on a course supported by NYT long after I performed with them; without their support I wouldn't have had the courage or confidence to try my hand at it. To this day Razia Mother is one of the most special parts I've ever played. Handle her with care, please!

Tallman

Dominic McHale

Tallman was written by Dominic McHale for a forum theatre tour about knife-crime awareness which NYT toured to schools and pupil-referral units in London and Birmingham. It examines the culture and context surrounding knife-crime and presents characters and situations that are both tragic and, in moments, darkly comic.

Under the surface of *Tallman* is a web of relationships, jealousy and anger, which ultimately leads to Jason and Sean being stabbed. At the beginning of the play, Tallman and Sean have both robbed someone at knife-point because they owe Naz money. Sean is angry with Tallman for apologising to their victim about having a knife during the robbery and the pair continue to disagree about what to do next. Tallman decides to hide the money at Sean's girlfriend Seanna's flat, and as the play progresses, we learn more about Seanna's family life and the difficult relationship she has with her mother and sister. Towards the end of the play, Tallman and Sean get into an argument with Jason, in the course of which Sean stabs Jason; after that Tallman stabs Sean. The end of the play is then left open – we don't know if Jason has survived, or what will happen to Tallman, and Seanna's family are unwittingly dragged into the situation.

Mum

Character A woman in her thirties.

Location Present-day Britain.

Accent Your own.

Scene *Tallman* has a quick-moving plot full of characters that have conflicting motivations. This speech by Mum comes towards the end of the play when a lot has already happened. She is sitting on the sofa talking to Seanna, her eldest daughter, and on the surface she is apologising for going out after work when she promised she wouldn't. Mum then tells Seanna that she knows her secret, at which point Seanna confesses that she is pregnant. This isn't the secret that Mum is referring to, however; she is talking about the bag of money that she has found under Seanna's bed... Just then, Naz walks in.

Who is she talking to? Seanna.

Where? In their living room, on the sofa.

What does she want? Mum is a complex character who appears to both love and resent her daughters. In this speech she is apologising for going out, but she also appears to be quite insensitive when she suggests that mentioning her daughters put off a man she was flirting with. Does she genuinely want Seanna to accept her apology, or does she want Seanna to know that because of her she can't have a relationship? Also, when she suggests that they all go away on holiday, is this because she cares for her daughters, or because she wants to spend the money she has found (which Tallman has hidden under Seanna's bed)?

Things to think about What time is it? If it is late, and Mum has both been at work and then out with a friend, how might this affect her? Is she tired? Has she been drinking?

Is Mum aware of the effect that saying 'Don't have kids, yer life's ruined' might have on her daughter? She might be, or she might not be, but what does this say about her?

Mum's relationship with her two daughters is complicated; look at the earlier scenes in the play and see how they might give you clues about this speech. Think carefully about how Mum feels about Seanna – try not to judge her.

■ **Where to find the play** This play can be read on the NYT website (www.nyt.org.uk/monologues, password: nytspeeches).

Mum

I shunt have gone out I knew it. I knew it. That fucking article tonight! I wunt mind but he was a right tight-fisted fuck as well. Sweating everytime he had to buy a drink. One of them y'know, he'd have found a fucking plaster him and cut himself. Know what I mean? And the speed of him! What? Soon as I said 'Yehh I got two girls – ' Bumb! That was it. Dint see him for dust. That's it though yer life's ruined with kids. Don't have kids, yer life's ruined. Yer'll never get a fella, they don't wanna know. Tell you the truth I don't want one. I don't want a man in here telling me what to do, telling you two what to do, I won't have it.

(*She squeezes her head.*)

Ohh. I should have stayed in. I said I wasn't going to go out. I came back, fully intended not to go and then I got a text from Sheila and suddenly it was there looking at me and I thought fuck it. And I'm sorry. I'm so sorry love you're gonna kill me aintcha? I know you are. I'll give it you back. And anyway all the shit you have off me. And anyway I might kill you. I think you need to tell me something dontcha? Yes? Mrs. You tell me what you need to tell me and then we'll take it from there. Here. You know what I was thinking? We should go away. As a family. Me, you and Mia. We've never been away have we? On a plane? Imagine that? Get some cheap flights.

Naz

■ **Character** A twenty-year-old man.

■ **Location** Present-day Britain.

■ **Accent** Your own.

■ **Scene** This monologue is spoken by Naz, and whilst not a main character in the play, Naz is certainly important. In this speech Naz makes three phone calls. First he calls Sean, and then Tallman; neither picks up though, so he leaves them a message. He is clearly frustrated and wants to speak to them both, and we later learn that they both owe him money. He then calls his mum and, surprised that she answers, has to sing 'Happy Birthday' down the phone to her. Coming near the beginning of the play, this speech contains lots of details that will then become important as the play reaches its climax.

■ **Who is he talking to?** First he is leaving a message for Sean, then for Tallman, and finally he speaks to his mum.

■ **Where?** The play doesn't specify where Naz is, so you will have to decide this for yourself.

■ **What does he want?** Naz wants different things from Sean, Tallman and his mum. It's clear that he wants to assert his authority over the two men, whereas he wants his mum to believe him that he has forgotten her birthday, and for her to think he's a loving son – whether he achieves this or not is another matter.

■ **Things to think about** Unusually, this speech features someone on the phone. Watch other people when they are on the phone: what do they look like? Where is their attention? How do they achieve their goals?

Also think about what his mum is saying to him – you have to make us believe that there is someone else on the end of the line.

Look at the rest of the play: what else does Naz do? We know that he loves his mum, but in the final scene of the play, how does he treat Seanna's mum? What does this tell us about his character?

Whilst *Tallman* deals with some serious issues and characters whose behaviour is morally questionable, there are darkly comedic moments throughout. Have a think about whether there are any moments of lightness in amongst Naz's anger.

■ **Where to find the play** This play can be read on the NYT website (www.nyt.org.uk/monologues, password: nytspeeches).

Naz

Sean. It's Naz. I'll keep this brief yeh cos I'm getting a bit bored of leaving messages. One word yeh? One word. Blouse. I'm serious. Don't wind me up y'get me? Y'know something I don't think you do. The idea behind a mobile is that when someone wants to get in touch with you they can get in touch with you. So how come every time I've rung you haven't picked up? Or it's gone straight to voice mail? And don't say it's because you hant got any credit cos if you hant got any credit then fucking get some! When you get this ring me. Don't text me ring me!

(*He ends the call, presses the numbers on his mobile phone, before placing it to his ear.*)

Tallbollocks. It's Naz. I'll keep this brief yeh cos I'm getting well bored of leaving messages. Are you and that shitstain doing this to wind me up? I can't get hold of any of yuz. And don't say it's cos you hant got any credit. Get some fucking credit! Ring me when you get this. Don't text me ring me!

(*He ends the call, presses the numbers on his mobile phone, before placing it to his ear.*)

Oh hello Mum. You alright? No I was gonna just – I dint think you'd answer, I was gonna leave you a message. It's somebody's birthday innit? Yeh. Eh? Aw come on Mum. Yeh but it's not the same though – okay (*Sheepishly sings.*) Happy birthday to you, happy birthday to you, happy birthday dear Muuumm, happy birthday to you! Eh? See. Pretty good that weren't it? And guess what? I've got you something really nice – You on about last week? I thought it was today! It's today innit? You're joking. You know something I've been stressed. That's what it is I've been stressed. Mum. Stressed. Don't stress me out now don't stress me out I don't wanna get stressed I dint forget it on purpose I dint wake up last week or whenever it was and think 'Whose birthday shall I forget this week? I know, HERS! She can do without!' I dint do that!… Hello?… Shit!

Tory Boyz

James Graham

Tory Boyz was first performed at Soho Theatre in 2008, and then revived in 2013 as part of the REP season at the Ambassadors Theatre. Originally written when Labour was in power, in 2013 James Graham updated the script to reflect the new power-sharing coalition government that had governed since 2010. The play asks two questions: firstly, did Ted Heath (the Conservative Prime Minister from 1970 to 1974) hide his homosexuality, and secondly, have attitudes to gay people in politics changed in the last forty years?

The play revolves around Sam, a young, gay parliamentary researcher for the Conservative Secretary of Education. Whilst not 'in the closet', Sam feels awkward about revealing his sexuality; when he visits a school to talk to pupils about the government's education policy he doesn't know how to respond when he's asked if he's gay. In his office at work, he is also unsure about whether to be out-and-proud or to keep his sexuality quiet. Sam's boss, Nicholas, is a big, brash character who enjoys winding Sam up (especially about his sexuality), and it is through conversations with Nicholas that Sam begins to question the Conservative Party's complex attitude towards gay people.

Nicholas

Character A man in his late twenties.

Location London, 2015.

Accent Your own.

Scene Nicholas has just come back from a job interview which he thinks went really badly. Despite being frustrated at his own job prospects, he suggests that Sam could get any job he wants, and asks him why he hasn't moved yet. Eventually Nicholas discovers that Sam may be thinking of running as an MP, and so he begins to explain to Sam how homosexuality is viewed by the Tory party.

Who is he talking to? Sam, his junior colleague.

Where? In the parliamentary offices in Westminster.

What does he want? On the surface, Nicholas wants to help Sam. He thinks that Sam is naive and so wants to enlighten Sam as to how being homosexual works in politics. Through telling Sam how it 'really is', he also wants to prove that he knows more than Sam, to keep his position of authority and ultimately to undermine him.

Things to think about How might Nicholas subtly undermine Sam in the speech? Think about *how* he says *what* he says, his tone of voice and his physical behaviour.

Nicholas is the boss of the office; think about how he might dominate the physical space.

How has Nicholas's interview affected his mood? In later scenes we witness how Nicholas can switch between jokiness and ruthlessness – in this speech, when is he being friendly and when is he being malicious?

The speech is full of broken thoughts (shown through ellipses); is Nicholas modifying his language for Sam? What does he *not* say? Think about what kinds of words or phrases he might use with his friends, as opposed to the language he uses here.

██ **Where to find the play** This play is published by Methuen Drama, an imprint of Bloomsbury Publishing Plc (www.bloomsbury.com).

Nicholas

Oh my God, I knew it. You want to be one of them don't you?

Hey, no, listen. It's not like it wasn't obvious, even if it wasn't to you. All this… benevolent extra-curricular stuff, like with the kids and shit. You're just, you're one of those that… you know. Want to. Make things better. I personally couldn't give a blind man's fuck and that's why I'm getting out. (*Beat.*) Sam. A 'politician'. (*Smiles.*) Ah, which now makes sense about the gay thing. I like your thinking.

You know, keeping it on the down low. No parties, no… you know, no really 'gay' stuff.

Around here. On *this* ladder, it makes no difference. Does it? Diversity? Uh, 'yes'. But on that other ladder. Politics in public. Out there. (*Indicates the window and the 'real' world.*) You know? It's different. You can't… 'flaunt it'.

Okay. I see you're getting… I was, I'm just trying to help. I've been in this party longer, I know what it's like.

Look. Just… yes, of course, we have gay MPs. Humphreys. Married. Yey. But they… they kind of have to wait till they're near the top before they 'announce'. Just let your work do the talking, and if you shine, you can be whatever you want. You like men, women, old people, goats, hey. As long as… I'm saying they don't… You know, they're not 'really' gay.

They've covered their tracks is all. There are no seedy stories, no pictures.

You might think the country has changed, but it hasn't all that. And you might think the party's changed but you know that isn't true either. We're different, the new intake are different. The young 'uns. And the front bench is different. Hurrah. But behind them, in the House and filling the hall of the conference are party members as rooted in the Right as they have ever been. And they will have a black, Islamic wheelchair-bound liberal as Prime Minister before we see a fella kissing his other half on the steps of Number 10. And you know I'm right. (*Pause.*) Christ, I'm just saying if you want to climb that ladder, don't make it an issue.

Daniel Ings was a member of NYT from 2002 to 2008, when he played the part of Nicholas in NYT's first production of *Tory Boyz*. Since then he has gone on to appear in shows including *One Man, Two Guvnors* and *Frankenstein* (National Theatre) as well as working extensively on screen playing Mike Parker in *The Crown* (Netflix) and Matt Taverner in *W1A* (BBC).

How did you prepare for playing Nicholas?

Most of my prep involved reading the newspaper and getting a greater understanding of British politics in general, but also the (back then) new breed of Tory politicians who were laying the groundwork to take office. David Cameron and Boris Johnson were both seen as young guns at the time and there was loads being written about their supposed green credentials, and we were keen to make fun of that.

I remember watching some of *The Thick of It* to try and get a sense of that environment – it's also still one of the best examples of super quickfire dialogue delivery and sharp wit. The actors in that are on fire but I knew if I could achieve even one-tenth of that I'd be on the right track.

What advice would you give a young actor playing Nicholas?

I always want the audience to like these kinds of characters even though essentially they're the villain. Let's face it; the devil gets all the best lines. But he's also charming, wily, seductive and persuasive. In a sense Sam's, journey relies on him being drawn into the world of slimy villains like Nicholas, and only later realising that actually there is no place for his kind of bigotry any more.

But for that to work we as an audience need to be carried along by Nicholas's comedically over-inflated sense of self and persuasive logic. Just because we don't like what someone stands for, doesn't mean we can't find them funny and charming. So shamelessly nick those laughs (pun intended) – and the more throwaway the better.

If you could give one piece of advice about auditions, what would it be?

Anything you can do to rid yourself of nerves is a winner. I try to think of auditions like I'm also auditioning the script/ director/producer to see if the project is a good match for me. In reality I know that's not what's going on, that I'm the one on the spot, but it helps make it feel more equal. A meeting of minds.

Also try to remember that you rarely have any idea why you didn't get the part. I was once told I was the best actor they saw but I didn't have the right 'look' – to which I thought, 'Well I don't really want to be in something where they don't hire the best actors!!' But equally it could be that you look too much like someone who's already been cast, or you're too tall next to the lead actor.

Go in there and give them the clearest, most dynamic version of what you would choose to do with the part and be willing to shape and change that if they have notes (it's as much about seeing how you take direction, even if you're first read is spot on). It's hard but try to be as 'in the moment' as you can – when I started out I would often go in with pre-prepared anecdotes or things I wanted to ask, just to seem switched on, but it always sounds weird. Let them see who you are. Then forget about it as soon as you leave. Most stuff is badly written anyway – you probably deserve better.

How did NYT affect your future life and career?

NYT changed my life. When I left school I genuinely thought I was destined for stardom because I'd been a big fish in a teeny tiny pond. NYT taught me to approach acting and working in a cast like being part of a team. It teaches unselfish acting and ensemble work as well a sense that plugging away, being a good company member and slowly building up your body of work can lead to bigger and better parts down the line when you've learnt your craft. I also signed with my first agent after she saw me in *Tory Boyz* and booked my first TV job through a casting director who saw the show.

UnStoned

Amy Evans

Performed as part of the Sextet season of plays at Soho Theatre in 2006, Amy Evans's *UnStoned* tells the true story of a group of 200 people who climbed over the Berlin Wall in 1988. Focusing on the intertwined lives of a group of anti-capitalist activists, *UnStoned* explores what lengths people will go to for love and asks what people are willing to give up to fight for something they believe in.

The 'notes' at the beginning of the play give a comprehensive précis of the political situation concerning the Berlin Wall, but in brief, the play takes place on a contested piece of land called Kubatstan. This stretch of land in West Germany was owned by the East Germans and in the summer of 1988 was being occupied by a group of environmentalists, hippies and anarchists. The play begins when the camp is about to be invaded by the police, and the characters are considering what to do next. Some, like Panne, think they should stay and fight, whilst Petra is beginning to lose faith that their occupation will change anything. Tilt, meanwhile, has come here to find Zoë – an old girlfriend whom he still has feelings for – but Zoë has started a relationship with Panne. Through the course of the play, as all of the characters start to confront their imminent eviction, relationships being to change and hard decisions about their futures have to be made.

Tilt

■ **Character** An eighteen-year-old man.

■ **Location** Germany, 30 June 1988.

■ **Accent** German or your own.

■ **Scene** Tilt has been living in the camp in Kubatstan for a month before he spots Zoë during a protest against the police. Having held back for a while, he approaches her once her current boyfriend, Panne, has left to get some breakfast, with the plan of reading her a poem he's written for her. When he tries to speak to her, however, she won't communicate with him, so he just talks and talks about his travelling and everything that's happened between them until that moment. Eventually she responds, but it quickly develops into an argument, and is stopped by Panne accosting Tilt, thinking that he's a spy.

■ **Who is he talking to?** Zoë, his ex-girlfriend.

■ **Where?** Kubatstan, next to the Berlin wall on the Western side.

■ **What does he want?** On the surface, Tilt just wants to give Zoë a poem that he has written, but underneath he may want much more. Tilt certainly wants to explain why he went away – that he hadn't forgotten about her and that he has been thinking about her a lot. When he tells the story about the skinheads, he may also want to impress her. Maybe he even wants to tell her that he loves her (even though he knows she doesn't feel the same), but he doesn't quite have the courage, so instead he gives her the poem.

■ **Things to think about** Tilt doesn't know that Zoë will refuse to speak to him, so when he enters the scene he might think that the conversation will be quite different. As a result, he is making this up as he goes along, and you need to make sure that the thoughts feel fresh.

There are no full stops from 'Italy and Spain and Turkey' to 'and all of a sudden there you were', which suggests that this speech pours out of Tilt. Make sure you can find the impulse to speak non-stop without pausing for such a long period of time.

If Tilt has decided to wait until Panne leaves, is there a sense that he thinks he might return at any point? This might help you raise the stakes for the speech.

The poem is very important to Tilt; so when he gives it to Zoë make sure the stakes are high enough.

■ **Where to find the play** This play can be read on the NYT website (www.nyt.org.uk/monologues, password: nytspeeches).

Tilt

So you still won't talk to me, that's cool. I've been travelling a lot. Italy and Spain and Turkey, yeah, Turkey, and France and maybe you heard about it, how we almost got arrested and how skinheads chased us and we fought them fist to fist and I got hit in the jaw and cracked a tooth, I'm okay now, but I came back and stayed in a house that Schrott said wasn't far from yours and I walked down the streets every day for a year hoping I might see you but then someone told me you were out of town, you were in Wackersdorf living in the woods and I wanted to live in the woods with you, but I remembered what you said, that I'd never be able to make you feel whole and I thought at first there's no point in being alive if I can't make you feel... but I don't think that any more, and it's okay if you never want to come back to me because you're free and you deserve to be free and sometimes I hear your voice in my sleep and then I saw you one day on the street and I was so shocked I started shouting and you didn't do anything so I thought maybe you didn't hear me so I followed you into the house and I knocked on your door and you answered and I talked but you didn't say anything so I decided I'd leave you alone forever and leave Berlin and Germany and the western hemisphere and the whole fucking world, but then Schrott, he told me about this place, he said come and take a look, so I did and for a month life was beautiful again... and then the cops went crazy and everyone was running and screaming and throwing rocks so I went running too and threw some rocks and all of a sudden there you were. This is for you. It's a poem I wrote. No one else has ever seen it, and after you hear it, I'm going to rip it up and light the pieces on fire. Okay?

The Volunteer

Michael Arditti

The Volunteer was first performed at the Shaw Theatre in London on 14 April 1980. The play is set in an assessment centre for boys who have been taken into care. By focusing on the character of Martin, a young and optimistic university graduate who volunteers at the centre, the play considers the extent to which our upbringing affects our life chances, and asks what the best way is to manage young people from troubled backgrounds.

The Volunteer explores the complex lives of a group of boys who have been placed in care for a variety of reasons: Andrew was left with family friends by his parents when he was four; Gareth was being abused by his uncle after his parents died; and David has been put into care after stealing from his school. Martin is an Oxford University graduate who has come to volunteer at the centre to give something back to people less privileged than himself. When he arrives he is greeted by Mr Nash, an ex-army man who is in charge of their care, and it quickly becomes apparent that they have greatly differing views about the best way to treat the young men: where Martin believes in kindness, trust and respect, Nash is an authoritarian who has little faith in the boys. As the play unfolds, the audience follows Martin as he tries to make a difference in the boys' lives – especially David's – and we watch as he experiences many challenges and frustrations along the way.

Mrs Small

■ **Character** The mother of a fourteen-year-old boy.

■ **Location** Gloucestershire in the 1980s.

■ **Accent** Gloucestershire or your own.

■ **Scene** In order to decide where the boys will be sent after being in the assessment centre, the authorities have what is called a 'conference' with various officials. Towards the end of the play, several boys, including David, are waiting to hear what course of action has been decided for them. Martin is astonished to hear that, when David committed theft, his mother hadn't fought to keep him at home, but instead requested that he be taken into care. In disbelief Martin decides to visit David's mother, Mrs Small, in Gloucester to persuade her to take David back; in this scene she explains the choices she has had to make.

■ **Who is she talking to?** Martin, a volunteer from the assessment centre who has insisted on coming to see her.

■ **Where?** In her front room during the day.

■ **What does she want?** She has been forced to defend herself, so she wants Martin to understand the reasons behind the difficult decision to put David into care. She also wants Martin to accept that David was a difficult child, and that she deserves happiness herself. The sooner she can give her reasons to Martin, the sooner he will leave her house and the whole ordeal will be over.

■ **Things to think about** This is the only time we meet Mrs Small in the play so you need to be a detective to find out as much information about her as possible. Look for everything that David says about her, and all the clues within this scene to work out what kind of person she is.

At the beginning of the scene it is suggested that Mrs Small has had run-ins with social services before. Try to think what these encounters might have been like, and how this affects her attitude towards Martin: is she wary of him? Resentful? Nervous? How does it feel to have him in her house?

Just before the speech she says: 'I told his Child Care officer. Why did you have to come?' This suggests that the speech is hard for her to say, that she doesn't want to go through the emotional turmoil of making this decision all over again.

Even though Mrs Small is clearly angry with David, you should also consider the pain and guilt she feels at rejecting her son.

■ **Where to find the play** This play can be read on the NYT website (www.nyt.org.uk/monologues, password: nytspeeches).

Mrs Small

It's asking too much. Please, you must understand. I've grown old looking after them all. Now for the first time I've another chance. To make a life for myself and for them too. The man who lodges here, William; he's a good man. Holds a steady job. Overtime and all. Pat and Susan and Derek; they act like he's a second father. They're glad to have him here. The other night Pat said to me, Mam, why don't you and William get married, so he can be our proper Dad. They get on that well. But not David. He's done nothing but make trouble since the day that William came. Bawling fit to burst if he so much as asked me out for a drink. Just round the corner. But you'd think it were the end of the world. One day I came home to find these two cases packed at the bottom of the stairs. He'd put all William's things in them. But so neat and tidy, not any old how. As if he really thought he'd go. I was at my wits' end. Then one night he went for him with a knife. Like a maniac. Cut him on the arm. William won't stay if David comes back. He says it'd be on his mind all the time. A man can't live with summet like that on his mind. David likes to think it doesn't matter. But it does to me. I've been on my own long enough. And loneliness spread between four don't leave all that much to go round. I want to do what's best for everyone. I have three other kids and a man who needs me. All I ask is the chance to forget.

When You Cure Me

Jack Thorne

When You Cure Me, originally called *A Bedroom*, was performed at the Lyric Hammersmith in 2004 alongside several other short pieces. A year later Jack Thorne rewrote the play and it was performed under its new title at the Bush Theatre. *When You Cure Me* deals with the brutal rape of a seventeen-year-old girl and the after-effects it has on herself, as well as on her relationships with her family, friends and boyfriend. The subject matter of *When You Cure Me* is challenging, and you should think carefully before choosing a speech like this. The introduction to the published play has information about the Rape and Sexual Abuse Support Centre, which might help you with any research you choose to do around the play.

The play takes place in Rachel's bedroom. She is recovering from a vicious attack in which she was led to a secluded shed on an allotment, raped, beaten and cut on the face. In the aftermath of the attack, she has inexplicably lost the use of her legs, and so has to be cared for around the clock – washed, helped to use the toilet and fed. Despite the unstinting subject of the play, what follows is a touching, sometimes funny account of how she comes to terms with what happened to her, and specifically how she rebuilds her relationships with both her mother and boyfriend.

Rachel

■ **Character** A school-age girl in her teens.

■ **Location** Present day.

■ **Accent** Your own.

■ **Scene** It is almost two weeks since Rachel described the attack in detail to her boyfriend, Peter; in the meantime, she has become increasingly difficult to deal with. She has started to resent both her mum and Peter, and in the previous scene she has accused them both of doing nothing to help her. In this scene, she sees how far she can test Peter: they try to get her out of bed, then she suggests going on a date, after which she asks him to give her a bed bath before physically attacking him when he tries to help her back into bed. Immediately after their fight, she begins to describe what she would do to the man who raped her, if she could.

■ **Who is she talking to?** Peter, her boyfriend of six months.

■ **Where?** In her bedroom.

■ **What does she want?** Rachel is an incredibly complex character who has been through a massive trauma, and her actions in this scene could be interpreted in a variety of ways. On the surface, this could be a speech about how much pain and suffering she wants to cause the man who raped her. You should also consider, however, what she wants from Peter. In previous scenes Peter is the only person that Rachel is willing to show any intimacy towards, by telling him what happened to her. You could decide that she wants to further share her pain with Peter by confiding in him again – and so she wants him to comfort her. Or you could decide that she wants to punish Peter by making him hear this graphic account, for not having been there to save her. Of course, you may decide that she wants all of these things at various points throughout the speech.

■ **Things to think about** This speech comes after a long build-up; make sure you have read the play to understand how Rachel has reached this emotional state.

She is exhausted from her tussle with Peter, and is lying on the floor – think about how you will stage the speech. You don't have to lie down, you could use a chair if you like, but try to find a position which helps you recreate her physical state.

Rachel's description of what she would do is very graphic – in order to really connect with her situation, you will have to really picture everything she describes.

It is an incredibly intense and emotional speech, so think about how you will prepare yourself, and be careful not to give a general 'wash' of emotion.

Think about whether this speech is right for you – the subject matter is very sensitive, and you should think carefully before you consider performing it. There are two other speeches in the play that you may want to look at, which you can find on pages 27 to 28 and pages 81 to 82 of the published playtext.

■ **Where to find the play** This play is published by Nick Hern Books (www.nickhernbooks.co.uk).

Rachel

I've worked out – I'd cover everything he could breathe with – his mouth and – you can do ears too, breathe through ears too. So I'd – just leave his nose. And then I'd stand there and I'd just watch him, tied up with tape over his mouth and his ears and anything he can breathe by.

I don't know whether you can breathe through the eyes – I was quite surprised about the ear thing. And I'd have a hammer with me, I'd just sit there mostly, but I'd have a hammer. And every now and again I'd just tap him, his nose, with the hammer, not to break it, just to remind him that I had it, and he'd know that he could only breathe out of his nose, because his mouth and ears are covered, so I'd just keep reminding him of it. And I'd tap it harder and harder but still tapping. Then I'd hit it harder, just so it'd sting or something, just so he really knew. It'd probably be really difficult for him to breathe then, but it'd come back to normal and we'd both wait for that, him and me. Just until it's completely right again. Then I'd break it. He'd probably still be able to breathe then but it'd hurt all the time. Then I'd hit it again until it was flat, his nose, and maybe that'd make him unconscious, the pain, or maybe he'd suffocate. But sometimes I think he's not too bad. I mean, just mixed up a bit, like you. Will you – bring your head down?

(*Pause.*)

I think I smell. I can smell myself, Peter. I can smell me, okay? My… I want you to wash me, I want you to see me.

Whose Shoes

John Hoggarth

Whose Shoes was a site-specific piece written by NYT's former Artistic Director John Hoggarth that was performed in and around the Lowry Theatre in Salford. Featuring a cast of over seventy performers, the audience was taken on an epic journey through different spaces and told the story of a mythical city and the people that lived in it.

Examining ideas of identity and belonging, *Whose Shoes* centres on the story of a fairytale city and its tyrannical ruler, Thelonious. The story goes that Thelonious was once a true and brave king, until he fell in love with a woman who could fly. In an attempt to prevent his love from escaping he built a city around her and declared that he would never let her fly again. However, after imprisoning her in a tower, his wife became so desperate that she climbed to the highest point and threw herself off. After this, everyone in the citadel became so scared of the king that no one questioned his authority and everybody lived in fear. That is until Ayotunde, an exile from the city, returned spreading hope and the promise of a better life.

Fin

■ **Character** Age and gender unspecified.

■ **Location** In an alternate universe.

■ **Accent** Your own.

■ **Scene** Fin's speech marks the climax of *Whose Shoes*, and tells of a great battle that happened between Thelonious and Ayotunde. Fin is Ayotunde's long-lost brother, and as such this story means a great deal to him. At the start of the play, Fin is working for Thelonious as Chief of Police, but he is stripped of his position when he lets Ayotunde escape death after realising that he and Ayotunde are related. When Fin tells this story to the audience, they have all returned to the same place where the play began.

■ **Who is he talking to?** The audience.

■ **Where?** An unspecified place.

■ **What does he want?** Fin has been on a big journey through the play – he used to be one of Thelonious's main supporters, but by the end he is loyal to his sister, Ayotunde. By telling this story, Fin is trying to come to terms with what happened, and make the audience realise what was lost through the deaths of Ayotunde and Thelonious, but also what might now be possible.

■ **Things to think about** At the end of this scene Fin says that even though the battle happened they are still living under an authoritarian rule – what dynamic might this bring to the speech? Might he be fearful that someone will hear?

Ask yourself where Fin was when the battle happened – did he see it with his own eyes or is he retelling a story he has heard?

Read the whole play and think carefully about how Fin feels about Thelonious. Is he sad that the king died? At the time of the battle, which side was he on? Has this changed since it ended?

Remember that straightforward storytelling can be just as compelling as a dramatic speech. Experiment with how simply you can tell this story, but make sure you can picture all the moments you are describing.

▩ Where to find the play This play can be read on the NYT website (www.nyt.org.uk/monologues, password: nytspeeches).

Fin

The days after the fleeting revolution were exciting times for Ayotunde. She couldn't be everywhere and so, when she wasn't, people told stories of her instead. The stories were translated and the word became true; a banner to walk behind; to belong to.

The gossip grew louder, events became stories, stories became myths and myths became real. Lines were drawn and vows and oaths and pledges and contracts and unions were made… two sides, two armies, two truths, too strong.

The flag of Ayotunde stood for freedom; the courage to make a move; to discover new horizons and tempt the future by walking towards it. Soon she began to crave danger and search for adventure. Search it out in the darkest places. She started to believe she was immortal, no one could touch her and the braver she grew the more reckless and risky she became, her exploits became legendary and her reputation shouted louder. In opposition Thelonious built numbers and quietly planned. His army grew and waited. Both resolute and both blessed. The clash would send the world into a spin, on one side the voice of freedom, the other the voice of control. And the lines were drawn and the people took choices; which side are you on?

Which side are you on?

On the day of the reckoning two armies stared across an open plain. Today was her death day. She knew it well enough, but she would approach it with honour. Blood was spilt and sinew torn. And when the fighting was over the dead lay ankle deep around her and nobody would rise from the twisted mess of skin and bone. Ayotunde wailed, not in joy but in sorrow for those who would not return. Nobody knew her pain. She looked around her for a friend to help her but nobody came. I believe in you, she said. Thelonious looked into her eyes and saw the love she was letting go. He saw he was wrong, wrong to hold so tightly; his armour slipped. Ayotunde thrust her sword, walked into his arms and onto his dagger and when the embrace was over…

When the embrace was over they both lay dead.

Paul Roseby, NYT Artistic Director

Learn out loud. Don't learn it in your head. Learn your speech so well that you can say it in your sleep.

The World's Wife

Carol Ann Duffy

The World's Wife was performed in an abridged version at Latitude Festival in 2015. At first glance, this is a collection of witty, tongue-in-cheek poems written from the perspective of greater- and lesser-known women (or wives) from history. Look a little closer, however, and they become theatrical monologues which delve deep into the female experience. Carol Ann Duffy's writing is so rich and imaginative, it invites you to see these women as so much more than just wives, and it is your job to bring them to life.

I have extracted two poems from the collection, the first of which is 'Mrs Tiresias'. Tiresias (the man that the speaker is married to) is the Greek prophet who appears in the *Oedipus* plays and many other Greek myths. As well as being blind and able to predict the future, Tiresias was said to have been born a man, then turned into a woman and eventually back into a man again! In this monologue Carol Ann Duffy has brought the character into the twenty-first century, and explores how Tiresias's change of sex might affect his wife.

'Pilate's Wife' is the second selection. The 'Pilate' of the title refers to Pontius Pilate (pronounced as in an aeroplane *pilot*), the man who presided over the trial and crucifixion of Jesus. Pontius Pilate appears many times in literature throughout history but his wife is mentioned only once in the Bible and has had much less written about her. So who is she? That is for you to decide.

Mrs Tiresias

■ **Character** A woman, of unspecified age, who is separated from her husband.

■ **Location** Present-day Britain.

■ **Accent** Your own.

■ **Scene** Mrs Tiresias begins by recounting the day that her husband turned into a woman. She goes on to describe the moment that she first saw him as a woman, and then how their lives changed as he began to embrace his new identity. Towards the end of the speech there is a shift, however; they split up, he gains celebrity, and then comes the moment when Mrs Tiresias introduces her new partner – who happens to be a woman.

■ **Who is she talking to?** As with all the speeches in *The World's Wife*, whilst we may know a lot about the speaker (or their husband), we aren't told whom the character is talking to. This is for you to decide.

■ **Where?** Once you have decided this, then also think about where she is when she's speaking, and how this might affect your delivery – if she is in her own home, is it the same house she shared with Tiresias, and if so does it remind her of her old life? Or is she in a public place and if so how does that affect her tone?

■ **What does she want?** Again, this will depend on whom you decide she is talking to. Take into account the fact that whilst her husband has changed sex, she herself has changed her sexual orientation. Mrs Tiresias is much more complex than she first seems, and so there are many choices to be made about her. Does she want to embarrass Tiresias and show him up for being shallow? Or does she want to gloat over him and humiliate him (especially at the end of the speech)? Or is it that she wants to prove that she tried to make their relationship work?

Things to think about On the page, this looks very much like a poem, but try to think of it like any other monologue in this book. Think about who she is, where she is, who she is talking to and how she is trying to affect that person (or group of people). Once you have explored these questions, then you can start to enjoy the richness of the text through the eyes of the character.

She begins the speech saying 'All I know is this', and goes on to tell us about the nitty-gritty of her marriage and its demise, so whom might she be talking to?

The poem throws up lots of questions about identity, relationships, gender and sexual orientation, which may or may not be of interest to you. It is important to remember, however, that while all of these ideas can bubble under the surface, if you perform this speech, you must firstly connect with the character and the situation she finds herself in.

Mrs Tiresias is obviously older, but don't worry about playing the physicality of her age. Instead try to engage with and explore the essence of her character, and think about where she is, who she's talking to, and what effect she wants to have.

Where to find the play This collection of poetry is published by Picador (www.panmacmillan.com/picador).

Mrs Tiresias

All I know is this:
he went out for his walk a man
and came home female.

Out the back gate with his stick,
the dog;
wearing his gardening kecks,
an open-necked shirt,
and a jacket in Harris tweed I'd patched at the elbows myself.

Whistling.

He liked to hear
the first cuckoo of spring
then write to *The Times*.
I'd usually heard it
days before him
but I never let on.

I'd heard one that morning
while he was asleep;
just as I heard,
at about 6 p.m.,
a faint sneer of thunder up in the woods
and felt
a sudden heat
at the back of my knees.

He was late getting back.

I was brushing my hair at the mirror
and running a bath
when a face
swam into view
next to my own.

The eyes were the same.
But in the shocking V of the shirt were breasts.
When he uttered my name in his woman's voice I passed out.

Life has to go on.

I put it about that he was a twin
and this was his sister
come down to live
while he himself
was working abroad.

And at first I tried to be kind;
blow-drying his hair till he learnt to do it himself,
lending him clothes till he started to shop for his own,
sisterly, holding his soft new shape in my arms all night.

Then he started his period.

One week in bed.
Two doctors in.
Three painkillers four times a day.
And later
a letter
to the powers that be
demanding full-paid menstrual leave twelve weeks per year.
I see him still,
his selfish pale face peering at the moon
through the bathroom window.
The curse, he said, *the curse.*

Don't kiss me in public,
he snapped the next day,
I don't want folk getting the wrong idea.

It got worse.

After the split I would glimpse him
out and about,
entering glitzy restaurants
on the arms of powerful men –
though I knew for sure
there'd be nothing of *that*
going on
if he had his way –
or on TV

telling the women out there,
how, as a woman himself,
he knew how we felt.

His flirt's smile.

The one thing he never got right
was the voice.
A cling peach slithering out from its tin.

I gritted my teeth.
And this my lover, I said,
the one time we met
at a glittering ball
under the lights,
among tinkling glass,
and watched the way he stared
at her violet eyes.
at the blaze of her skin,
at the slow caress of her hand on the back of my neck;
and saw him picture
her bite,
her bite at the fruit of my lips,
and hear
my red wet cry in the night
as she shook his hand
saying *How do you do;*
and I noticed then his hands, her hands,
the clash of their sparkling rings and their painted nails.

Pilate's Wife

■ **Character** A woman of unspecified age.

■ **Location** First-century Judea.

■ **Accent** Your own.

■ **Scene** The speech tells the story of the arrival of Jesus (referred to as 'the Nazarene'), and the reaction Pilate's wife has when she sneaks out one day to see him. We then hear of a dream she has, after which she writes a note to her husband instructing him not to convict Jesus. This plea falls on deaf ears, however, and the poem ends with her considering Jesus's claims to be the son of God.

■ **Who is she talking to?** This is for you to decide.

■ **Where?** Again, this is up to you. Depending on who you think she is talking to, she might be in her bedroom, or conspiring in a noisy café. What time of day is it? Or maybe this is an imaginary space and talking to the audience gives her a chance for her to reflect.

■ **What does she want?** 'Pilate's Wife' lets us into her innermost thoughts – especially about her husband. Is she talking to a close friend? Or does it feel like she is confiding in someone she doesn't know well? Could you imagine she is being interviewed – if so, by whom? Or maybe she is talking to a lover? Once you have thought about this, then consider: is she focused on Pilate? Or the Nazarene? Does she want to convince the listener that her husband is useless and not worthy of her? Or does she want to excite and inspire them about Jesus? Maybe she wants to do both in different moments. Perhaps she wants to elevate herself above both of these men, dismissing them both as being beneath her.

■ **Things to think about** Why does she start talking? Is it in response to a question? Why does she feel the need to tell the story?

Her encounter with 'the Nazarene' has a profound impact on Pilate's Wife – when she talks about these things, how does she change?

Is she being honest with herself when she asserts that Jesus *isn't* God? Or is it more complicated than that? Does she feel conflicted about who he is?

Who is Barabbas? And where is the Place of Skulls? Can you picture what they are like?

The language is modern, but try to imagine the character 2,000 years ago.

What can you find out about women of the time? Or would you prefer to think of a modern equivalent? A politician's wife perhaps? It is important you get a clear idea of who she is.

■ **Where to find the play** This collection of poetry is published by Picador (www.panmacmillan.com/picador).

Pilate's Wife

Firstly, his hands – a woman's. Softer than mine,
with pearly nails, like shells from Galilee.
Indolent hands. Camp hands that clapped for grapes.
Their pale, mothy touch made me flinch. Pontius.

I longed for Rome, home, someone else. When the Nazarene
entered Jerusalem, my maid and I crept out,
bored stiff, disguised, and joined the frenzied crowd.
I tripped, clutched the bridle of an ass, looked up

and there he was. His face? Ugly. Talented.
He looked at me. I mean he looked at *me*. My God.
His eyes were eyes to die for. Then he was gone,
his rough men shouldering a pathway to the gates.

The night before his trial, I dreamt of him.
His brown hands touched me. Then it hurt.
Then blood. I saw that each tough palm was skewered
by a nail. I woke up, sweating, sexual, terrified.

Leave him alone. I sent a warning note, then quickly dressed.
When I arrived, the Nazarene was crowned with thorns.
The crowd was baying for Barabbas. Pilate saw me,
looked away, then carefully turned up his sleeves

and slowly washed his useless, perfumed hands.
They seized the prophet then and dragged him out,
up to the Place of Skulls. My maid knows all the rest.
Was he God? Of course not. Pilate believed he was.

Wuthering Heights

Emily Brontë
adapted for the stage by Stephanie Street

Stephanie Street's *Wuthering Heights* is a bold re-imagining of Emily Brontë's novel, reframing the action around the meeting of Cathy and Heathcliff in a space somewhere between life and death. Exploring big themes like love, mortality and the nature of the human soul, *Wuthering Heights* is a challenging and moving piece of theatre, which was performed as part of the 2015 REP season.

Adapted many times (there are several films and TV versions you can watch), *Wuthering Heights* has inspired artists ever since it was first published. It tells the story of Cathy and Heathcliff; when Cathy's father finds Heathcliff homeless, he decides to take him home and bring him up as one of his own children. Cathy and Heathcliff grow closer and closer and, during their adolescence, begin to fall in love. Due to social expectations, however, they cannot be together and when Cathy receives a marriage proposal from Edgar Linton, a societal equal, Cathy and Heathcliff's relationship breaks down. They can't live with each other, but they can't live apart and both their lives are destroyed when Cathy dies, heartbroken. This adaptation imagines a conversation between Cathy – now a ghost – and Heathcliff in a graveyard somewhere between life and death. As they try to make peace, they remember their lives, and the audience sees the action play out, beginning when they first met.

Cathy

Character A seventeen-year-old girl.

Location Yorkshire, eighteenth century.

Accent Yorkshire, or your own.

Scene This speech comes approximately halfway through the story; Edgar has proposed to Cathy and Cathy has said yes. But in this scene she confides in Ellen, her housekeeper, that she doesn't know if she has done the right thing. Cathy is also angry with her brother Hindley, who she suggests has 'ruined' Heathcliff. She is trying to work out how she feels and what she should do – should she follow her heart and leave with Heathcliff, or stay and accept Edgar's marriage proposal?

Who is she talking to? Ellen, the housekeeper.

Where? In the kitchen.

What does she want? Cathy says she wants Ellen's help, but is very confused in this speech. She is unsure whether or not to marry Edgar and she is angry with her brother, Hindley, who she thinks has turned Heathcliff into a beast; she does not know how to describe the depth of her love for Heathcliff. She wants for the situation to be resolved, but knows this isn't possible.

Things to think about What is Cathy's relationship with Ellen like? Do they get on? What is the status relationship between them in terms of social class, and how might this affect the way she speaks to her? Or are they speaking on a level – woman to woman?

When Cathy says 'After Daddy died... what Heathcliff said... I understood it', what is she referring to? Look at the conversation they have earlier in the play.

She says that she wants to be with Heathcliff forever, but can't be because of society's expectations. Explore how helpless and frustrated this must make her feel.

We learn in the play that Cathy has become interested in poetry, and the way she expresses herself in this speech could be described as 'poetic', but make sure you are clear about what she is saying and how she is using imagery to express what she thinks and feels.

The stage directions suggest that Cathy enters into an altered state of mind and at the end of the speech she has to ask Ellen what she has just said; think about how Cathy's feelings and emotions might be expressed physically.

■ **Where to find the play** This play can be read on the NYT website (www.nyt.org.uk/monologues, password: nytspeeches).

Cathy

Where's the problem? Where?

(*She brings her hand up to her chest.*)

Here.

Or here.

I'm not sure where it is, my soul. But I'm sure it's telling me I've made a mistake.

AHH!!! (*She doubles over with the pain and then slowly recovers.*)

After Daddy died, what Heathcliff said... I understood it. Daddy's soul had left his body but I knew I could still see it in the stars or feel it in a glass of cold, cold water. It hadn't gone.

(*And then on her stomach.*)

But then one day Joseph said, yes, yes it had gone, His spirit was in heaven – I don't even know what heaven is! I don't want my soul to go anywhere; I want it here always! Here... with Heathcliff.

But Hindley fucked it. Hindley's... ruined Heathcliff... So I can't marry him. It would... degrade me.

I had everything and then Hindley wrecked it all. He ruined him... So Heathcliff can never know how I love him.

(*Turning to Ellen.*) You want me to leave here, where my whole life is. Etched into these rocks and these trees...

But, you see, we won't ever have to be apart, will we? We're... I mean, you don't thank the gritstone for being under your feet, for holding you up. But without it, where would you be? You can live without leaves on the trees – you do in the winter, don't you? – but not the soil, or the earth.

Or without blood... running through your veins...

(*She rolls up her sleeves, takes out the knife she had earlier and starts cutting into her arm the initials CH. The blood runs freely.*)

Here, somewhere... he's here... In here. Aren't you?

(*Her consciousness wavers. But she stands nonetheless, deeply distressed.*)

It's raining, why's he gone out in the rain...?! What did I say? Did I say something awful? Joseph, go find Heathcliff and tell him to come. I have to speak to him.

Heathcliff! Come home! Heathcliff!

Zigger Zagger

Peter Terson

Zigger Zagger was the first ever play commissioned by NYT especially for the company, and they have performed it eight times in the last fifty years. Written by Peter Terson in 1967, it harnesses the full force of a fifty-strong company to create epic ensemble theatre; in many ways it set the precedent for the company's work. It tells the story of Harry, a football-mad young man who struggles to find a sense of purpose when he leaves school. With a chorus of football fans punctuating scenes with chants and songs, *Zigger Zagger* pulses with a raw, youthful energy, and charts the journey of a teenager beginning to make their way in the world.

Structured like a morality play, *Zigger Zagger*'s protagonist is named Harry, an everyman character whom we meet at the age of fourteen, just as he is leaving school. The play then presents scenes from his life and the various moral dilemmas he encounters as he enters the adult world. We watch as he turns from an enthusiastic fan who dreams of getting an exciting job, into a small-time hooligan who shouts racist abuse on public transport, before reassessing his life towards the end of the play, and choosing a path towards a more secure future. A mercurial character named Zigger Zagger accompanies us through the play; sometimes as a narrator, sometimes as a character in the action, and sometimes acting as a tempter of Harry, drawing him back to the thrill of the football stadium at the expense of the rest of his life. As Harry begins to resist Zigger Zagger's temptations, the play asks us to consider the choice we all make between taking responsibility as we grow older and the excitement of youth.

Harry

■ **Character** A teenage football fan.

■ **Location** An unspecified British town in the 1960s.

■ **Accent** Your own.

■ **Scene** This speech comes in the middle of the play, and in it, Harry describes the feeling on a Saturday afternoon before a football match, from the build-up in the town right through to kick-off. In the previous scenes, Harry has been turned down by the army and is feeling dejected about his future. Despite the efforts of his brother-in-law, Les, who attempts to persuade him to knuckle down and learn a trade, the draw of Zigger Zagger and the match are too much; Harry is unwilling to become a grown-up, instead choosing to focus on the match on Saturday. Up until now, the scenes have been punctuated by crowds of supporters chanting, but this is the first time we get to feel the tension and excitement of match day.

■ **Who is he talking to?** The audience.

■ **Where?** In an imaginary space.

■ **What does he want?** Harry wants us to feel what he feels: the excitement, the anticipation, the camaraderie. He wants us to see what he sees, smell what he smells, feel what he feels, and be with him in that moment as he heads to the stadium. At this point in his life, going to the football is the most meaningful thing in his life, and so he wants the audience to understand the depth of feeling and emotion that being a supporter gives him. When he delivers this speech, nothing else matters, only being there and soaking in the atmosphere.

■ **Things to think about** The match means everything to Harry – he's been beaten up by one of his mum's lovers, and

383

turned down by the army, and he's decided that the rest of his life doesn't matter – only Saturday afternoons. Make sure the stakes are high for Harry – this has to be about more than just a game.

Make sure you fully imagine all of the things he describes: the sights, the sounds, the smells. By seeing and remembering everything Harry describes, you will be able to transport the audience to the football ground.

Pay attention to where the full stops are – there aren't that many, so don't break the pace of the speech too much by pausing at the end of each line. Use the poetic rhythm of the speech to give you energy and a sense of anticipation.

▨ **Where to find the play** This play was published by Penguin Books. It is now out of print, but you should be able to find affordable, second-hand editions for sale online.

Harry

Come Saturday,
The whole town comes alive.
People are going one way,
From all the streets,
They are going the one way,
And meeting and joining,
And going on and meeting more and more
Till the trickle becomes a flood.
And men are so packed tight
That the cars have to nose their way through.
And you come to the stadium,
And it's humming,
A hum comes from the bowl.
And the people inside seem to be saying,
Come on in, come on in,
And you jostle at the turnstile,
And the turnstile clicks and clicks,
And you push nearer and nearer,
Through the dark gap,
Then you're in.
And the great stand of the City End,
It's like a hall,
A great hall,
And you go on,
Through the arch
And you see the pitch,
Green, new shaven and watered,
And the groundsman's made the white lines
As straight as a ruler
And the ash is pressed.
And you find your place among the fans,
The real fans,
The singers and chanters and rattle wavers.
And a sheet of tobacco smoke hangs over the crowd.
And the crowd whistles and hoots,

And the policemen circling the pitch
Look up and know they're in for a rough day of it,
And the stadium fills up,
The open End first, then the City End,
Then the paddock, then the covered seated stand,
Then, last of all, the fat directors
With the Lord Mayor and cigars.
And the reporters are in their little glass box,
And the cameramen position themselves
By the goal,
And there's a looking down the tunnel,
Then a hush.
Then out they come.
The lads,
Like toy footballers on a green billiard table.
And then the roar goes up…

Glossary

Context: The situation that the play sits in; this could include the historical time, or geographical place, or the relationships that already exist before the play begins.

Direct address: A term used to describe a character talking directly to the audience.

Dynamic: A force that produces some kind of change. Sometimes I may have described a character as being 'dynamic', meaning that they are positive or energised in some way. I have also talked about 'the dynamic' in a speech, and I am encouraging you to identify a specific energy which is driving change in a character – this may be the dynamic of anger or hope or pain, for example.

Elizabethan/Jacobean: Plays that were written during the reign of Elizabeth I and James I (James VI of Scotland), between 1558 and 1625.

Ensemble: The French for 'together', which when used in a theatre setting can describe the whole cast. For NYT, 'ensemble' and the idea of the group coming together to work, play and create is at the heart of what we do.

High-stakes: A phrase that I have used to describe a moment when a character *really* wants something – the situation is at a turning point, and the outcome of this moment will have a big effect on the course of the action.

Metatheatre or **metatheatrical**: Something which draws attention to the unreality of what is happening in a performance. Something that is 'metatheatrical' acknowledges the fact that this is a play or artifice within the performance.

Naturalism: A type of theatre which emerged in the late nineteenth and early twentieth centuries and has become the mainstay of British theatre. At its heart, naturalism tries to create the appearance of reality on stage (the opposite of a **stylised** or **metatheatrical performance**).

Playing age: The age of character you are most suited to playing. So if you are a mature fourteen-year-old, you might be able to realistically play characters up to the age of eighteen, whereas if you are a young-looking twenty-year-old, your playing age may be younger, and you can get away with playing someone who is sixteen.

Playing Up: An accredited ten-month drama-training programme run by NYT. It offers young people aged nineteen to twenty-four who are not in education, employment or training (NEET) the opportunity to gain an Access to Higher Education Diploma in Theatre Arts.

Published plays: Plays which have been chosen, edited and produced on paper or as an e-book by a publishing house such as Nick Hern Books. We have recommended always choosing a speech from a published play, as it will have gone through a certain amount of quality control.

Site-specific performance: A performance that was made to be performed in a specific, non-traditional theatre space, for example *Whose Shoes*, which was made to be performed on the Salford Quays, in and around the Lowry Theatre.

Stream-of-consciousness: A term used to describe a continuous flow of multiple thoughts, feelings and reactions that pass through a character's mind.

Stylised performance: A type of performance that isn't naturalistic – it is heightened in some way.

Subtext: Something that isn't said by the character. This might be because they don't feel they can be 100 per cent honest, or because they are holding something back in order to achieve their objective, but it is a feeling or thought that bubbles underneath the spoken lines or actions.

Superobjective: The main goal the character has in life. Their superobjective exists from before the play begins and continues on afterwards. It is a big, overarching ambition that encompasses everything they do, for example 'to achieve happiness' or 'to succeed above all others'.

Acknowledgements

The editor, the National Youth Theatre and Nick Hern Books gratefully acknowledge permission to quote extracts from the following:

Electricity by Miriam Battye, *UnStoned* by Amy Evans, and *Zigger Zagger* by Peter Terson, all reproduced by permission of The Agency (London) Ltd. *The Volunteer* by Michael Arditti, reproduced by permission of Michael Arditti. *Harm's Way* and *Skunk* by Zawe Ashton, both reproduced by permission of Zawe Ashton, c/o The Artists Partnership. *The Class* by Luke Barnes, reproduced by permission of Luke Barnes, c/o 42M&P Ltd. *The Holyland* by Daragh Carville, *The Life and Adventures of Nicholas Nickleby* by Charles Dickens, adapted by David Edgar, *Tory Boyz* by James Graham, *Killing Time* from *Barbarians* by Barrie Keeffe, *Pigeon English* by Stephen Kelman, adapted by Gbolahan Obisesan, *Blood Wedding* by Federico García Lorca, translated by Gwynne Edwards, *Oedipus the King* by Sophocles, translated by Don Taylor (enquiries for all rights to *Oedipus the King*: info@steinplays.com), all published by and reproduced by permission of Bloomsbury Methuen Drama, an imprint of Bloomsbury Publishing Plc. *Dumped* by Daragh Carville, *Razia Sultan* by Jamila Gavin, *Blue Moon Over Poplar* and *Stars Over Kabul* by Rebecca Lenkiewicz, *Prince of Denmark* by Michael Lesslie, and *Flood* by Rory Mullarkey, all reproduced by permission of Casarotto Ramsay & Associates Ltd. *Fluffy Rabbit* by Paul Charlton, reproduced by permission of Paul Charlton. *Out of Me* by Jane Bodie, *Cold Comfort Farm* by Stella Gibbons, adapted by Paul Doust, *Relish* by James Graham, and *Balls* by Sarah Solemani, all reproduced by permission of Curtis Brown. *Murder in the Cathedral* by T. S. Eliot, and *Dancing at Lughnasa* by Brian Friel, both published by and reproduced by permission of Faber & Faber Ltd. *Little Malcolm and His Struggle Against the Eunuchs* by David

national® youth theatre

The National Youth Theatre of Great Britain is a world-leading youth-arts charity. We inspire, develop and showcase exceptional young people aged fourteen to twenty-five from across the UK. We were established in 1956 and have nurtured the talent of hundreds of thousands of young people.

Every year we reach out around Great Britain to audition over six thousand young people at over sixty audition centres. We believe that young people should have access to our opportunities regardless of their background, locality or ability to pay – and strive to represent the diversity of Britain's youth in all its forms.

We deliver free and affordable talent-development courses all year round at key partner venues and believe that the best way for young people to learn is by doing, and by engaging with leading artists and industry professionals. Our opportunities give young people the competitive edge and support their practical career development. We champion and develop the best in emerging talent, including directors, writers and backstage staff and commission brave and relevant new work, providing creative pathways that enable young people interested in all areas of the theatre industry to progress, from backstage technical talent to creative leadership and direction.

We produce brave and relevant new writing, retell classic stories for our time, and are renowned for our innovative mass-ensemble productions. We are as ambitious as the young people we serve, platforming young talent on leading West End stages, in stadiums worldwide and at iconic sites both home and abroad. Our outlook is international, understanding what it means to be a young person today, addressing issues of social responsibility and global citizenship.

Our world-renowned alumni include Helen Mirren, Daniel Craig, Chiwetel Ejiofor, Rosamund Pike, Daniel Day-Lewis, David Oyelowo, Orlando Bloom, Andrea Riseborough, Gareth Pugh, Catherine Tate, Ben Kingsley, Ashley Jensen, Matt Lucas, Hugh Bonneville, Matthew Warchus, Matt Smith, Zawe Ashton, Michael Grandage and many more.

www.nyt.org.uk

Supported using public funding by

ARTS COUNCIL ENGLAND

National Youth Theatre is proud to acknowledge our principal supporters Arts Council England, The David Pearlman Charitable Foundation and the Pureland Foundation.